Vienna's Will

A True Story By

Mark McCullough

ISBN: 1496012771
ISBN 13: 9781496012777

Chapter 1

(APRIL 1992)

I sat in the backseat of my parent's station wagon and watched the world go by as we crept down Interstate-95 south towards our destination. I watched the trees gently blowing in the warm sun outside my window and gazed at the people driving by, going about their daily lives. Heading to work, heading from work, heading wherever their minds pleased. Watching my parents from the back, they knew no such luxury. I couldn't see their faces from where I was sitting but their slumped shoulders and complete silence except for the occasional small cry from my mother told me what was in their thoughts that day. They knew, as did I, that each mile we drove, each state line we passed, brought us closer to the endpoint of a journey that may as well have been the passageway to hell for them. In a way, that was exactly where they were headed.

This hell, was in no fault their own though you would have been hard pressed to convince them otherwise.

Though not deserving of the pain to come, I'm sure in their own selfless, faithful way wished that only they would have to suffer. If that were true, they could protect and defend me, their twenty-five year old son from whatever unknown evil I would encounter in the following days or months, perhaps even years if things took there likely course. As much as I feared the end of our journey, I worried more about them. I felt that this would likely be the end for me, in one way or another, but they would have to continue. I knew they would endure countless years blaming themselves for the outcome and having lost one child already many years earlier, I could only hope that their strong faith and belief in their God would see them through. That was difficult to fathom though, for their faith had already been pushed to its outer limits and quite honestly, things were likely to get much worse.

Throughout our journey my mother would occasionally turn her head to look at me and her eyes would always bring me to tears. It seemed as if she was trying to remember me. My face. My expression. Like she wanted to forever lock my image in her head. My father never turned back to me, and never spoke but I could see him responding the same way in the rearview mirror. I felt like I could hear the words spoken over and over in his head. "How did this happen? How could this be happening?" The one thought I heard most from my dad on that trip was, "Son, how did I fail you?" He didn't of course. And even though he was an imposing man and could outwardly appear to be even more formidable especially with his bald head and full beard, at heart he was a gentle man consumed only by the love of his family. So with the events that had since past, and the outcome they had produced and all the uncertain future actions that would follow, he felt all the guilt rested squarely on his broad shoulders.

I had witnessed throughout the recent days and weeks when he thought he was alone, this larger than life, exuberant man, reduced to a blubbering child. No one copes well with this visual of a loved one, especially in that state of pain and duress regardless of its cause. In this case, I knew its origin started and ended with me, and my actions on February 27th, 1992.

I knew we were close to our destination when we turned off the highway and my father took out the map and read the last of the directions to where we were headed. The words spoken from my father brought simultaneous tears from my mother. "We're almost there." he said. A long, straight road led us to a turn-off which contained a series of one story, concrete buildings. The atmosphere and surroundings led to near euphoria from my dad. "This doesn't look so bad." he said. A long, deep breath from my mother echoed the same sentiment.

We pulled alongside the curb and my father quickly rolled down his window, calling out to a man headed in our direction. The mood was further heightened by his broad smile and easy demeanor.

My dad asked, "Are you one the docs'?" The man leaned down into my father ignoring the question and said, "Can I help you Sir?"

"Yes, we're here to drop off our son."

The man's puzzled expression elicited a feeling of fear and fore-boding that started deep within my stomach and reached my brain just as he spoke. He said, "You must be looking for Butner." He pointed back toward the highway. "Go back up to that turn off and make a left. Go down a ways, not too far, then turn right and you'll see it. Can't miss it."

My father rolled up the window without saying a word. His gaze was void of any emotion or expression. The man tapped on the window but it was as if my father didn't hear. He had heard all he needed to. He simply put the car in drive and followed the direction the man had spoken. My anxiety of course returned. Maybe it was the see-saw of emotion that transpired or the anticipation of what was to come, but the short drive up the road seemed to last forever.

Up the road a ways and turn right, you can't miss it is what he said. No truer statement has ever crossed a man's lips. I'm sure there were plenty of signs and people and buildings when we finally arrived, but all we saw, all the three of us could absorb was wire and fence. Maybe twenty feet tall, wire snarled around the top, a small strip of land at its feet, then more fencing and more wire. There was no more quiet tears coming from my mother now, she sobbed openly. I looked away from the fence and read the sign directly in front of us. BUTNER FEDERAL PRISON. I looked past the fence. I watched the trucks roaming the perimeter and the guards coming and going for the day. Free to leave, to go home to their loved ones, secure in the knowledge that at least for the night, they were safe from the inhabitants that lurked behind the fences. I wanted to scream out. I wanted to tell someone that this was wrong. That I would never survive inside those fences or the walls they surrounded. Blonde hair, blue eyes. Maybe 140 pounds dripping wet. No way. I wanted to open the door and run from everything that brought me there. Everything that made this a reality. But I knew I couldn't.

I distinctly remember saying to myself, this is home now. For the first time in months, it was my turn to cry.

The walk to the main entrance felt like how I would imagine walking the plank would feel. You knew once you got to the end, no matter how slow your pace, the outcome wouldn't change. Save for some last minute reprieve, a stay of your sentence, your final step would be your last.

When we reached the processing desk after passing through the main entrance doors, I knew, just from a quick glance, that we were about to encounter one huge asshole. My radar was spot on. We went through the surrender process and handed in all the necessary paperwork then he said something to my parents, he really directed it more towards my mother, he said, "Is there a number we can reach you at?"

"It's on the paper work. Our home and business are right there."

"No, I mean later today."

My mother didn't know how to answer that so my father asked, "We don't understand sir. For what?"

His reply came with a little smile curled up in the corner of his mouth and a glint in his eye.

"In case something happens to him."

He let that sink in then he stood up and pointed in my direction. "Step over here."

He cuffed me and led me away. I told myself I wouldn't look back. But I did. I had to. My father had already turned and walked away but my mother, she just stood there, tears streaming down her face. Weld up with pain, and the anguish of knowing for the first time in her life, she couldn't make things better. This wasn't school where she could talk to the principal, or an angry parent whose son I had a problem with. For the first time, there was nothing she could do or say to save me. As the guard and I headed further down the hall, one thought focused in my mind, and will forever be imprinted within me. That is the image of how sad, how small, and how fragile she looked, and that

I was its cause, is something I knew would bring a feeling of torment and misery for all the years to come.

I was shuffled into a small room with an orange jumpsuit folded neatly on a wooden bench topped with a pair of blue slip-on shoes.

"Take off your clothes. Someone else will be right in." I did as I was told and sat naked on the bench feeling for all the world as exposed and vulnerable as I had ever been. Another guard entered soon after and spoke low and clear. "Stand up."

What happened next is something that stays with you forever. Burned into your brain and branded as a memory to be locked away somewhere far and deep into your thoughts and chained up with a lock and tossed key.

"Bend over. Spread."

I stared at the wall. Is this really happening? Is another man really prodding and manipulating my body this way? I thought I knew what shame was but this was an indignity so horrific and lacking in human nature, it almost didn't register as a reality in my mind. Almost.

"Turn around. Look at me. Open your mouth."

This has to be a mistake is the thought that kept circling my brain. I'm not a criminal. I've never been in trouble in my life. I come from a good family, no, a great family. I'm educated, well read. I respect my parents and my elders. Yet someone, a stranger is demanding that I spread my ass in half and telling me to cough. He pointed to the jumpsuit.

"Put that on and put your clothes in here."

He handed me a bag. "Tap on the door when you're done. You have two minutes."

"Yes, sir."

I was led down the hall and passed off to another guard. I could see outside now. It was gray and dreary and the clouds were low and dark and shifting quickly in the sky above me. The outside world looked shaded and out of focus. A light rain began to fall across a long, open field and I could see buildings and pathways leading people hurriedly along their way. An overweight man with a large, round, pitted face and an unkempt mustache grasped my arm. Oddly, I remember thinking he had a kind face.

"This way son."

The walk of shame. The walk of regret. The walk of years of isolation and inner turmoil. Throughout the years as I think about that walk, that first day, an array of different emotions come to me. All of them full of fear and punctuated with remorse.

He didn't speak at all as we walked. Maybe he wanted me to look around, to take in my surroundings, to see what I had done and where I was. Perhaps his intention was to make clear my fate for the actions I had chosen. Not that they were actions really, more like steps on a journey that seemed set on a one way course, and had no true direction. The absurd notion to run was still in my head. Maybe I could clear the fence even with the cuffs on. Maybe he would just let me go and not tell anyone. Maybe no one would notice I was missing. Yeah, and maybe Elvis was playing in the cafeteria that night.

We approached a series of doors, then descended down a long set of steps and walked through a maze of never ending corridors. It felt as if we were plunging into the dark depths of hell, like we were headed to someplace that once you entered, you would never find your way back. A one way ticket to nowhere. Everything was concrete and steel. The light was bright in my eyes and showed every stain and blemish that had accumulated over the years. It all seemed unfit for an animal, never mind anything associated with the human race. The guard grabbed my arm and finally spoke. "Stop right here."

I turned to face a door with a single keyhole and a small, narrow slit. It was marred with deep scratches and riddled with dents. I knew for sure that I didn't want to know how any of it got there, nor the likely aggression needed to make its presence known.

"I'm gonna take these cuffs off. No funny business, hear?"

He started to loosen the cuffs.

"How long do you have son?"

"I'm not sure. I'm here on an evaluation."

He paused with the key still in the cuffs then said, "Opened ended, pending?"

"Yes, sir."

He whistled and I could see him shaking his head from the corner of my eye. He keyed the cuffs, then the door, then he spun me toward him. I can't imagine that was protocol but I'm sure in his eyes, I didn't present much of a danger.

"What'd you do?"

"Robbed a bank."

He paused.

"Armed?"

"Yes."

"Gun?"

I took a deep breath and exhaled.

"Yes."

"And you're here on evaluation?"

"Yes, sir."

"Bank robbery with a gun and you're here on evaluation?"

He shook his head, and sighed quietly.

"Things didn't go quite as planned." I said.

"What's that mean?"

I didn't answer.

"Damn shame. It'd be better to have 5-10, at least then you'd know where you stand."

He led me inside and closed the door behind me. As he did he said, "Look through the slot son. Down here."

I knelt down and listened as he spoke through the opening that I would later learn is how my meals would be dispersed to me.

"I'm gonna give you some advice whether you want it or not. Understand?"

"Yes, sir."

"Tell the docs' you want to do your time down here, got me?"

"Why?"

"Have you ever been in prison son? In any jail of any kind?"

"No, sir."

"Then believe me when I tell you this, anything down here is better than everything up there. Understand?"

"No sir, I don't."

7

"Just trust me. I don't understand why you're here, and I don't much care to understand it. That's not for me to judge. That's not the man I am, but listen…. the yard is no place for someone like you. Good luck son, and God bless you."

I heard his steps grow softer as he left me alone with his words. I knew what he meant but tried not to allow myself to process its true meaning. I turned to face my surroundings. My new home was approximately eight feet by ten feet. The bed was on my right and appeared to be molded straight into the wall. The mattress was thin and coated with stains. A stainless steel toilet sat to my left. I wasn't certain, but it appeared that some type of satanic emblem was etched into the floor directly beneath my feet. I could hear screaming and pounding from somewhere down the hall and a guard screaming back telling whoever it was to shut the fuck up. I slid down the wall and slumped to the floor and for the first time realized my shoes were two different sizes. One a nine, the other an eleven. I looked back up at the setting before me and leaned back on the door and thought that I could actually hear my heart pounding. I was sure it was going to burst.

I imagined my parents driving down the highway. I thought of my family back home, and random things like fast food and ice cream. I drew a picture in my mind of the lake we lived on and knew without question that I would gladly trade years left of my life just to feel the warm sun on my skin and listen to the birds calling out and soaring high above me. I wanted to feel the breeze on my face and cast out a fishing line not much caring whether I caught anything or not.

I had been incarcerated for less than an hour and the idea of freedom, or lack of it made we want to scream much like the guy down the hall. Maybe that's why he was screaming. Maybe he too so badly wanted to taste freedom and the sense of peace only one's home can bring.

I remember crying and thinking to myself, what have I done? How did I get here? If I was to be honest with myself, I knew how, I just didn't know how I could have changed the outcome. It was like my life was some fucked up, foregone conclusion. An unlucky karma if you will. A destiny set on a certain path that nothing, and no one could alter its direction. Maybe I did something horrible in another life and this was my punishment. Maybe my sentence was to live a life inside my own head. Condemning someone to live within their own mind when depression is its controlling inhabitant, is truly an act that is free of mercy and lacking any form of human empathy. Depression is not blind to you, it's not something beyond your mind's eye. Instead it's something you fully retain and grasp both its power and ability to paralyze you. You see it all, it's right there in plain sight, but you are incapable of doing anything about it. I thought, as I had many times throughout the years that this was just the cards I was dealt. I assumed these dark thoughts and feelings that crisscrossed through my brainwaves were just my fate, that's all. I believed that to be true, but even I would have to admit, some of the people I met along the way, fueled what was already at work inside me. I crawled into bed with that thought to lull me asleep the first night I found myself in prison.

Chapter 2
(JUNE 1976)

As we grow older, regardless of background, ethnicity, race or intellect, we think back on our youth and are forever linked with certain memories and aspirations. In college, maybe we believed we were destined to become the lawyer that had doctrines named in our honor. In high school, maybe we would be the doctor who cured cancer or even be the first scientist to truly solve or justify the Big Bang theory. Or, perhaps we would be the one to unlock the mysteries surrounding God and religion and all its uncertainties. In grade school though, that's where we really dreamed big. We could, on any given day, be anything. President, Secret Agent, Star Quarterback, maybe an Award Winning Actor. There were no limits to our imagination. We were young, and with youth came all the world's possibilities. We could climb any mountain, and defeat insurmountable foes. In those days, we could rule the world.

For me, at 10 years old, I was sure I would pitch in the World Series. There was no doubt in my mind. I loved baseball. I felt like I belonged. Even then I knew things were different inside me but not on the field. There, I was equal to everyone. Actually no, I was often better. Not because of talent necessarily, but more because, even at that age, I was lost. But on a baseball field, on a bright, sunny Saturday afternoon, all was well in my mind. That, and an absolute love for the game seemed to set me apart from the other kids.

If we were fortunate enough at that age, we had people to influence us, to mold our minds toward a positive path that our primitive, undeveloped selves are hopefully open to. We looked up to and leaned on those who guided us. We assumed they were wiser and smarter, making us both susceptible and vulnerable to those who teach us.

I was no different. I listened to my siblings, obeyed their wisdom, and assumed that all the adults in my life would point me in the right direction as my family did. We are, after all, wide eyed and entrusting to the ones we assume, because they are older, must somehow be more knowledgeable about life. I would later learn how wrong that theory was. I would also learn, even at that age, about trust and the expectation of relationships. People were rarely what they seemed to be.

I often, even to this day, some thirty-five years later, go back to the same fields I once played on as a child. I can close my eyes and remember the chattering of young boys encouraging their teammates and the parents in the stands shouting out words of inspiration to their kids on the field. I can remember how the dirt would crunch under my new cleats and how happy I was my father found the time, and the money to buy them for me. Most of the memories are good ones and usually each time I go I remember something new and different from the time before. My favorite field was always field #2. It had lights and a booming P.A. system. When they called your name, you felt like a star. It also had a big scoreboard that beamed brightly down onto you and a fence in the outfield close enough to hit one over its limits and make the dreams you had of your heroes come to life. On those occasions, life simply couldn't get any better.

My parents never missed a game and although baseball wasn't my dad's favorite sport, he would always seem to find both the time to be there and the encouraging words to lead me on. I knew he was proud of me, and that knowledge, meant as much if not more to me than the game itself. Even back then, my dad wasn't hard to spot in the stands. Six foot two and over two hundred pounds with a glistening bald head and a thundering, baritone voice. If I sit in the stands at field #2 even now, I can still hear…"Atta way to go Marcus Aurelius!!!!"

It never ceases to bring a smile.

There is one field though, that I rarely visit. Field #5 sits in the back, away from the rest. A long, dirt road leads you to it and it sits separated and isolated from the others, packed away and hidden from view. It sits alone and to all the world, it's no different or any more special than the others around it. For me though, it was and never would be the same. There came a time where I wouldn't even play in games that were scheduled at that field. I would pretend to be sick or I would make up an injury just so I didn't have to play there. On occasion, my parents wouldn't have any of it, and they made me play regardless of any tantrum I would cultivate. On those days, the game I loved so much, was anything but enjoyable. To the outside observer, field #5 would neither impress, nor strike anyone as anything more than ordinary. To me though, it was anything but typical. It held a secret that I have carried with me for more than 35 years. That field, and the history it possesses has been stored in my mind, hidden, but never far from view. It will stay with me forever like a chronic illness. An emotional affliction on my soul. Even at that age, I knew to suppress it and keep it somewhere deep inside me but I also knew, even then, that it would always be there with me. It would always be like a wound that would scab over, but never heal.

I had a morning game on a Saturday that I remember as a perfect day to play baseball even all these years later. Warm with a light breeze and a sky that didn't possess one cloud on its canvass. It was deep blue and beautiful. The type of day I knew would keep me outside long after the game was over. When I got older, whether through my lack of interest or my skills peaking, I was an average player. But at ten years old though, I was a very good player, one of the best. With that, came special treatment from coaches and parents alike. Even at the ice cream shop after games it seemed an extra scoop or two found its way to me. A slight wink or a small nod from my coach and I would have a pile of chocolate so high, it would be a dripping mess long before I could get halfway through it.

On this particular Saturday though, a Saturday which started with such promise and possibility, I was being treated in this same manner, but for a very different reason. I blew the game. I walked three batters then gave up a homerun. That had never happened before. I let myself, my parents, and my teammates down. My teammates had their ice cream, so the game, not even an hour out of sight, was a long forgotten memory. I also knew my parents would get over it quickly. They knew it was just a blip, a minute event so insignificant in the larger scheme of things that would occur in my life that they wouldn't give it much thought by the time they hit the driveway.

For my coach though, it was a different story. He had a son named Michael on the team and Coach lived and breathed for those Saturday afternoon ballgames. What made that day so particularly painful in his eye was his son, who wasn't an especially good player, struck out the following inning after I gave up the runs. There were kids on base and he could have saved the game for us, for me, and more importantly, for his dad. Michael cried openly after striking out then hearing the jeers coming from the opposite bench, and also from some of his own teammates. I was sure I saw tears in his dad's eyes that morning as well.

Michael was often picked on and teased by the other kids and was socially awkward. He had a pudgy appearance, round face and a haircut ill-suited for a kid who was constantly defending his honor and existence on this earth. When he would run his legs would rub together so he would attempt to spread them out which more often than not, resulted in a spastic, awkward style that usually ended in a face first nose dive. I would always pick him up and attempt to distract him from the cruel taunts coming from the other kids. I liked Michael. I understood him. I understood how hard it could be, just being a kid. I also knew, even then, how sensitive and emotional I was. I saw it in myself, and I saw it in Michael.

Although we couldn't have been more different to the outside observer, I was rail thin and gangly, I felt I knew what it was like to be Michael. What it was like to live inside his head, and I think he felt the same about me. I knew it pleased his father that we were friends and I often felt the same pride he had in me as I felt with my own father. So on this particular Saturday, real or imagined, I felt his disappointment as well. As we sat alone at a table, I realized how much he treated me like his own son. I guess he probably saw the same insecurities and flaws in me that he saw in his own child. My own father, as great a man and dad as he was, was busy going to school, running a business, and doing whatever he had to, to keep our family afloat. So an additional sense of fatherly guidance brought more security to my unsteady psyche. It pleased me to have someone like Coach to look up to. There were things I could discuss and open up to him about that may have been too difficult to reveal to my own flesh and blood. He was a funny man also. He would do these odd voices and had this ridiculous walk often pretending to trip into things. Anything was fair game. A pole. A wall. There were no limits. The result often ended with everyone around him being reduced to tears. The tears on this day though, weren't from joy or laughter.

"Why some glum?"

I didn't look up over the bill of my cap.

"Cat gotch yer tongue?"

He pushed the cap back and lifted up my chin.

"What's up slugger?"

"I lost the game for us."

"Yeah and…?"

He took my hat and placed it backwards on his head. I looked up at him and laughed at the image.

"Something funny?"

"You look ridiculous."

He pulled back in mock shock and surprise. "I am truly and deeply offended."

I started laughing louder. I knew what he was doing and I appreciated it. He was replacing the tears with laughter. He turned the cap so the bill was resting flush on his left ear.

"Is this better?"

I don't know why it struck me as being so funny but he looked so comical plus he kept crossing his eyes and pretending to pick his nose. I nearly peed myself with laughter.

"My wife likes it, watch."

He turned to a table to his left where his wife and Michael sat.

"Hey Honey, don't I look good like this? I'm going for my own sense of style. What do you think? Is it me or what?"

She looked at him and pretended to not hear a word he said. Michael did the same.

"Jeez. Tough crowd goin' down at the ice cream palace."

He took the hat off and his face changed. He did what he set out to do, to get me to loosen up and smile.

"Son, look around you. Look at all these kids here. Do you see them? Most of them will never be able to do the things you can do."

He looked around the room, and I'm pretty sure his eyes rested on his own son.

"I've watched you since you were eight, and all I can do is shake my head."

He was a father to me now, the class clown was gone. He leaned closer.

"I see how easy things come to you, like you're not even trying. But I'm shaking my head for another reason, do you know why?"

"No, sir."

"It's because you only see the failure. How many games have you won for us between this year and last?"

I shrugged.

"Today was a fluke. It could happen to anybody yet it's all you can set your sights on. I bet if we win every game for the rest of the summer, this will be the only game you'll remember. Am I right?"

I just shrugged again. He leaned into my ear and kept his words just above a whisper, not wanting to be heard by the other kids.

"I see these kids try and try but they're never going to get any better. Sounds harsh I know especially when we're talking about ten year old boys, but the truth is the truth." He leaned in even closer and said, "You have the potential to do anything you can dream of, anything. Do you hear me? Figure that out right now, right this minute. Decide today that that's who you are, how you're going to think."

He tapped my temple. "If you do that, you will do many great things. If you don't, life will surely show you the rough road."

He slapped my back and dipped into my ice cream.

"Hey."

"It's melting."

15

We sat in silence and stuffed ourselves full. When the bowl was near empty, Coach dropped his spoon, rubbed his belly and said, "Finish up and we'll head back to the field. I think I know what happened out there today."

I was more than happy to go back. The ride over, looking out the window, the day was still beautiful. The sky was still clear and free of any blemish or imperfection. I couldn't wait to get there. I was so quick to ditch the rest of my teammates and get in the car, I didn't even realize Michael wasn't with us until we pulled into the park.

"Where's Michael?"

"He said he didn't want to come. See what I mean? Remember what I said before? You have to decide what you're gonna be. You've decided you want to get better. To learn from your mistakes. My son, God bless him, I love him with all my heart and soul, but he has decided he'd rather read comic books and watch television."

"I like comic books and television."

He smiled down at me and tussled my hair. "Don't sass me boy, ya hear me?"

"Yes, Master."

He laughed. "Now that's better."

The car barely came to a halt and I was already out the door. Coach called out, "Jesus H. Christ son, slow down before you get yourself killed."

Too late, I was off. I tore down the hill and made a beeline for the pitcher's mound. The day's games were now over and the field, the entire park was all ours. Coach parked the car and scrambled down the hill after me, nearly stumbling and falling in the process. I knew my own father had already headed back to work and had stretched all the free time he had out of that day, so my appreciation for Coach and the extra time he took for me swelled my heart, and made for the best of days for this particular ten year old boy.

"Slow down Hot-Shot." he said.

It was all I could do to contain my enthusiasm. It was too late to undo the failure of that morning, but maybe, as Coach said, if I set my mind to it, I could get better. Maybe through practice and patience

I could assure myself that I would never fail again and never have to feel the way I did earlier. I realize now how foolish and irrational that logic was, but I truly believed that if Coach said it, then it must be true. I stood on the mound and looked all around me. I was happy. Truly happy. Maybe it was going to be a great day after all.

"Perfect, that's perfect. Okay, now throw the curve but use the same form as the fastball. Gotta disguise it."

Coach was standing behind home plate barking at me. His energy and enthusiasm were relentless.

"Okay now, high and tight. Gotta be able to shake 'em off the plate. Know what I mean?"

I did and I obliged him.

"Nice. Very nice. You're dropping down too far though on your delivery. Remember, you have to repeat the same motion over and over. Repetition is the key."

I buzzed in another pitch.

"Shoulder in, I like it. That's the way it's supposed to be done. Keep it up son."

We did this for hours it seemed. "Putting in the work." That's what Coach called it. After a while, I must have been feeling pretty good about myself and he saw it.

"Okay Hot-Shot, let's see what you got. From there, on a line, straight to the backstop without a bounce. Up for it?"

"No problem."

I knew I could, I had done it many times before with my brother.

"I'm waiting Golden Boy. Let's go."

I wound up and would have bet all I had in the world that I could, and would meet the challenge. Coach would be proud and I would feel that sweet, indescribable emotion of knowing something I did, gained approval and admiration from someone I looked up to and respected.

I believe that all of us have certain memories that no matter the years that pass between them and our daily lives, we can remember them with such detail and accuracy that it's as if we can relive them to the point of feeling it was but a few hours past in our history. I remember that day much that way, and one thing I remember so clearly, is how badly I felt when the pitch fell short of its target. I guess my expression made for an easy read because Coach quickly said, "What's with the long face, son?"

Even with my back now turned to him, I could hear the exasperation in his voice. He jogged out to me and knelt down to face me eye to eye.

"Look at me, son."

He tipped my chin up.

"Remember what I said before at the ice cream shop? Remember how I said you have to be all in, in here?"

He tapped my skull.

"You have to believe you can do anything, I mean anything you set your mind to. I believe in you, your folks, your teammates, they all believe. That means a whole lot of nothing unless you believe it too. You're special son, and I don't mean donkey head special like some of these kids out here. You've got it right here."

He grabbed my left arm.

"But you gotta feel it in here."

He tapped gently again on my temple.

"One more time but with feeling. The sooner you see it-"

"The better off I'll be." Then he said, "Now you're talking. Let's put this aside a minute and take a load off. Sound good?"

"Sounds good to me Coach."

We strolled over to the dugout with Coach's arm draped around me. It felt like he was protecting me somehow. From what, I didn't know. Maybe in his eyes, from myself. Either way, it felt right, and it felt safe. We reached the dugout and sat down on the bench inside. It felt good to be out of the intense sun on the field and rest a while. He opened up two cold sodas and sat down next to me.

"How do you guys like the new uniforms?" I took a sip from my can and said, "They're okay I guess. My feet are killing me though."

"Your feet? Why?"

"My dad got me new cleats but they're not broken in yet."

"Gotcha."

We sat in silence. I looked out at the empty field before me. It was everything I could ask for in a Saturday, minus the disastrous last inning from earlier that morning. Baseball, a cold soda, a beautiful sunny day, and someone to enjoy it with. I didn't have many friends back then and I often struggled to fit in, to see my place with the other kids. At that age, that can be a devastating revelation to yourself. When you have that knowledge, and you carry it around with you, life can be very lonely. That day at least though, I was not alone. Coach finally broke the silence. "Michael says he doesn't want to play anymore."

"How come you didn't mention that earlier? Is that why he didn't come?"

He nodded.

"Didn't want to spoil your day."

"Thanks."

He took a sip of his soda, then looked down at me. "You know why he wants to quit?"

"Uh-huh."

"Because of you."

I spun my head around fast to look at him. I could feel my face getting flush with anger and adrenaline.

"What does that mean?"

"It means, that he's jealous of you."

"Why?"

"Says I treat you more like a son than I do him."

"But he's my friend." Tears started filling my eyes.

"I'm afraid not anymore son."

His tone and manner were different than just moments earlier and his words almost seemed as if they were intended to bring harm. He simply blurted them out without concern or hesitation despite knowing the pain it would bring to me.

I started to get up and walk past him. He held me up with an arm and sat me right back where I was. I was crying freely now when he said, "It's okay, everything's gonna be okay."

"No it's not. He was my only friend."

He knelt down in front of me, and again his tone was different.

"What am I?"

I didn't answer him. He grabbed my cleat and pulled it off my foot. He began to bend and twist the leather around in his hands skillfully and with great care.

"What I'm about to do, you can show no one. Understand?"

I nodded. I began to squirm in my seat, unsure why things seemed to change so suddenly.

"The secret is… are you ready? The secret is to twist this way, but have the tongue out loose like this, see? Breaks in the leather without compromising the support. Wise old trick passed on down from my old man."

I looked at him, but I felt as if I was seeing someone else, someone unknown to me. His eyes were wide and dilated and he appeared older, meaner. His mouth was dry and cracked, like the sun had baked it crisp and brittle. My voice trembled when I spoke. "Do you…Do you want some of my soda?"

I had always known Coach to be a jolly, at times, a silly man. It was nice to see grown-ups behave that way. They always seemed to be so serious and self-absorbed. Not Coach though. He never seemed to have a care in the world. Always cracking jokes, always smiling. But he wasn't smiling as I watched him manipulate my cleat over and over. He looked unsure, uncertain of what to do next. Finally, his eyes showed an eagerness, a hunger that he had to satisfy and the consequences were no longer a factor in his indecision.

He spoke softly. "Remember now, what happens here, stays here, understand? Can you do that for me?"

I couldn't move. He ran his hand slowly up my left leg and rested it on my groin. He spoke even softer. "No cup son? Not even a jockstrap?"

He pulled down on my pants with his left hand and parted my legs with his right. He ran his tongue over his lips as beads of sweat formed, then fell from his scalp and onto the dugout floor. I remember thinking that somehow I had forgotten how to breathe. The simple task of just drawing in air and exhaling seemed alien to me. I felt as if a weight was centered squarely on my chest and that consciousness would soon slip away.

He began to perform oral sex on me. He had loosened his own pants and was masturbating. He didn't hold me down or threaten me in any way, yet I couldn't move any part of my body. As he continued, I imagined myself floating away, drifting harmlessly back into my house, and landing softly by my mother's side. Wrapped safely in her arms, knowing only her warm and unconditional love. I don't know exactly how long it lasted, but to this day, the deep, guttural noises that came from within him are as clear and distinct in my head as they were that day.

I lived several miles from field #5 but I ran all the way home after he was done with me. I don't think I stopped until I saw my mother. Despite her warm embrace, all I could think about was what he said to me. "What happens here, stays here with us." And it did, I never told anyone. I learned that day about pushing everything far and deep inside me. Into a place where no one could ever reach. I also knew that all the innocence and naivety a ten year old boy possesses was gone from me forever.

Chapter 3

"Hey, wake up in there. Let's go. Let's go."

It took me a minute to remember where I was. I sat up slowly in bed to the realization that I had slipped out of one nightmare and into another. I was in my cell, in seclusion, and it was some time in the middle of the night. The banging got louder as I stumbled to the door. I opened the flap and could only see the torso of a body outside. The light from the hallway was bright and blinding.

"What's going on?"

"Put your hands through the slot."

I did as I was told, and just as quickly cuffs fastened my wrists together.

"Step away from the door and turn around."

I turned and heard the door jar open. The corridor was quiet now, making the heavy, steel door all the more unsettling to hear at that hour.

A guard entered and quickly patted me down, which I found a little odd considering I was presently cuffed and had been sufficiently violated with a full cavity search prior to being placed inside my cell. He led me out and into a room with several people wearing hospital type gowns. Their faces were masked and gloves were already placed on their hands. No one spoke as I was guided to a chair and a tube was wrapped tightly around my bicep. It seemed oddly inappropriate to ask what they were doing. I mean, it was obvious what was about to take place but the fact that I didn't offer any resistance nor did they propose an explanation seemed somehow, the proper path for this event to take. They took their blood, for reasons I did not know, then I was quickly led back to my cell and shut in. The key turned and I broke the silence through the door slot and toward the guard who guided me in.

"I need help. Please. I need your help."

To my surprise, he didn't turn and walk into the night. He also, didn't answer.

"Could you get me a piece of paper and a pen?"

"No outside amenities allowed until you're out of seclusion."

"I know and I understand. But just listen to me, okay? Just listen. I don't belong in here."

"No one does. I hear it every day son."

He started to walk away.

"No wait, please. Just listen. Please, just listen to me."

He didn't walk any further, but he didn't come back either.

"I need to write to the doctors' upstairs. I need to explain to them. I need to make them understand. Please, I'm just asking for something to write with. Give me a fucking crayon I don't care but please, you have to help me."

He walked away. I slid down the wall and rubbed my face. My hands were black from the grime and filth of my mattress and the room smelled of sweet antiseptic. The floors were damp with moisture that filled the gaps around the toilet bowl, and the seat was slapped with a residue from some type of sanitizing liquid. Someone must have come to clean my cell when the night time vampire crew were draining the blood from my body.

I stood to relieve myself and as I did, a small pencil and a single piece of paper dropped in from my slot. No words were spoken. The only sounds were of the guards' steps as he moved quietly away. Perhaps he felt sorry for me. Maybe he felt compassion for another human being. Maybe he saw something in himself through me, or maybe he had just witnessed too many people who had simply given up. Perhaps he was tired of witnessing the day in and day out display of lost souls riding out their time in this world going in and out of the system no longer seeking a life, but rather, some twisted form of existence. Most people in prison I would later learn, particularly those down in isolation do not dream of picket fences and job promotions. Their reality is one of endurance. A perverse survival of the fittest. I respected the risk he must have taken. I knew what he had done was completely against prison rules. I could have hurt myself or someone else, although that was highly unlikely considering the pencil was an equivalent to the type you keep score with at a mini golf course. Regardless, I took his kindness as a small bright light shining through the darkness that was now part of my existence. Then I began writing.

I don't know who to write this to or if it will even mean anything to the reader, or, if it will even reach you. Maybe it doesn't matter. I'm sure this place gets the best of everyone, staff included. I know what I must be to you. Another case, another number. Another person with some sad story about how it's not their fault.

I hope I can help you understand me. Understand what brought me here. What led me to the crime that I myself understand but have much doubt that I can find the words, the proper ones anyway, to make any sense of it for you. It was an act I never intended to turn out the way it did. If it went the way it was thought out in my mind, this letter wouldn't be possible.

I'm sure you are aware that clinical depression is defined as so severe as to be considered abnormal, either because of no obvious environmental causes, or because the reaction to unfortunate life circumstances is more intense or prolonged than would generally be expected. I believe all that to be true but in the end, I prefer the anger turned inward interpretation. Anger, frustration, loneliness all forced deep down inside and into a place where I know and live. Every day, every hour. Throughout my life I have heard people say they wouldn't wish a certain illness or ailment on anyone. Me? I wouldn't wish depression on my worst enemy. It would be far better to be diagnosed with something you can see on an x-ray or some test result. People understand and sympathize with that. They get it, it's tangible to them. They can touch it and see it. Tell them you're depressed, the reaction is "snap out of it" or "stop the nonsense". Either one of those, believe me, would suit me just fine. As I sit here, I'm not sure what I'm trying to say or what the intention of this letter is except to try and express that I feel lost in here, down here, and most of all, in my life and I'm asking for your help. I can only leave hope that it's not too late. That is all I have to give.

    Mark

    Inmate-1161993

I drifted off to sleep. A fitful, tossing and turning would be a better description. Life moved differently down in seclusion. There were no clocks to gauge the present or the future. No way for your body to assess how it should feel or react to your surroundings. The only way to know the approximate time was regulated solely by when meals arrived. There was nothing to do, no way to pass the time except to whittle the minutes and hours away in your head.

That was a grueling endeavor for me even in the best of circumstances. There is no worse existence in my opinion, no place of confinement, no dwelling of abuse be it physical or emotional that is worse than when someone can't live within their own thoughts. You can try drugs, a temporary reprieve to dull the roller coaster of emotions cultivating in your intellectual mind, but time would inevitably bring you back to where you were, back to negotiating and pleading with your troubled soul.

There is of course, always an option to permanently shut out those feelings. There's an absolute solution to the pain. An eternal respite from all the suffering. That decision, the ultimate and most permanent one any human being can make, has been chosen by many who feel there is no relief, no reprieve that will release or even diminish the pain trapped in their head. I cannot blame or judge anyone for coming to that conclusion. It's a decision I had made more than once in my life and as I laid staring into the wall of my cell searching for sleep I hoped would come, it was one I assumed, would be made again. The timing was all that remained a mystery.

Chapter 4

(SEPTEMBER 1980)

I stepped off the school bus and into the parking lot on my first day of high school. Standing five feet eight inches tall and busting the scales at a whopping 114 pounds, I may as well have landed on the moon because that's exactly what it felt like. Just a few months earlier, I was the Captain of my grade school conference winning basketball team. I was looked up to and respected. That warm September morning, I felt anything and everything but admired and accepted. The kids were older and bigger and louder. Looking back, I wouldn't imagine I looked much different than a lot of the new kids, but standing there in my dress slacks, sport coat and tie, I felt like the proverbial sore thumb.

My dad, probably sensing my apprehension and anxiety that morning, offered to help me get ready for my first day. I appreciated his expertise and precision in tie knotting and I welcomed his words of wisdom and advice concerning all things pertaining to the world I was about to encounter. That being said and with all due and deserved respect, I made a mistake that fateful morning. One I promised myself, and all those who would listen, that I would not make again. My error was that I let him comb my hair. It had been awhile since I had allowed such a violation to my insecure, unstable pubescent psyche but yet, here it was again. My father had a way, a patented skill almost, of both parting and matting your hair in such a manner, as to resemble a hardened, immovable helmet. He was so enthusiastic about it that morning, as he was most things, that I didn't dare disrupt or discourage his positive outlook. Needless to say, between my stiff, hurricane proof hairdo and my goofy, clean cut face, I was ill prepared to leave the house, never mind start high school.

Walking slowly and with my head down and my duffle bag strapped to my back, I ventured on. I crossed most of the parking lot, passing windows and side stepping fellow students when it occurred to me, I had no clue where I was going. A bell rang, for what purpose I had no idea, but what I did know was that panic was starting to set in. I dropped my bag and sifted through papers I had seen my father stuff inside earlier that morning. I must have been quite a sight to the older kids. Slacks a little too hemmed, brand spanking new Tom McAn shoes, and my tie up so tight and straight, with papers strewn about all around me. But hey, on the bright side, there was a stiff late summer breeze brewing, yet my hair still hadn't moved. I heard a voice behind me, a deep, baritone voice that I didn't think was intended for me. The voice said, "Lost, my good man?"

I continued nervously scouring through my bag, looking hopelessly for that one single piece of paper that would magically tell me exactly where I needed to go. I heard the voice again, and this time I spun around. The voice said, "Deaf?"

"Huh?"

The man behind the voice had a sizeable belly that hung over his belt, highlighted more so by the shirt he tucked so tightly into his waist. He possessed a shocking head of red hair, and a beard that was neatly trimmed and bore the same outstanding trademark shade as those on his head. He had a round face and an easy smile that immediately set me at ease. The white collar around his neck only added to my comfort level. He tapped my papers and spoke again, "Speak Lad, speak."

"I'm lost Father."

With a twinkle in his eye he began. "All that is gold does not glitter, not all those who wander are lost;

The old that is strong does not wither, deep roots are not reached by the frost."

I cut him off.

"From the ashes a fire shall be woken, a light from the shadows shall spring;

27

Renewed shall be blade that was broken, the crownless again shall be king."

He smiled wide and pulled the papers from my hand. As he sorted through them he said, "A man only learns in two ways, one by reading, the other is by associating with wise people."

I said, "So I guess that rules you out."

I turned the papers right side up for him.

He squinted and said, "A fool thinks himself to be wise, but a wise man knows himself to be a fool."

"Better a witty fool, than a foolish wit."

"Alas!" he said. "There is many a man that has more hair than wit."

I laughed and said, "That's the smartest thing you've said." Then I added, "Hell is empty, all the devils' are here."

His smile faded and he seemed to struggle with those words, presumably confused with its content and meaning coming from a child of just fourteen. He focused his attention back on one particular page then brought it tight to his face and moved his head quickly side to side mumbling its content.

"Got it! Come with me!"

We entered through a set of doors leading to a long hallway where kids were wandering aimlessly. Some were locked in mindless conversation. Most were split in their expression. A few seemed excited at the prospect of a new, and hopefully exciting school year, while others showed the slow and anxious manifestation of both panic and sadness that one exhibits when they come to the realization that their rush to the toilet will fall terribly short of its mission.

"Over this way!"

We pushed further down the hallway. Older students were high fiving him and smacking him on the back. He appeared to know everyone. Students, teachers, whoever we passed got a slap or a shake. As we continued, I realized he hadn't told me his name. I yelled through the noise and banter around us.

"What's your name?"

"Casey."

He stopped and rapped on a locker with his knuckles.

"Right here my good fellow." He pointed down the hall. "Your first class is right around that corner."

"Father Casey?"

"Common sense is not so common. What gave it away, the collar?"

"You are just a verse machine aren't you?"

"Is there anyone so wise as to learn by the knowledge of others?"

"It's experience, learn by the experience of others. It's Voltaire."

"Go fuck yourself by Father Casey."

He rapped on the locker again and started away from me. As he did he said, "Your name?"

"Mark."

"Nice to meet you Mark and remember, the first step which one makes in this world, is the one on which depends the rest of our days."

Just like that, he was gone. I didn't see Father Casey again until basketball season rolled around and I went to try out for the team. I stepped into the gym and spotted him immediately. Looking back, that wasn't very hard to do. He was shooting at a side basket and would best be described as wearing clothing you would likely find in a bag marked 'save for salvation army'. He looked ridiculous in all bright, mismatched colors and black high top sneakers. What made things worse, or better, depending on your viewpoint, was how serious his expression was. It was in stark contrast to the outrageous attire that clung tightly to his round frame. He was focused and determined, and seemed unaware of anyone or anything around him. If I didn't know better, I would have fully believed that his next shot would not only win the state championship, but also decide the fate of the entire free world. I walked up behind him and said, "All the world's a stage and we are merely players."

His reply was, "They have their exits and their entrances."

"And one man in his time plays many parts."

He finished with, "His acts being seven ages."

His focus and determination paid off with a shot that found all net. I realized then that I had missed talking to him. The months leading up to that day were filled with the same emotional unrest and nameless anxiety I always felt back then. Truth be told, the few minutes on that first day with him were probably the best I had experienced within the walls of my new surroundings. He took another shot at the basket as he asked, "How are things?"

The ball clanked off the rim.

"Must be the first one was lucky."

"Hey, I'll have you know, I made All-Catholic last year."

To which I offered. "Yeah? Was it a Jewish league?"

He paused, then bowed to me. Sarcastically he said, "Hold up folks. Listen up, we have a comedian in our midst. Was it a Jewish league he says. Too funny. You have a future in comedy son. I'll have you know it was a hardcore group of the Lord's finest."

I said, "I'm sure."

"I do believe I sense some form of mockery in your tone young man."

I slapped the ball from his hands and scored.

"You do. And that sir, is how it's done."

We went on and on like that, not just that day, but for many days to follow. He became my best friend. He would get me out of science class, take me to the movies, to ball-games. We went for French fries and ice cream more times than I could possibly count.

He was more than just a friend though. He became a mentor, an advisor, and an outlet to vent and release whatever was stored in my usually impenetrable, aimless mind. His friendship, and the effect it had on me both mentally and emotionally, freed me to feel and speak things that no therapist, regardless of training or experience, would ever get out of me. Because of our time together, I had begun to see changes in myself. I became more assertive, more open to show more of myself both to others, and, more importantly, to myself.

The great philosopher Aristotle spoke out extensively about friendship. It was said he felt it was of higher value and stature than justice. He stated that friendship was necessary for life, for existence to be of value to mankind, regardless of creed or stature. I would have vehemently argued against that point only months earlier because although I had friendships, they were simply for friendships sake. I neither felt compelled nor obligated to share in this kindred spirit. People, in my thought process, were a source of pain. They were never as they seemed and would show their true color and ultimately, their selfish motivation. I would have reasoned that trust and acceptance within one's own family was all that was necessary. Their love and understanding from my point of view was the true meaning of friendship, and the only type that was crucial in one's life.

That philosophy and the sound structure on which it was based had no bearing or value when it came to Father Casey. It may have seemed to most around us to be an odd relationship to say the least. I was a kid, a freshman in high school, and he was a man of the cloth more than twice my age. I reasoned that he saw in me not a simple child, but rather, someone that although lacking in the maturity age brings, was, in some ways, an old soul. Seasoned and aged not by years, but by experience, both good and bad, but as I assumed he knew, mostly bad.

My parents loved that I was spending so much time with him. They saw his effect on me and witnessed first-hand how his influence was slowly pulling me out the shell of self-reflection and internal brooding that had become my way of life. He wasn't by any stretch of the imagination, your typical priest. He cursed and yelled, and he pointed out and even tried to set me up with the prettiest girls in school. He could break wind with the best of them and wouldn't hesitate to display this talent in even the most public of arenas. Once, at a basketball game we attended, he threatened to "moon" a ref, if he didn't "get his shit together and rub the crap from his eyes." He would later insinuate to that very same ref that lack of breast-feeding was perhaps why he sucked so badly. I believe he saw his need for my friendship too. He didn't really seem to fit in with most of his colleagues. I believed it mostly bordered on a deep level of misunderstanding and confusion for what I thought he was trying to do. I was convinced that he felt, not just with me, but also with other students he befriended that understanding our lives, not just on some superficial, one-dimensional level but rather at its deepest core was a more relevant and substantial way to reach us and help us grow.

He never openly preached religion, nor did he quote gospel or wave the ways and beliefs of the Church in your face in any way. He was far more subtle in that respect. He seemed to try to reach us more through self-reflection and a foundation of trust and awareness, rather than through the moral teachings of any higher power.

He would come to my house often to visit both me, and my parents. There was one such evening that will forever stay with me. It was an evening my father and I discussed years later and at the very same table at which it took place.

Father Casey was coming for dinner before we were going to go to a ballgame so I decided to wait for him on our front porch. It was the dead of winter and it had snowed a few nights earlier. I always loved the house we lived in, especially after a storm. Our landlord had so many different species of animals on the property that an evening on the porch watching chickens or wild turkeys attempting to navigate the fresh snowfall was better than any show broadcasting from our television inside. The moon was full and bright and the air had a crisp, refreshing boldness to it. It was the kind of night that made me think of times that my parents would reminisce about their days and nights growing up in the Midwest during the winter months. There were always tales of ice-skating and snowball fights. My father was even known to shoot baskets after shoveling the driveway in temperatures most people wouldn't think of even stepping outside, never mind engaging in sport. It always made me smile when they would talk of their young love. They met as freshman in high school, married at eighteen, and remained so happily their whole lives. I cherished those accounts of their unconditional commitment and acceptance of one another. It was hard to grasp that at the age I was right at that moment, they were already deeply in love and it would continue through all their years together. Their love story, and the offspring of unquestionable devotion and acceptance of me is what I clung to each day when I woke up. Their relationship gave me hope that I too would someday feel that way with someone in my life. Even at my age, I knew genuine love and approval would be a difficult task for me to conquer. Unconditional trust, would likely amount to a responsibility and commitment I was already too derelict to accept. Nonetheless, I felt good that night. My friend was coming and that was good enough. I can honestly say I was actually happy. I watched Father Casey as he wound down our driveway and closer to me in his big four door sedan and I looked forward to the evening ahead of me. Even before he came to a complete stop, he was waving me toward the car. I stepped down to greet him and heard him say, "Get in quick."

I jumped in and landed on a cardboard box and as I did, he said, "Get up, get up. You're crushing it!"

I lifted myself up off the seat and he grabbed the box from beneath me. He examined it closely before saying anything, but quickly deemed it damage free.

"This is for you."

"What is it?"

"Just open it and see. I wanted to give it to you before we went to the game so you could set it up."

I opened the box and pulled out an alarm clock. I was sure my puzzled expression led to the spirited explanation he gave of the content.

"It's an alarm clock."

"I can see that."

Then I got it. It was the kind you could set to music to wake you up. I had mentioned to him a few weeks earlier how awesome a classmate's alarm clock was because he could wake up to his favorite radio stations and listen to music before he dragged himself out of bed. I told him I thought that would be the coolest way possible to start the day and that if I had one like that, I would never be late for school again. He remembered those words.

"Thank you, thank you so much."

"You're very welcome. Can't have you running late for the school bus anymore now can we?"

I turned it over and over in my hands.

"No, no we can't."

"You can pre-set it for whatever station you like."

"Classic rock it is."

"Then classic rock it shall be."

I sifted through the wrapping and found a sealed card at the bottom.

"What's this?"

"It's something else for you but don't open it just yet okay? Hold onto that for a while. After all, how poor are they who have no patience! What wound did ever heal but by degrees?"

"Othello. Does it have a snooze button?"

"A what?"

"It's this button you can hit and it shuts off the alarm but then it comes back on like ten minutes later I think."

Before he could answer, my mother opened the front door and waved us in. It seems silly now to be have been so happy about an alarm clock but I was. He was always doing things like that. He knew the days I most needed a pass to get out of class, or money for lunch, or just an ear to listen. He seemed in touch with my moods and knew how to bring me out of the bad ones, and as important, how to keep the good ones rolling. He was aware of what that simple offering, a genial gift of an alarm clock of all things would mean to me, so he didn't hesitate to bring me that simple pleasure.

I burst into the kitchen eager to show my folks what he had given me. My mother said, "You didn't have to do that Father."

"Please, it was no trouble at all. He's a wonderful young man."

My father walked in to see what all the commotion was about.

"Look Pops, it's a radio you can wake up to. It plays all your favorite songs."

I quickly ran down the hall to my room, and set it down on the table by my bed. As I did, I could hear my parents talking in the kitchen. My father echoed my mother and said, "You didn't have to do that Father."

"It's no problem, I was just telling Rosemary what a great son you have. He's growing up into an outstanding young man. You should be very proud." My dad said, "We are, and we appreciate you taking him under your wing like you are."

"It's my pleasure really. The kids keep us young don't they?" My mom said, "That they do."

There was a pause in my dad's voice before he said, "How is he doing at school? With the other kids I mean?"

"He's doing just fine. Mark is a sensitive, emotional, wonderful kid. You shouldn't be concerned about him in the least."

I knew my father was then, and had always been worried about me. He was now a trained therapist and I'm sure he saw the warning signs in my behavior. I was withdrawn, quiet, and often indifferent to the world around me. It was such a contrast to his outgoing and gregarious personality, so I knew he struggled with my detached attitude and demeanor.

"He doesn't talk much to us Father." My dad said.

"Don't let that bother you. I have to pull things out of him myself. He's just being a kid is all."

"We really appreciate you spending so much time with him. It means the world to us to have a man like yourself giving so much time to our son."

"Please, it's no trouble at all. It's my pleasure, really."

There was a pause of silence, then I actually heard Father Casey say, "Do you think he can he hear us?"

They were quiet for a moment and then Father Casey said, "He will come around, I'm sure of it. But I will say this, I have been around kids for quite a while now and I've never seen someone at Mark's age have such a bleak, almost tragic outlook on life. Do you know where that comes from?"

My father's tone seemed to imply that he felt threatened by the question. He said, "No, we have no idea."

"I didn't mean anything by that. Please. I'm sorry. You took that the wrong way."

My mother jumped in. "It's fine Father, and we know what you meant."

Father Casey added, "He talks about things you don't often hear from a young man his age is all I meant. Sometimes his thoughts are very profound and worldly, and sometimes they trouble me a great deal."

My mother's voice was changing now. I could hear it clearly in her tone. "Should we be concerned Father?"

"No, I don't think so. I just...I'd like to know how such thoughts can be so precise and so thoroughly cultivated in the mind of essentially, a child."

The room grew quiet again before my mother broke the silence. "Come on, let's eat before everything gets cold."

When I came from my room I could see that my mother's eyes were red and moist. Father Casey attempted to change the atmosphere in the room by saying, "Got the radio all hooked up?"

All I could manage to say was, "Yes."

I was quiet all through dinner as was everyone else. I went from feeling overjoyed at the simple gift my friend had given me and the possibilities the evening brought to just wishing the night was over. I wanted to just go back to my room, close the door and shut everyone, especially Father Casey out of my mind.

I sat quietly, barely touching my food. I wished I hadn't heard the conversation about my behavior. It's not that I didn't think my parents were already contemplating the thoughts they voiced to Father Casey, but to hear them out loud, to get a glimpse inside their anxieties over my detached attitude and daily temperament was especially difficult to hear. Although the conversation was short, it got directly to the point, and was expressed by the people I cared about the most, my parents and my best friend.

My emotions at the dinner table swung wildly in all directions. I was heartbroken that Father Casey viewed me the way he did. It's not that I could blame him. I told him so many of my deepest thoughts. He knew about my most private and protected views and speculations on life, and my place in it. I was also angry. Maybe because I did reveal so much to him. Someone now knew almost everything I knew about myself, and was discussing it openly with my parents. The realization that he was actually exposing or even discussing any of the secrets I had entrusted to him, was yet another saddening emotion spinning inside my head.

Dinner seemed to last forever. I was quiet the whole ride to the game, as was Father Casey. I was sure he was assessing my mood, and perhaps coming to the conclusion that I had heard at least a portion of the conversation between him and my parents. I kept my eyes directed towards the window to avoid even a glance from his direction, and I didn't speak a word before, during, or after the game.

We ended up at a diner, pushing around French fries and avoiding eye contact when he finally broke the silence. "It is a wise Father that knows his own son."

"You're not my Father."

I still wouldn't look up at him. I knew if I did I would burst into tears. He said, "That's right, I'm not. I'm your friend, remember?"

"No, you're not."

I finally did look up at him and I could tell that my words were like a knife to his heart.

"Well, that's a news flash. What happened?"

I focused my eyes back on the table and didn't answer him.

"Can I assume you heard us talking earlier?"

I continued to avoid his stare and instead focused all my attention on the words he had spoken earlier in my parents' kitchen.

"He who has injured thee-"

I could feel the anger rush to my face. "Please, just shut the fuck up. Stop quoting Shakespeare. You sound like such a pompous asshole."

The entire restaurant stopped to look and listen in our direction. I'm sure the realization that those words came from a child, and were directed towards a man of the cloth humored some, and disgusted others. I didn't care either way. I knew I was losing control, and that I was, in a way, outside my own body and watching the moment unfold much like the people around us. I had always focused my attention on blending into any situation, hoping to be invisible and as inconspicuous as possible, but that was not the image I was portraying as I stood up to face him. It didn't matter that I was being watched or making a scene. What mattered is what happened, and how it made me feel about him, and about everything that I valued. It was obvious that he didn't share my disinterest in the attention we were receiving. He looked around us, then back to me and gently grabbed my hand and said, "Please sit down. You're making too much out of this." I pulled away from him. I couldn't hold back the tears anymore and I blurted out, "I did never know so full a voice issue from so empty a heart, but the saying is true. The empty vessel makes the greatest sound."

He grabbed my arm again, and again pleaded for me to sit and calm down. I jerked away from his grasp. I must have fallen through some

37

crack in my conscious mind because I started shouting, "I FUCKING HATE YOU DO YOU HEAR ME!"

I backed away as he stood up but everything was coming out of me. I continued to shout and curse at him as I knocked everything from our table onto the floor. Looking back at that night, I'm convinced it wasn't specifically the words that passed between him and my parents that enraged me, it was what it represented to me. I felt as if the one true person in my life outside of my family, the person who I looked up to for friendship, guidance and unconditional support, betrayed my trust.

I ran out the door and he followed right behind me. He grabbed my arm and spun me around to face him. "Listen to me Mark, would you please just give me a chance here?"

I pulled away from him. "NO!"

I started walking away from him and I could see that everyone from inside the restaurant was starting to come outside so that they could continue to watch the commotion. He saw them as well, and seemed visibly uncomfortable that we had an audience around us. He took a few steps towards me and lowered his voice.

"Please son, just give me a chance. Don't I deserve that much?"

I stopped without turning around to look at him. I was so exhausted at that point and I realized that I had nowhere to go, and nowhere to hide.

"Come on Mark, just get in the car. Okay?"

I relented, but I still hadn't looked at him. When I finally did, I could see he was crying. He turned to the people gathering around the entrance and said, "Show's over folks."

We drove in silence until we reached the high school parking lot. He shut off the ignition and rubbed his face in his hands. Maybe he was thinking of the right words to say, or the proper action to take to make things better. I couldn't imagine any words in any language that would make that possible.

"I wasn't trying to hurt you Mark. I was trying to explain to your parents that they need to have patience-"

"Why, because you think I'm crazy? Because you think I belong in some looney bin strapped to a bed?"

"Is that what you think you heard? I never said anything like that."

"You might as well have. You talked to them about stuff you swore was only between us. I trusted you."

"And you still can Mark. You can trust me." With those words, his hand fell to my knee.

As much as I cherished our friendship and couldn't wait to see him every day, there had been times that he did things that made me uncomfortable. He had pushed, almost outright forced me to ask this girl from my English class to the freshman dance. I finally did, and to my amazement, she said yes. She would eventually turn out to be my very first true kiss. A memory that made me smile for a week, and still does to this day. He asked me about it but I wouldn't tell him and that made him extremely angry. He pestered and annoyed me until I finally gave in and described a more dramatic and outlandish version than what really occurred. The fact that he clung to every word so intently, seemed odd to say the least.

He would also tell me of his sexual experiences prior to committing to the priesthood. Sometimes, they were detailed to such a degree that I believed they would make even the most hardened and experienced adult blush. To a fourteen year old boy, they were just thoroughly grotesque. When he would share them, he looked to be gauging my reaction to his words, watching for my response or opinion on the matter.

Also, every time I got out of his car he would say "I love you." It came out unlike the way that a parent or family member would say it and it always sent an uneasiness throughout my body, but I always, just let it go. He was after all, my best friend and he had accepted my quirks and deficiencies, so the least I could do was offer the same consideration and approval.

One thing he did though, that I constantly struggled to overcome and had many times tried to find the proper words and mindset to discuss with him, was when we were driving he would put his hand on my knee and rub it. I would eventually push it away, giving whatever excuse came to mind, but it always made me extremely uncomfortable. He would either tease me about it, or just get angry, then he would usually grow quiet and withdrawn at what he perceived as some form of rejection of his love for me. The nature of that discomfort paled in comparison to the fear I felt as we sat alone in his car. His hand wasn't resting on my knee. It was now further up my thigh, with his fingers drawing circles and designs across my pant leg.

"I know you're upset with me Mark, but you shouldn't be. I would never intentionally due anything to hurt you."

He moved his hand further up, still weaving spirals across my thigh.

"Do you know why we are such good friends Mark?"

My world was spinning fast now, but his words seemed warped and slow. His face had become like an image in a broken mirror. His expression, one that was always so jovial and pleasing, now seemed menacing and cruel. Past experience meant I understood the consequences. It was the second time in my life I had seen that face on an adult.

"Answer me Mark. Do you know why we are so close? Do you? Do you know why I know your thoughts? What's going on inside that head of yours?"

He slid his hand further into my groin, and with each passing, he would manipulate and finger my testicles.

"It's because I understand you. We are the same you and I. When I was your age I thought much like you do now. The same thoughts and fears. The same desires. Your thoughts are my thoughts. Your dreams are my dreams. You don't ever have to worry or be afraid with me do you understand that?"

I sat frozen and rigid while he groped and caressed me.

"Just relax Mark. You know I would never hurt you. You know that right Mark?"

He quickly changed hands and turned my head towards him. I pushed away from him, but his lips still met mine.

I'm not sure to this day how it happened, whether it was a fortunate circumstance, or a hidden strength I was not aware I possessed, but I pushed him hard in the face and spilled out of the car.

I got up quickly and heard these words before I took off running.

"You misunderstood me Mark." He called out.

What he said next remains with me to this day. Both the words and the timbre in which they were spoken, came not from a friend or trusted companion, but rather from some morose beast, a sinister monster who invaded my life, and my mind. He said, "Tell anyone and I will deny it. Tell anyone and you'll regret it."

I continued running, not even aware of my direction or surroundings. I knew then, regardless of how fast I ran or how far, I would never erase the memories of that night. My mind kept spinning. Can I tell my parents? Should I tell my parents? Should I go to the police or the school? One thought though, that was steady and clear in my head was, how had things gone so wrong so fast? How had my friend and confidant, the person whom my whole life revolved around, turn so quickly into the scheming, sickening predator of that evening? The truth was there with me, but I tried hard to push away. He wasn't my friend or my confidant after all. He was a manipulator. An imposter. A fraud. A monster focused solely on his needs and desires and highly skilled on how to best obtain them. The desperation he showed that night, and the risk he took exposed to me that he knew his calculated plans for me were beginning to crack. He knew all the weeks and months of preparation were falling short of their intended target.

I pretended to be sick the rest of that week, and then, when I ran out of excuses I made my way back to the bus stop, and back to school. I didn't see him for weeks, and when I did, he acted as if what happened was just a minor event. If anything, he seemed angry with me that things happened as they did. Like I was the cause of the position our friendship was now in, and that my actions, not his, were the reason for our lost relationship.

For the rest of the school year and through the summer that followed, I continued with what I did best. I buried everything. Every thought, every emotion even remotely tied to him, I tucked far away, somewhere deep within me and into a place that no one could ever enter. I knew that place within myself well. It was becoming a much bigger part of me, and how I viewed both myself, my life, and my place in it. What wasn't lost on me, is that place, and the space and the effort required to keep it hidden and secret from the outside world, was growing larger and more difficult to live with each passing day.

That being said, I started my sophomore year with a new resolve to not just get through, but to thrive in my life. I worked hard with my grades and spent my days after school working towards the upcoming basketball season. All things seemed to be heading away from the past, away from what happened, and towards a bright, maybe even optimistic future. That is, until I saw him.

He was leaning against a bike rack with his leg up and one arm resting on his knee. He was wearing shorts despite the cool fall weather and his eyes were locked intently on a young man. Skinny and clearly nervous, he looked both uncomfortable and yet forever grateful for the attention he was receiving from such a prestigious faculty member. There was no doubt in my mind he was a freshman, and also no question as to where the conversation was headed. I was too far from range to hear the dialogue, but no matter, I had heard it all just a year prior. His body language was both charismatic and enticing. He knew what he was doing, and he knew just how to do it. I felt for that kid. He was a son, a nephew, perhaps someone's brother. What he was soon to be without question, was a victim. I walked away and put the entire scene with him out of my mind. Or tried to anyway. The rest of the afternoon I did all the things needed to complete a day in high school. I went to class, I interacted with other students, and I pushed forward, attempting to block out what I had seen earlier.

As each hour passed though, I knew I was losing the battle. I'm not sure why on that particular day seeing him affected me the way it did. I suppose it could have been because he was a consistent poison, hopelessly trapped in my mind. He was there with me constantly. Never leaving, never giving me peace.

Then it happened. The bell rang sounding the end of the day, and also, the end of my time in high school. At least the one that had Father Casey lurking and working in its halls.

I walked to the building I knew housed the faculty and the administration. I tossed a rock back and forth between my hands while I looked up at the third story window I believed to belong to the principal, Sister Maria. My uncertainty was quickly dismissed when she poked her head outside, perhaps gauging the weather, or maybe to look out over the school grounds under her rule before returning to her office and shutting the window and blinds behind her. A girl from my science class walked up from behind and started to speak to me but quieted quickly when she looked into my eyes. I'm not sure what she saw, or how I appeared to her, but the best explanation I can give was, she looked mortified.

I felt strangely calm, almost relaxed, despite knowing what I was about to do. Maybe it was because I knew it would all finally be over.

Weary and seeming uncertain, she spoke quietly. "What are you doing with the rock Mark?"

My response was to throw one up toward Sister Maria's window but I missed badly.

"Are you crazy? Do you know whose window that is?"

Kids started gathering around us when they realized what was happening. I still felt so composed and at ease, not the least bit concerned or worried about my actions, or the consequences that were sure to follow.

I threw another rock and again I missed. The crowd was larger now, and I was aware of the mumblings around me. Despite my almost serene nature, I was aware that I was having a severe meltdown. The girl tried to grab my shoulder before my third toss but it had already found its target. The kids all erupted with a yell of approval, then quickly scattered knowing what was coming next. I didn't move and I didn't react to the girl trying to pull me away. The attention I sought for my actions didn't keep me waiting long. The window rolled up and out of it appeared Sister Maria. She didn't say anything at first, perhaps assessing what had just occurred and how to best sort out its origin. When she saw me, she summoned me up to her office with the crook of her finger.

She was surprisingly calm despite the cool air blowing through her office and the bits of glass scattered about on the floor. Maybe she was too stunned to yell, or maybe she was curious at how at ease I appeared despite the nature of my actions. She seemed to be weighing all of that, and sizing me up before she sat down and instructed me to do the same. I ignored her and walked over to the window and looked down at the very spot I stood just minutes earlier. Pieces of glass had landed on the sill outside and small fragments made it down to the pavement below. The girl from my science class was still standing there. I wasn't sure why, we weren't particularly close. I suppose she needed some explanation, some answers to what she had just observed.

From behind me I heard, "Why?"

I didn't answer. The coolness coming through the window was a welcome relief from the heat and suffocation surrounding the room. She kept her voice low and soothing as she spoke. "You're Mark, right?"

Again I kept my gaze out the window, declining to speak.

"I'm going to have to call your parents. What will they think?"

I broke my silence. "They won't think. My mom will cry and my dad will kill me."

"Maybe if you just told me-"

I picked up a paperweight bearing her name and slapped it into the palm of my hand and cut off her words. "I'll do it again."

I moved away from the window and toward the one on my right. She said again, "Why Mark?"

I parted the blinds and again looked out. The girl was gone now. Probably off somewhere trying to make sense of, or perhaps forget the event she just witnessed. The calm, almost tranquil feeling I possessed that morning quickly faded with Sister Maria's next words. "I see you with Father Casey all the time am I right? What do you think he'll say?"

"Fuck him."

"Watch your choice of words young man."

I didn't respond. She grew quiet for a moment. Unsure I suppose, how to continue. When she spoke again, the simple sentence she expressed would leave her with no choice but to expel me from her school. That suited me just fine.

She said, "Is this about him?"

I slammed the paperweight through the window, and calmly walked to the next one and did the same. I can only imagine what I must have looked like standing there with her, just the two of us, alone in her office, glass everywhere, and essentially a weapon in my right hand.

"Mark, answer me. Is this about him? Is there an issue with Father Casey I should know about? Mark, is there?"

I dropped the paperweight on her desk and continued to stare out the window. I watched the cars on Broad Street drive by. People on their way to everywhere and nowhere seeming oblivious to the monsters that lurk all around us in this world and do their very best to keep their identity concealed from view.

"I can help you Mark."

For the first time I turned to face her and said, "There is no helping me Sister. Please call my parents."

I walked passed her and out the door toward the street.

A week later I was enrolled at the public school that educated the kids from my hometown. My father tried to get me into some of the other catholic schools in the area, but once they learned of what happened, there were no takers.

It is not without exaggeration that my father, with the exception of the most basic dialogue people that live under the same roof must communicate to each other on a daily basis, did not speak to me for three months. Even when I made the basketball team later that fall at my new school, he went to every game, but would leave before I came out of the locker room when it was over.

The following year a close friend who was a priest came to him and confided that Father Casey was rumored to have been involved in an inappropriate manner with some students and perhaps that was the cause at least in part, for what happened at the high school.

That day when he came home, he walked into the kitchen where I was sitting and it was clear in his eyes that he had not just been crying, but instead, openly sobbing. He sat down next to me, his hands trembling, and asked me if it was true about Father Casey. When I told him, he cried like a child. His tears falling on the same table where they had shared so many meals and impassioned dialogue together. To this day, I wonder what hurt him more. What happened to me and the reality that he didn't recognize it, or the fact that I couldn't come to him and share what had occurred with Father Casey. I knew he felt he was somehow to blame for what had happened, but he was simply far too good of a man to understand and grasp that type of evil in another human being.

Chapter 5

I awoke on my third day in seclusion to the sounds of screams and cries. The room was damp and cold and had the feel of being hidden within the walls of some desolate cave. The cries echoed with the same pitch and duration over and over again.

The second sound I heard was made by a tray being slipped through the door slot. From behind the door I heard, "Breakfast."

I waited for the sound of footsteps to fade down the hall but the echo never came. A moment passed and fear crept over me. I knew someone was standing outside the door and my boundless imagination started running into overdrive. My fears turned to joy when I heard these words whispered through the door. "The docs' got your letter."

"Thank you."

Then he was gone.

I have tried, and I'm sure failed miserably throughout the years, to adequately express what time is like in seclusion. Time, even in our normal lives can have periods that pass by slowly and leave us with a sense of wanting more, of feeling that things are somehow unfinished or incomplete. We fail to appreciate the simple gifts that surround us and often analyze and even criticize their lack of substance and adventure. The world is often boring and bland when seen through the eyes of most people. There is little recognition given to what we have. The focus more often, is on what we don't have and what we are convinced we must obtain. I admit, I have also been guilty of this crime of disregard for life. I too, have failed to pay the proper respect to the simple, yet precious moments that our 'ordinary' life provides us.

I hoped, as I sat on the edge of my bed doing my best not to gag on my prison issue breakfast, that no matter what the future held for me, those precious moments would be, perhaps not lived in a state of bliss as one would hope, but at least would receive the recognition so richly deserved.

I found out later in my stay that some individuals, whether deemed too violent or just simply too unstable to co-exist with others, did their entire sentence in the isolation unit. I can't imagine nor would I care to let my mind entertain the concept of it being a permanent residence. When the guard told me to consider doing my entire stay down there, I admit that I contemplated the idea at first, and its significance to my health and safety. But just days into my time there, I knew the Devil and a band of his finest couldn't keep me down there. I was terrified of the unknown that awaited me upstairs, and having never been in jail my only reference points came from television and movies. But I knew if I didn't leave there soon I would most surely lose what was left of my sanity. I went in a depressed, suicidal twenty-five year old man, if my time down in isolation were to last much longer, twenty five would be the best I could do.

I fully understood why you were not allowed to have anything down in there. Everything was bolted steel and smooth to the touch for a reason. The risk the guard took even giving me the pencil was far clearer to me now. Just hours had passed from that moment, and I'm sure, if it were now in my possession, I may have actually found a way for it to serve a darker purpose. The concept of accepting and appreciating the simple pleasures in life simply didn't exist down there. There was only existence itself, and that was all.

I passed the day away doing push-ups and counting how many times I walked from one end of my cell to the other. I did my best to avoid thoughts of my family and if a thought were to find its way to the front of my mind, I quickly beat it back. I knew I needed to start accepting the realization that I might be in prison for a long time. That concept, and its consequences were of little real concern to me though. I knew I could never survive in there, and I knew even if by some bizarre and fortunate course of events I did survive, what would I be? I was already going in a lost, depressed soul. Were years in prison going to rectify that reality?

Like the others, the day moved with minutes feeling like hours, and hours seeming to last a full season. I finally laid my head down to hopefully sleep and dream for a better day.

As I drifted off, I thought of other times in my life that felt like a prison sentence. Not in terms of deprived freedom, but still a punishment, a handed down verdict of confinement all its own.

I also reflected on stretches of time in my life, if guided just slightly down a different path, perhaps if their direction was just skewed ever so slightly, maybe a different conclusion may have found its way to me.

Chapter 6

(BOSTON, 1986)

My source of inhabitance during the winter of 1986 actually consisted of two residences, if you could call them that. Some nights I would sneak into my former college and sleep on a chair in a closet meant to hold suitcases and other amenities.

I was fortunate that the closet was meant to be sized and equipped enough to comfortably suit six residents and their belongings. That meant that a recliner, while not able to realize its full extension capabilities, still fit well enough alongside some milk crates, a few magazines, and a small television.

It was a far cry from the home from which I rested my head just months earlier. Prior to my then current residence in a dorm room closet, I lived and even thrived at another school nearby. The months that followed me from that state of being to where I was I currently located, were a steady and swift decline into a period of darkness and a time in my life where to this day, I have no idea how I survived.

My former roommates, whether out of loyalty to me, or more likely, because of a sense of compassion and empathy, initially aided me on most occasions.

On the evenings when I couldn't get inside the dorm, my second choice of residence was outside. I would sleep wherever I found a spot to close my eyes. This usually led me to a bench on campus or the park nearby. I don't know why I chose to live this way, or what is even more puzzling to me is why it didn't seem abnormal or odd in the least bit way.

I assume this was a complete state of denial. I suppose too, if my mind had been clean of the large quantity of drugs and alcohol I was indulging myself with, the prospect of facing my father and seeing the disappointment in his eyes at the poor choices I had made, was not an exchange I cared to face any time in my near future. So denial would once again, win out.

The opening day of classes that September I went to my first class, sat down and just as quickly got up and walked out of the room. That was the last time I set foot inside the school hallways, at least as a student anyway. I kept up the pretext throughout most of the first semester and right through the Thanksgiving holiday that I was a willful, even eager student. I never led on to anyone that I was no longer attending classes, even my roommates were unaware of my deception. It wasn't until I returned after the winter holidays that my counterfeit life was forced to show its true face. That's when living inside a closet became my reality.

The amount of marijuana and alcohol I was consuming, even for me, was clearly getting out of hand, and beyond my control.

It was easy to convince myself and those around me that it was normal and acceptable to consume the quantities I did, and to portray it as almost a noble deed. Something to be proud of and to strive for. That was all manipulation of course, not really meant to fool those around me, but more so, to deceive my own self.

The days were designed strictly for sleeping and eating. I didn't work so finding alternate means of survival was a consuming process. The nights were solely intended for enough consumption to all but guarantee slipping into a booze and weed filled comatose state. It seemed obvious and certainly appropriate that the best means to serve both my drug and alcohol requirements as well as a need for cash, was to sell drugs myself. It seemed, from all angles to be the perfect plan to allow myself, and my lifestyle to continue without delay or interruption. What was a sound plan, at least on the surface, and one that appeared to be relatively harmless and void of any real grave consequences, would turn out to be anything but innocent in nature. It would set in motion a direction in my life I wished I could have simply passed on, just let it go right on by. But unfortunately, I didn't.

When I returned to school after the winter break I was completely out of control. I made it a point to keep things together for my folks during the holidays, so when I got back into my swing at school, I went in full force.

During the second week, I was nearly asleep in my chair when I heard the voices of my room-mates and some other students from the dorm right outside the door. I'm sure they thought I was unconscious because they did little to conceal what they were thinking. One of them lived next door. Her name was Kelly. She was one of those perfect specimens who possessed both beauty and intelligence, but more, she was blessed with the gift of making you feel somehow better about yourself just by being in her presence. A bright smile, a loud boisterous laugh, and a warmth that attracted most everyone she encountered.

I knew I was in no condition to ever see her as anything more than a friend, but there were times I felt changing my current lifestyle, and having her in my future, were worth a complete renovation of my existence.

I heard her voice first through the door, followed by Steve and Mike who went to high school together and followed their friendship to the University. They seemed to have been pressed up against the door trying to listen, to what I wasn't sure. I had a joint in between my fingers and was rather enjoying this little sideshow when I heard Kelly say, "Ssshh."

I envisioned her ear pinned to the other side of the door. I also imagined her pulling back her blonde hair and listening intently for any sound. I so loved that she cared about me. She saw only the good in everyone, especially it seemed, when it came to me.

"Do you think he's alive?" That was Steve's contribution.

"He must be, I can smell the weed." Mike said.

"Doesn't mean he's not going to burn the place down."

I could picture Kelly punching him in the stomach when I heard her say, "You guys are assholes. Remind me to never look to you when I'm down."

"Down? Really? He's fucking wasted Kelly. Every single fucking night. It's insane."

Steve agreed and said, "He's right Kelly. Are you're kidding me? You're defending him? Come on. The guy is living inside a fucking closet. A fucking closet for Christ-sake. Come on Kelly, that's not completely nuts to you?"

She was quiet at first, and I couldn't blame her. There wasn't much defense for the case they were building. And they were right. It was fucked up to be living in a closet. And they were also correct in their assumption that I presented a potential danger to them.

One night, just a week earlier, I came in and turned on my television and settled in for a night of fuzzy screened, late night entertainment. Not long after getting comfortable, and soon after nodding off, I was dousing my blanket with a beer. I had actually burned through the fabric and set fire to the chair while smoking a joint. A little longer, a little more blacked out, and the whole place may have gone up in flames.

Finally I heard Kelly again. "I'll talk to him."

Steve said, "And say what?"

"Just stop okay? I'll take care of it. You guys can go now."

I knew I was completely stoned out of my mind, but I was pretty sure she was crying when she said, "He just doesn't realize-"

Mike cut her off. "What? That he's whacked out of his mind? This is not normal or acceptable behavior Kelly. No rational human being lives this way. I'm sorry, but he's got to go. You're right. You do have to talk to him. You need to tell him to leave." Steve spoke softly and added, "We love the guy too but, Mike's right. This is nuts. Someone needs to contact his family."

I heard Kelly twist the door handle. "Just go."

I didn't open my eyes when she quietly squeezed into the room. Nor did I acknowledge her hand gently rubbing my arm or her soft voice talking quietly and sweetly into my ear. What I did do is lay still and fully enjoy, even through my warped and altered state, her unconditional concern and care for me. She stayed with me, stroking my hand and face at least until I passed out.

53

I woke the next morning consumed with the knowledge that I knew I had to leave soon. This existence couldn't go on indefinitely, but, where was I going to go? Home was not an option, at least not in my twisted vision of things and I had no source of steady income, a legal one anyway in which to support myself, so where could I possibly go?

The days continued as they had been except I kept myself out of the dorm as much as possible, and started moving with a different crowd.

Jake, a friend from my first day on campus, had also grown tired of me and my abnormal approach to everyday life, and also joined the revolution to extradite me from the lives of the others in the dorm.

One night though, in an effort to soften his stance on me and my living arrangement I convinced him that we should hang out together. It was a Friday and I had gotten paid for an eighth of weed with a few blotters of acid. I nagged him to drop with me and he finally relented. We decided to do what we thought was the wise thing and only take a half blotter each, and that we did.

The night was incredible. We got served alcohol at a club despite being under age, we danced and met girls from all over the city, and we smoked weed in the bathroom with women twice our age who were willing to exchange sex for a few hits from a joint. We had the time of our lives.

We staggered around town and every situation, every encounter seemed to go our way. Nothing could go wrong, and nothing did. The town, and the night were ours to be had, and have it we did.

The following week, all we could talk about to anyone who would listen, was about the tales of our adventure that night. The places we went, the women we met. We held nothing back. It felt good to brag and feel a part of something, even if it was just an acid induced night of stupidity.

We decided the following Friday that we would take what we had experienced that night, and take it to a new level. Several other students decided to join the festivities. The logic agreed upon within the group was, if a half of a blotter caused such an arousing night of pleasure and celebration, could you imagine what a full blotter would do?

We started the evening mellow and low key, with the only thing on the menu to start being beer and weed. Later, when it seemed as if the big night was going to go bust and everyone was settling in to their own zoned out fantasies, someone spoke up. I didn't know who it was, but I clearly remember the words spoken. "Who's ready?"

We all dropped our equal portion and set out for what was sure to be the greatest night of our lives. Better, more exciting, and filled with stories and accounts both true and embellished. We were young and felt the night was fit for kings, and we were more than eager to fill the role.

The night started much the same as the week before. We found a club to serve us and I danced in front of hundreds of colorful fish to the sounds of music so loud, I imagined it to resemble a handgun being shot off somewhere inside my skull.

Sadly, that sensation was the highlight of my night. To say things went down in a fast and equally disturbing direction is a subtle way to say I was fucked.

By the time we made it to Faneuil Hall, I was a complete mess. In and out of consciousness and reality, I stumbled around having no idea where I was. If someone had approached me, I was sure I couldn't have spoken a complete sentence or even stated my own name. My mind was a melting pot of mush. The buildings ebbed and flowed, and the streets were bubbling and crumbling all around me. I kept shaking my head, trying to clear the fog and bring everything back into focus but it didn't work. I had come loose from my group and felt even more disoriented. My head kept shooting up and out and sideways as I stumbled in a different direction each step I took. I knew I was walking into people and I remember staggering and swinging my arms wildly. Everything grew wide then narrow. Everything swayed and collapsed. People. Doors. Benches. Trees. They were like liquid but with a silvery substance and shape. I started to shout and confront people passing by me, and I cursed at them for making their faces change in appearance and texture. Eyes were black or colorless. Lips were bright red and moved in slow motion and spoke words I couldn't understand. I swung viciously at what I saw, and also, at what I couldn't see.

I'm not sure how long this lasted, but I eventually found myself trying to wrestle away from someone's grip but instead being lifted and carried away. Somewhere, in my drug soaked brain I came to the conclusion it was the police and I was going to be arrested. In hindsight, that wouldn't have been the worst of conclusions I could have encountered that night.

I couldn't bring my eyes to focus, but my mind was lucid enough to contemplate the reality that if the individual dragging me was the police, they were leading me away from society, and into a park.

I tried speaking but the words wouldn't form. I knew, or believed so anyway, what I wanted to say, but the translation wasn't to be made. I numbly wondered why whoever was carrying me wasn't speaking. When they laid me down on a bench and started rooting through my pockets, I understood why. I was being robbed. I probably had ten dollars total in my possession, but I had left the dorm with at least an ounce of weed tucked into my jacket.

Some dirt bag scavenged through my pockets and took everything I had, which seemed an appropriate punishment for being such a drunken, drugged out waste. The problem with this painful turn of events was not the loss of some recreational material, it was the awful truth that it wasn't mine to possess or to lose. It was intended first for disbursement, then profit for someone other than myself.

There were two individuals I had an arrangement with pertaining to the handling and allocation of their property. One was a dorm student living on the same floor as me. He didn't care if I pinched from his bags and overcharged his clientele, as long as he got his money. It was simply a way to pad his pocket between care packages from home.

The other individual whose merchandise I lost that evening, did not offer the same laid back approach. He did not see it as seed money for beer parties or Celtic tickets on a Friday night. It was his livelihood.

It paid his bills, his alimony, and I'm sure fed his habit for a substance a bit more substantial than weed. His beliefs about his 'business' as he put were based on law. His law. He was an ex-con on parole for some 'trumped up bullshit' he called it. Although we spoke every day, and his existence in my life had become substantial, I didn't much care for him. What I did feel for him, was an undeniable fear and an abundance of suppressed loathing.

We met on the subway. As it turned out, we were both headed to a frat party at a nearby University. I was on my way at the request of an acquaintance for a night of excessive alcohol and overall indulgence while he on the other hand, was en-route for the soul purpose of financial gain. He introduced himself as Ronnie, and we initially hit it off. He had an easy manner, and a laid back attitude that I liked. The fact that he exposed his coat pocket and displayed a zip-lock bag of what appeared to be some of the finest green weed I had ever seen didn't lower my opinion of him much either.

We would glance around, then take quick hits off a joint as we watched the stops pass us by. He said he was once a Harvard student but had to drop out do to hardship. I knew that was complete and utter bullshit. Not to say he didn't possess the charm and charisma to pull that off on an unsuspecting sorority girl, but when the topic of the SAT's came up, he said they were optional at his high school. "Not a mandatory doctrine" is what he said. I wasn't sure what doctrine he was speaking of, but yeah, I'd heard Harvard didn't much care about GPA's and diplomas either. Grades? Nah, not that important to the staff and faculty at an Ivy League school I'm sure. Regardless, who cared? He had weed and he seemed harmless.

We spent the evening getting wasted and hitting on rich society girls. He had a way with women and I was impressed with how skilled he was at talking them up. He would look so pensive and sincere as they would discuss their majors at school, and their projected career paths once they graduated. He would elude to his brief tenure at Harvard but would become vague if the name of a particular student or faculty member came up. He owned the place though I must admit. Inevitably, every girl he spoke to ended up in his lap, laughing and pretending to fend off his advances. He offered not the gift of language per say, but the smooth and easy banter that they seemed to love whispered in their ear. He carried on that way all night. He worked the room like a veteran emcee. If I didn't know better, I would have thought it was a party he was hosting within his own home.

Much later in the evening, it was obvious he decided it was time to do business. I guess he felt he had laid the foundation and could now charm and manipulate his way into their pockets. It could have been not only the large quantity of alcohol I ingested, but also the variety that threw off my assessment, but his easy smile and awe shucks demeanor had turned into a cold, no nonsense posture. He was doing business, and I would later learn another of his mantras that evening. "Time for play, time for business. When money is at stake, there ain't no play." That was his motto.

He sold bags of different proportions, and varied grades of product to anyone willing to open their wallets. He stood behind a small table and distributed his merchandise much the same as the guy behind the counter at the local pizza parlor or the ice cream truck that cruises through the neighborhood blaring ridiculous circus music.

His true personality presented itself when one unfortunate soul reached over and grabbed a bag from out of his hand. The slap he received to his face was not so much the kind meant to knock a man cold or senseless, but rather to show who was boss and that respect was warranted and would be granted or more affliction would surely follow.

"You just grab shit? Is that how it is? No askin' or nothing?"

His demeanor had completely changed now. He transformed from exhibiting a clean cut, almost wholesome persona, to that of some malevolent street thug. The free and easy smile was replaced with a threatening, and somehow revolting image. He wasn't a particularly big guy, and at first sight you wouldn't think much of his appearance in regards to strength or toughness, but right then, he seemed larger and meaner than any monster anyone could conjure up in their mind. All over someone touching a bag of his weed.

Just as quickly as his venomous demeanor erupted, it was gone. Back was the pleasant, fatuous grin.

"I'm sorry man. Did I hurt you? I'm such an asshole. You alright?"

And just like that, he was back in their good graces. Humble and self-effacing. He was quick to sample his stash with everyone to ease the moment, and sold out before the night was over.

It had to be close to dawn before we left the party. Feeling so good about his financial gains from the evening, and not wanting to wait around for the subway, he offered to pay for a cab.

"My treat." Were his words as he wrapped an arm around me and guided us to the outside world. We walked out laughing and joking, like we were lifelong buddies. I was so shit-faced and exhausted, I was more apt to just lay down at the party and sleep it off, but he insisted.

The whole ride back, he never stopped talking. I had no idea where he got the energy. He drank and smoked as much as I did, and it was all I could do to formulate a complete and coherent sentence, yet he was rattling off information about buildings and street signs and anything that appeared within his line of sight. His spirit and endurance were a complete mystery to me until I heard these words. "Try some of this."

He checked the driver in the mirror, then pulled out a little black box and a small plastic straw.

"No thanks man, I'll pass."

"You sure? This wasn't for the general population back there. This is my secret ingredient. Keep you wired and fired all day and all night long my friend."

"I can see that."

"Damn straight."

He peaked out the window and looked up and down the street, both in front and behind us.

"Last chance. You sure?"

I waved him off.

"I'm good, thanks."

"Well, alright. Don't say I didn't offer."

He took a long pull with the straw then smacked the seat in front of us and instructed the driver to pull over.

"Hey Mohammed, this is good right here. Stop, stop, stop. Christ, what are you a fucking douchebag?"

The driver ignored him and stopped the cab. Then he said in his best broken English, "That will be eight dollars please sir."

"Eight fucking dollars? Jesus Christ, we just drove down the street for fucks sake. Are you trying to rip me off you fucking piece of shit, huh? Are you?"

Things were rapidly getting out of hand. The Hyde side of Ronnie was showing its ugly head again. I said, "I got a few bucks dude. We'll split it. Come on."

"No, no that's not my fucking point here Mark."

"Look, you said you were going to catch the cab didn't you? Here, I'll chip in. Four bucks each, five with tip."

He looked at me, clearly seeing two heads.

"Tip? You think I'm tipping this fucking sand nigger? Are you as crazy as he is?"

The driver, to his credit stayed calm and tried to keep the situation from escalating. He seemed to be experienced in this practice, like it was almost a daily ritual for him. I'm sure being a foreigner in a strange city in a far-away country could not have made for an easy everyday life, and he certainly didn't need the likes of Ronnie first thing in his day. Unfortunately, that's just what was on his calendar that fine morning.

"Please sir, I don't want any trouble. Eight dollars please. That is all I'm asking."

"That's all he's asking. Do you believe this shit?"

He started mocking him and spoke in a weak imitation of his accent. "Please sir. Eight dollars sir. I'm just a raghead sir. Please sir."

The driver turned back around and grew quiet. I'm sure taunts about his ethnicity were not new to him, but I don't think that was the reason for his silence. He had seen the look in Ronnie's eyes, the rage and hostility in his expression, and understood what that most often led to. Ronnie smacked my arm and said, "Did you just hear that?"

The driver stared motionless and straight ahead.

"I didn't hear anything Ronnie."

I started to count out ten singles when he shoved them back towards my pocket and said to the driver, "Did you just say something? Huh? You- turn around and look at me."

As he did, Ronnie slapped him hard in the face, then once again. The driver spun away from him towards his window and spoke words I could not understand. I grabbed Ronnie, who was now trying to reach into the front seat and I said to him, "Come on man, let's just go."

He swung wildly hitting the driver across the shoulder and arms. I pushed hard towards Ronnie's window and found the door handle. The door swung open and we both spilled out onto the street. Ronnie stood and started kicking the side of the cab and punching the windows.

"Go back to your fucking sandbox asshole!"

Ronnie slammed on the hood and continued his verbal assault, then stepped away and howled loudly into the early morning sky like a wild animal after a satisfying kill. I stood by the window and motioned the driver to roll it down. He seemed unsure that was a wise choice but must have decided that I was of no threat to him because the window slowly came down and I handed him the crumpled bills.

"I'm sorry." I said.

Those words were in no way befitting the scope of apology necessary to atone for the violent mistreatment he endured that morning, but that was all I had.

I shook hands with Ronnie and had no intentions of ever seeing or speaking to him again, so when I stepped outside the dorm a week later and nearly tripped over him sitting on the steps, I wanted to simply turn around and go back inside, but it was too late.

"Hey Buddy."

The radiant, almost angelic smile was on full display, but he also looked exhausted and unkempt. His clothes appeared slept in and he was unshaven and his face had a greasy shine to it. I tried my best to not show my perception of his appearance and said to him, "Hey man, how have you been?"

Even the smile he projected, the one that wooed and entranced all the girls from the party, looked forced and worn.

"I'm just fucking peachy. You?"

"Hanging in there. You know how it is."

"Yes I do, yes I do." He pulled out a cigarette and lit up while he scanned the streets trying it seemed, to find the proper words. He started with, "You got a minute?"

"Actually, I don't. I was just about-"

"Come on Dude, five minutes. Trust me, you're gonna want to hear this."

As he spoke those words, and as much as I had seen what I believed to be the entire scope of his erratic and unpredictable personality, he was exposing a new and in some ways more disturbing side to himself.

He was now showing all the signs of being the calculating and conniving con man he had already displayed, but now it seemed, he was seeking and somehow finding a new level.

We walked a bit, him smoking and glancing around nervously, and me wondering how I was going to quietly and without provocation, end both the conversation that was initiating between us, and the relationship all together. He stopped and glanced over my shoulder, then spoke softly.

"Listen, I've got a little problem that I may need your help with."

I didn't like that he had come unannounced looking for me. The fact that it concerned some type of favor, turned my stomach in six different directions. I said, "May need? What's up? What's going on?"

"Actually no, I do need. I do need your help."

"Ronnie, listen, I had a blast last week but I really don't even know you. I mean, we just hung out that one time is all." He smirked and took a long hit off his cigarette. "Is this about that fucking cab driver? Is that what this is?"

"No man, no. But, that was pretty fucked up." His face had this ability almost on command to appear like that of a child. Like he flipped a switch somewhere inside himself.

"I know, I know. That was way outta line. I get stupid sometimes when I'm all jacked up. I didn't mean nothin' by it. I'm sorry man, really. Okay?"

"If that guy felt like calling the cops on us-"

He cut me off and hung his head like some kid being scolded for not doing his homework.

"I know, you're right. What can I say, I'm a big fucking shitstain."

He was letting me be in control and it was making me increasingly more uncomfortable.

"What is it? What do you want?" He flipped his cigarette high with his middle finger and followed it to the street. "I've got a little proposition for you."

"Yeah? What is it?"

"I know you like weed right? Like to smoke and get all fucked up."

"As much as the next guy I guess. Where is this going Ronnie?"

"Well, how would you like to have more at your disposal than you could possibly smoke between you and all your dorm buddies plus, make a grand a week easy, tax free."

"That's it? That's what this is about? Dealing? Listen dude, I don't remember exactly what I told you last week at the party but I'm no drug dealer. I sell a few bags for a guy and a little gets tossed my way and sometimes he throws me a few bucks and all but, no man, no way. Not interested."

I started to push past him but he stopped me.

"I got pinched."

"Shit. When?"

"Day after the party."

He let go but I didn't get the sense that I was free to leave. "They only got maybe an ounce plus some of my own private stash. Kicked down my fucking door man. There I am passed out on my couch with my girl beside me, next thing I know they're tearing my place to hell. Bull-shit. Total fucking bull-shit."

"That blows man and I'm sorry, I really am but-"

"Here's my problem, Mark. These cops, these fucking mutant cock-sucking ass-fucks are pissed off. Someone put them on to me and they knew to come looking. They all came through the door with huge hard-ons for big score, got me? If they'd come a few hours earlier, I had enough in my possession to get the whole city of Boston shit-faced for a week. With my history, I woulda been looking at twenty easy state time. Know what I mean?"

I was the one glancing up and down the street now.

"Just hear me out okay? Just clear your head for a second and just listen. Can you do that for me?"

He must have taken my lack of response as an okay to proceed.

"You won't have to weigh it, cut it, bag it, nothing. You don't have to do anything."

"Except?"

"Just pick it up and drop it off where I tell you. That's it. Keep some for yourself and bring me the cash. Simple as that. Plus a grand for your trouble."

I'm not sure why I let the conversation continue. Maybe out of fear of him, or maybe it was the idea of having some real money in my pocket for a change. I'm still not sure to this day.

My life held little value to me at that time, and a thousand dollars sounded like a million. I wish I could say I thought it through more, or that my integrity as a human being was struggling with the opportunity presented to me but it wasn't. I had come to the conclusion that I would never see age thirty. Whether it be an accident, an overdose, or by my own hands, my days were numbered. There would be no golden years for me. No two car garage or family vacations. No first house or car payments. I had convinced myself that I was fine with that. That I didn't want those things anyway. Life was, in my eyes meant to be lived day to day in a drunken fog of existence until such time as it was over. The party eventually ends for everyone anyway, mine would just come sooner than most. I followed that thought with, "When?"

It was just one word, but it was the first one to come to mind when I woke up lying in a shallow ditch of water and mud the night I decided dropping a full blotter of acid was an intelligent and constructive way to spend a Friday night. Whoever he was, whoever carried me into the park that night, took everything. The weed, what little money I had, even the change I had left over for the subway.

It's not that losing an ounce in itself would be such an issue to Ronnie, it's that I shouldn't have had it in my possession in the first place. They only way that would be possible, is if I opened the package I was to deliver the next day. That was not something that would be explainable or acceptable to him. The recipient of the delivery decided how much I was allowed, so going through the package in Ronnie's eyes, would constitute betrayal. He lived in a world of paranoia and suspicion and this turn of events would only serve to fuel his ever increasing irrational behavior.

I pulled myself up and checked for signs of trauma. My head felt like a freight train that was uncertain of its true destination, so going in circles and tooting its whistle repeatedly was the only choice of record. My knees hurt I assumed from falling and stumbling all along the cobblestone walkway earlier that evening and my lips were swollen and blood had caked with mud under my nose. A likely retaliation from some undeserving individual innocently enjoying their night with family or friend.

I took further stock of myself. I was covered head to toe in mud and filth. At some point I must have vomited because there were chunks of some unknown substance congealed with beer on my pant leg. My hair was matted and striped with sticks and debris. I was a fucking mess.

It was still dark when I started the long walk back to the dorm. In an effort to ignore both my inauspicious situation regarding Ronnie, and the foul stench of my clothing, I began to fill my thoughts with what was next for me. As I continued on, it became clear to me I had either a choice or a decision to make. They may seem on the surface, to be one in the same, but not in my eyes. It was obvious that I could not continue on this way. I was living in either a closet, or outside on some random bench. I had no job, unless you include my failed attempt at being a half-ass drug runner a worthy occupation. I was addicted to those same drugs and was using them solely to mask my depression and a total lack of attention to myself both physically, and emotionally. I had dropped out of school and had no prospects or aspirations for my future, and quite honestly, didn't care to have any.

I had rationalized and ultimately concluded, that my life would eventually cease entirely on my terms. I didn't know for sure when or how, but I believed it to be simply a formality. That was the decision I made years prior and one which odd as it may sound, gave me a sense of peace. I knew the time would eventually come to pass, that on a particular day, whether it be from lack of will, or a resolve to end my pain, I would take my own life.

As I moved closer to my destination that morning, I wondered if that was the day. I couldn't begin to imagine how to set about turning my life into anything resembling a worthwhile existence or one full of promise. Just months from my twenty-first birthday, and my only expectation was failure.

That being said, there still was a choice I could make. I could try. Be it ever so futile and lacking any real chance for a positive outcome, I still could attempt to create something out of my life. No matter the odds, or the perceived rate of success, it was a choice I could make. Even the concept, and the amount of energy and effort I knew would be needed to make the attempt were exhausting in my head. So to make that choice, would take a commitment that was not likely to be in my character at that stage in my life.

It seemed every stride I took, I would switch from my decision to my choice, then back again. I had very little on the list to represent a transformation to a promising and optimistic future but I did have one item whose presence and importance, made the list need no further detail. It was complete and needed no further assistance. It was my mother.

I cleared the park and with each passing step, my choice was finally clear. Even if I could find no true value in my continued existence, or speculate a rational reasoning to continue it, I could find worth in trying for the sake of someone else, and there was no better choice than her. I concluded that the decision not to end life, was not nearly as important as the choice to live it. Simply deciding not to end one's life without speculation or some type of inner accountability would eventually lead back to where one started. Making the choice to live, if joined with reflection and attitude, would bring life's possibilities a more meaningful directional curve. That theory and all its positive potential was the easy part, the force and energy needed to make it reality, especially on a day in day out basis, was both intimidating and overwhelming to me.

The walk had done little to alleviate the effects of the drugs still flowing in my system, but as I left the park and hit the pavement just blocks from the dorm, I knew more than anything, my mother, although with much sadness, would have accepted my decision. But my choice, that would have melted her heart.

The sky had turned from black to gray when I cautiously guided myself up the steps and squatted down to wait for someone to enter or exit the dorm. I dreaded the thought of seeing anyone. I doubted a rational conversation was plausible at that moment, but I'm sure the sight of me, and the foul odor I was eliciting would likely distract and deter any form of communication anyway.

I weighed that thought, and let the hallucinations from the acid still lingering inside me be guided toward the notion of just how good a warm, cleansing shower was going to feel when I heard commotion coming up the street to my left. As the noise came closer to me and grew louder, I saw its source. A crowd of six to eight white kids were taunting an African American man as he made his way down the street towards me. He walked backwards while facing them and although he was moving away, he had just as much to say, and was every bit as aggressive in both language and action as the pack stalking him. What they were actually saying wasn't clear to me, but it was obvious the words came out of anger and hostility.

I watched them grow closer, yelling and shouting and inciting one of the members of the group forward. A blonde kid pushed ahead and slapped the man in the face. He took the hit and continued to back up, but not back down. The kid, feeling the adrenaline of his first blow and the confidence it brought, attempted to step around and in front of the man. What happened next, made me vomit on myself for at least the second time that night. As he tried to gain ground, the man punched him with such force that I'm sure he was knocked out cold before he hit the pavement. I further believe that to be true because he did little to protect his fall. The sound of impact, and the visual of his skull slamming into the street was the most nauseating thing I had ever seen in my life. The sight of his head hitting without recourse, and then rebounding off the pavement was something I had hoped was simply drug induced. Perhaps, a hallucination left over from the night's festivities, but I knew it wasn't. The crowd immediately grew silent. The man continued running backwards up the street and away from the crowd, all the while jeering and mocking his assaulters. He needn't have run though, no-one was about to chase him down.

The stunned group gathered around their friend. He finally sat up and blood was pouring through his nose and into his mouth and when not held up from behind, he would start to fall over, unable to control or hold his own weight. I watched the crowd eventually pull him to his feet and drag him off toward what I hoped was some form of medical assistance.

I saw him a few days later in the cafeteria and his nose was heavily bandaged and both eyes were circled in black. His wounds would eventually heal, but the shame of that type of event will likely last him a lifetime.

I removed my jacket and was attempting to clean off my fresh load of projectile when the door opened and a well-dressed man carrying a briefcase came towards me. He didn't seem to notice me or maybe he did and chose to divert his eyes. Muddied, rumpled, and covered with smeared vomit tends to bring that out in people. Even in the state I was in, it wasn't lost on me how strange it was for a man of his age and obvious stature to be coming out of a college dormitory. But in regard to the condition I was in and my overwhelming desire for a shower and some sleep, I really didn't much care about the man except for the fact that he was my ticket inside.

I stabbed out my foot to catch the door and staggered through into a vestibule. I nearly walked into a second set of doors, then it occurred to me, I wasn't in the dorm. I was in the wrong building altogether. I started back through the doors, but then I looked out to the street, then down at myself. I never really minded the nights I slept outside, but that night was a different story. That night, it was not an option. I followed a short hallway to my left that led me down a small set of steps then opened into a laundry room. It was bare and basic with just two pairs of a washer and dryer, a utility sink and a small table jammed in the corner away from view. I took a set of sheets that I assumed had simply been left behind, and put one over the table for cover then climbed underneath. I pulled the other one tight to me and pressed myself to the back and corner of the room to where I hoped that no one could see me. My last thoughts before passing out were that of my mother, and the prospect of a new life ahead. I hoped for the best but as always, feared the worst.

Weeks came and went after that morning, and although I wasn't exactly clean, sober, and spewing about all that life has to offer, I also wasn't waking up in ditches and tripping on acid either. I hadn't seen Ronnie for weeks and I didn't know what to make of it. I wanted to get past the inevitable confrontation concerning the weed I had lost. I thought his absence to be doubly strange because I hadn't picked up the last three deliveries and yet I still hadn't heard a word from him. Unfortunately, all good things really do come to an end.

I was standing in line for breakfast one morning at the school cafeteria and getting an earful from a woman working the front door. She was citing campus policy about using someone else's meal card and how it was in direct violation of the by-laws. I lied and told her that I had lost mine and I promised her that I would correct the situation right after breakfast. She proceeded to grill me about which dorm I was in, and what meal plan I was set up for, and whatever other protocol I was failing to follow.

I was about to give up when I heard these words from behind me. "What do you have to do, give DNA to eat in this shit-hole?"

I knew who it was the second the words hit the morning air. I turned to face my fate, and the inevitable. The voice belonged to Ronnie. The woman looked at him and said, "Young man, please watch your language."

"Yeah, yeah. You got a conscience Lady?"

"What do you mean?"

He wrapped his arm around my shoulder and showed his dazzling smile first to me, then turned to her. "What do I mean? You're denying my good buddy here a nice, warm breakfast is what I mean."

"Young man-"

"You'll notice I didn't say nice warm 'tasty' breakfast because I happen to know that shit you dish out ain't fit for a fucking dog."

"It's no problem. I'm not really that hungry."

I tried to pull away from him but he kept me right there and said, "No, no. Let's figure this out."

The woman was clearly uncomfortable now, and was scanning the cafeteria looking for some form of assistance.

"Hey Lady, look at me. Listen, tell me. Honestly, would you eat that shit they're serving in there?"

A student walked by heading toward a trash can to toss what was left of his breakfast. Ronnie stopped him and said, "Hang on Pal. Let me have that." He slapped him on the back. "Thanks Buddy."

He took the tray and started toward her. She shrunk back as far into the doorway as she could. He dropped the tray on her stand and said, "I'm asking again cause I guess you didn't hear me the first time. Would you eat this shit? Yes or no?"

I started to speak, but his hand came up and his voice rose.

"Are you fucking deaf? Eat this. Fuckin' eat it bitch."

He shoved the tray toward her. "You hear what I said? You expect people to eat this shit but you won't? You know what you are Lady? You're a piece of shit fucking hypocrite bitch is what you are."

He pushed the tray off the stand and toward her. Bits of egg and syrup exploded at her feet. He stared at her as she appeared, unable to move. The moment seemed to last forever.

I felt for her. I knew what it was like first hand to be on that side of a confrontation with Ronnie, and I knew the fear he induced. His glare just as quickly turned to a big, bright smile as he said to her, "I'm just fucking with you Lady, I wouldn't eat that shit either. Have a splendid morning you hear? I mean it okay? Hey, you hear me?" Meekly she whispered, "Yes, I hear you."

"Well alright then. Now she hears me."

He turned to me, smiled, and slapped my back like we were old pals. The best of friends.

"Come on, let's go get some real breakfast. Sound good? Good."

His grip on my shoulder was a signal to let me know his question was strictly rhetorical, that any answer was pointless and held no value.

"It's on me. Whattaya feel like? Eggs? Bacon? Some pancakes?"

We made our way to a diner nearby and he grabbed us a booth by the window.

"So, how you been Mark?"

"I'm okay."

The waitress arrived and he ordered coffee and a full breakfast. She turned to me and said, "And for you Honey?"

"Just coffee please."

"Come on, eat with me. I hate to eat alone."

"I'm okay, really."

She smiled kindly to me and said before turning away, "If you need anything just give a yell. Name's Connie."

Ronnie said, "Thanks Connie. Hey, my name's Ronnie. Ronnie and Connie. We rhyme."

I believed it to be true that people could sense the violence just beneath his surface if he wasn't careful with it. She seemed to be having that type of intuition right then and left us be without responding to his attempt at dialogue.

"Bitch."

He looked me over hard before asking, "Are you sure you're okay Mark? Because I gotta tell ya, and please don't get angry or nothing but Buddy, you sure don't look okay. No offense."

"Just trying to figure some things out is all."

"Yeah, like what? Anything I can help with?"

"No, just bullshit stuff is all."

"Yeah, I hear you."

We sat in an awkward silence until the waitress brought our coffee and his plate. Ronnie said, "Thanks Connie."

She just turned and left his words out there.

"Bitch probably hacked one up in my food. What the fuck I ever do to her, huh Mark?"

"She's just doing her job man. Let it go."

He dove into his plate and scoffed down whatever he could fork into his mouth.

"You're right Mark, and when you're right, you're right. Whore don't even know me, right?"

"Right Ronnie."

"Ronnie is right about Connie."

He smiled at me, but now it was my turn for intuition. The next sentence came out with the same lilt and tone as if he was asking me to see a ball-game, or to move furniture.

"Hey Mark, what's your plan?"

"What do you mean?"

He slammed down on the table, then let out a full belly laugh. "What do I mean he says. That's rich Mark. I like it. Seriously though, how we gonna do this?"

"Do what?"

He slammed the table again, but no laughter followed after. He lowered his voice and said, "Please don't insult my intelligence okay, is that clear?"

"Yes. It's… yes, it's clear. I just don't under-"

"Say it. Say you don't understand to me. Say it."

People were starting to notice us, and were ending their conversations and listening to ours. He lowered his voice more and leaned into me. "You don't understand Mark, huh? A little foggy are ya? Then I'll spell it out for you. You took over an ounce of product from me which I'm sure I can be safe in assuming you smoked all up in a fucking blaze of glory. Then, and this is my favorite part, you stopped doing drops like we had arranged."

"I'm trying to change some things Ronnie. I couldn't-"

"You couldn't what? You got that brain of yours so fucking scrambled you don't know your dick from your asshole. You gotta know when to pull off the gas with that shit you know? It's fucked you up man. Made you all loopy in the head."

"I know, that's what I've been trying to say-"

He cut me off and changed his tone and the direction of the conversation quickly and said, "You know what Mark, I don't care about the weed. Really. Forget about it. Probably should have been staking you more anyways for your troubles."

"It's not that Ronnie, I-"

"You know what though Mark, you know what really chafes me? You know what really hurts me deep down inside? I came to you and asked you to perform a service. A service you knew I needed. It's my livelihood. It puts food on the table, feeds my kid. You didn't know that did you Mark. Didn't know there was a little junior me out there did you?"

"No, you never mentioned it to me."

"Well, I'm sharing it now with you Buddy."

I had no idea what to say, all I could think of was, "What's his name?"

He ignored me and sipped his coffee.

"You missed three drops Mark. Three fucking drops. Do you know what that cost me?"

"I figured you'd do them yourself."

"You figured that did you? Huh... That's interesting. Have you forgotten why I came to you in the first place? Have you?"

"No, I remember. Like I said, I just figured-"

"You gotta stop figuring Mark and start planning how you're gonna pay me back."

"I can get a job."

"Get a job? Look at you. You're a fucking mess. That's gonna be your big plan? A job he said."

He let out a strong laugh again and rubbed his belly to show he was full from his breakfast, and had his fill of me as well.

"Keep brainstorming Mark, cause that ain't no fucking plan my friend. That's just you talking out your ass is what that is."

"I don't know what else to say. I don't have anyone to borrow-"

"You know what, fuck all that. Don't sweat it. I think I know what you can do and I tell you what, I'll even help you. What do you say to that? Sound good? Everyone gets what they want. Sound like a plan?"

"Sure Ronnie. What is it? What's your plan?"

"Finish up your coffee, and I'll show you."

I had no doubt that whatever his intentions were for us that day, they involved something, someone, or someplace where I did not belong. Likely, all three.

I was both surprised and pleased that the subway was taking us outside the city limits, and into some of the nicer housing developments that surrounded the greater Boston area. My mood was further elevated by the fact that Ronnie had evidently talked himself out at breakfast. He was quiet and withdrawn. He stared out the window and said nothing during our ride to a destination unknown, at least to me.

"This is it. This is our stop."

Those were the first words he spoke since we got on the subway. He waited for me to step off first, never losing sight of me as if he thought I might make a run for it. That was a foolish and unfounded thought of course, because the reality was that I had no place to go. Whatever the plan was for that day, I needed to see it through and hope that when it reached its conclusion, it didn't go so deep, or so far downward that moving forward with my life was no longer an option, or a choice.

The day was cold but the sun was warm on our faces as we walked through the streets and neighborhoods of an area outside the city I wasn't familiar with, but if life had ever set me there at any point, I would have welcomed the notion of spending my days within its town limits. Kids were playing in the streets and running in and out of houses that although tight in proximity to each other, appeared well kept and cared for. The cold winter months had done much to diminish what I assumed would be small gardens full with plants and flowers lush with color and appeal that would be carefully tended to when the warm spring weather arrived. As the days grew longer, I assumed it would be commonplace for front doors to remain open without concern for one's property or personal safety.

I wished I could just walk inside any of the houses we passed and sit down to enjoy a good meal and conversation with its rightful owner. I longed to tell them why we were in their neighborhood, and how much I wished to just stay with them, and let the day's events play on without me as one of the main characters.

That was not an option I knew, and when Ronnie stopped and stared up at one particular residence, that reasoning was further verified. I knew we had reached our destination when Ronnie said, "Remember I told you about Reese?"

I could feel my face get hot and red, and my whole body start to tremble at the sound of his name. Ronnie had told me the first night we met about his connection as it related to his business activities. He used "scumbag" and piece of shit" often during the conversation, but the matter of topic being an ex-convict and known gang affiliate prone to outbursts that would seem to make Ronnie's notable and erratic behavior seem like child's play was not someone I wished to meet that day, or any day in the near or distant future. Ronnie once told me he witnessed him beat a man near to death, and then sliced above both eyelids with a knife. When Ronnie asked him why he did that, Reese said, "So every time that asshole blinks, he will think of me." Ronnie somehow found that amusing.

From the street, the house looked much like the others. Clean and neat. The paint looked fresh, and the porch seemed like an ideal place to waste away a Sunday afternoon lounging in a comfortable chair. It was a one level ranch style with a fence enclosing the entire property.

It also appeared to be a house set up for outdoor festivities. A barbecue pit was situated along the side of the house on a narrow stretch of land stripped bare and littered with holes dug up from the family dog. Toys were strewn about and bikes rested neatly in the shade under a tree carved with initials that likely represented several generations of past residents. In no way did its appearance suggest anything that would inhabit a ruthless drug dealer.

"I'm not going in there Ronnie. What the fuck are we doing here anyway?"

"I told you, you're getting my money and I'm gonna help you."

"Forget it, no way. I'll get you the money some other way."

He grabbed my arm and said, "Let's go."

That's all he said before he opened the gate and we walked down a pathway leading to the front door. I had never seen Ronnie look nervous before. His range of emotion flowed back and forth between some twisted form of elation and explosive anger. There was no in between, until that morning anyway. He drew a deep breath, and knocked on the screen door.

"Ronnie, come on. We don't have to do this. I can get the money-"

He knocked again, harder this time and his nerves were now replaced with some form of resolve. He was focused now, determined to carry out whatever ill-conceived plan he drew up in his delusional, fucked up mind.

"It's not just about the money." he said. "I hate this motherfucker and its time he learned his place. Treats me like some fucking pee-on. Like I'm some fucking lackey he can spit on. Fuck him. Here take this."

He tried to hand me a small gun.

"Have you lost your fucking mind, man?"

"Just take it."

I pushed it back towards him.

"I'm not taking anything. Let's just go man. You have done some crazy shit before but this is just way the fuck out there even for you. I'm going."

He pointed the gun at me. The same eyes that could seduce and disarm, now were occupied by some type of savage animal. He didn't say anything. He knew he didn't have to. The power he had in his hand said it all. He opened his jacket and showed me another gun in his waist, then extended the one in his hand to me.

"I said, take it."

The door started to open and as it did, he said quietly, "You better have my ass in there."

Just a face came into view when the door finally came open. A chain kept it mostly hidden but you could see it was pale and pock-marked. Patches of facial growth meant to cover up its defects only served to make it seem more grotesque.

"Fuck you want?"

"Just a word is all." Ronnie said.

"Fuck off."

Ronnie shoved his hand in the door as it began to close. The face said, "Best get your hand outta there less you comfortable losing some fingers."

"Just hold on, hold on. I, we have a proposition for you."

"Whatever you got, I already have so fuck off."

"Hey, just hold up. You're gonna like it okay? Just trust me. Could you just listen to what I have to say? Come on man, please? "

The face peered out through the crack in the door. Its eyes passed back and forth, analyzing the two of us, then said, "Move your fucking hand."

Ronnie pulled back his hand and the door shut. I could hear the chain unlatching and then the door re-opened.

He was dressed in a worn red robe and showed bare feet. His hair was sparse and scattered on his scalp, and showed no signs of care or attention. He wasn't quite fat, but he carried a considerable amount of girth on a frame that appeared to bother little with any exercise regime or health minded lifestyle. He backed up and led us into a space that betrayed the likeness the outside perimeter portrayed. It was smoky and hot and smelled of weed and cat piss. The floor was blotched with stains that appeared both fresh and stale, depending on where your eye settled. Ronnie introduced us. "This is Mark. Mark, this is Reese."

He didn't bother to turn and greet me, or even acknowledge my presence. Instead he plopped himself on a couch more soiled and spattered with filth than the floor beneath our feet. He stabbed a hand into a bag of chips, shoveled them into his mouth and spit out, "Five minutes. My show is coming on."

"That's all we need." Ronnie said.

His response was to grab more chips and lay them in his lap, picking the choice ones out of the pile.

"Nice place you got here."

"Yeah, it's the king's palace. Get to it. I'm busy."

"Yeah I know, your show is coming on."

Ronnie pulled the gun from his waist and showed it to him. Reese didn't speak, he simply removed his robe and continued to munch on his chips. His vulgar nature was now punctuated with the portrayal of him in shorts and a tank top. His stomach exposed itself, and he rubbed it mindlessly. He stared back at Ronnie, then the gun, and finally said, "Dumb fucking move douche-bag." Ronnie said, "I know what I'm doing."

"No, you absolutely do not know what the fuck you are doing. You haven't a fucking clue. I can fucking assure you of that."

He turned to me and said, "Who the fuck are you again?"

"I'm no-one."

"Okay no-one, am I safe in assuming this little soiree we have here was all dickheads' idea?"

Ronnie countered with, "He's the one who ripped you off."

"It wasn't my intention-"

He cut me off with the wave of his hand and turned back to Ronnie. "You've got it all wrong my friend, he didn't rip me off. He ripped you off."

"How do you figure?"

"Well, the way I see it, I'm your boss. You answer to me right? And you're his boss. Correct me if I'm wrong but really, he ripped you off because I don't have to worry about what he does. It's you I deal with. He's your problem, not mine."

He casually reached into the bag of chips not seeming to have a care in the world that a gun was pointed at him. I hadn't moved since we entered the room. I watched everything unfold in front of me hoping it was all somehow, just some bad dream. Reese turned to Ronnie. "Oh, and by the way, for every second you keep that gun on me it's going to cost you an extra minute of the long and agonizing beating you are going to endure. It's gonna be slow and it's gonna be painful."

He started laughing after he said it and I could see Ronnie was shaken by its weight and assumed consequence.

"So I'm asking-" Ronnie said. "Where's the money? Where do you keep it?"

"Oh boy, gettin' serious with me now huh? Gettin' right down to it. No funny business with you is there?"

He looked at me with the slightest hint of satisfaction on his face, almost like this whole scenario was amusing to him, like it was a game he loved to play, and was sure to win.

"You packin' too boy?"

I showed him the gun on my waist and hoped my expression offered the insight that I had no intention of ever using it.

He was playing with me now, clearly enjoying himself. He pretended to lunge toward me then said, "You ever used one of those before?"

I didn't answer. I just stood there watching him.

Ronnie answered for me. "Doesn't fucking matter if he has or not. Last time man, tell me where it is."

"Fuck you."

Without taking the gun or his eyes off Reese, he said to me, "Mark, go through his shit. Go to the bedroom and look around."

Reese said, "Be a Pal and make the bed for me while you're in there would ya Buddy?"

Ronnie moved forward and squared the gun on Reese's temple, as he waved me toward the back of the house. Reese was all smiles again. "Well look at you two would ya? A couple of fucking commandos is what you are. Real fucking gangsters. All tough and shit. Guns all ablazin."

He screeched like a little girl scared by some imaginary monster hiding in her closet and then laughed. I will never forget that laugh. It echoed down the hall as I made my way from room to room.

I pushed open what I believed to be the master bedroom door. The room was more revolting than the rest of the house. The bed was unmade and plates of food sat at its foot. Beer bottles were scattered all around and a litter box sat in the corner. Its contents had spilled on to the floor, and were spread throughout the room. A commode sat open and full to the left of the beds headboard.

I started to search through his closet and nightstand knowing full well, however crude and disgusting a human being he may have been, he was not stupid enough to leave bundles of cash just lying around. I heard Ronnie call to me just as a little boy, no more than six, pushed open the door. I was delicately sifting through a dresser drawer more out of disgust than consideration when he came upon me. He was both dirty, and disheveled but his eyes still wore the innocence and naivety of youth. A soiled blanket was pulled close to his face, and his fingers were stuffed in his mouth. He looked up at me and stuttered, "Where is my daddy?"

Reese yelled out as the boy posed his simple question.

"You touch my kid I will fucking kill you, you understand me? Hey, Michael, come to Daddy son. Come to Daddy, Michael."

I couldn't see Ronnie, but the timbre in his voice told me that he was quickly losing control of the situation. He shouted over Reese. "Sit the fuck down now! Mark, what's going on in there?"

"Michael, come to Daddy son."

The moment was slipping away into something, or more accurately, someplace I had experienced all too often before. Violence has a smell, more like a stench that is something you can both feel and taste its presence all around you if its strength bears enough weight. That moment had that aroma, and it was something fully realized by the participants of the occasion, and was clear and abundant throughout the house.

I made a decision that I was aware of, and acknowledged to myself right then in front of that little boy that I knew I would regret all of my years looking forward. My only excuse, if one were even to apply, was simply, self-preservation.

I could hear movement coming from the hallway as I looked down at the boy. He peeked out the door and into the living room, then back at me. Ronnie yelled louder. "I said sit the fuck down."

"You hurt my boy I will fucking kill you understand? Hear me in there? Hey No-one, you fucking hear me?"

All the humor and whimsy were now gone from Reese.

"MICHAEL, COME TO DADDY SON. RIGHT NOW OKAY? IT'S ALRIGHT. DON'T BE SCARED."

I took the gun from my waist and gently pulled the blanket from his hands. I wrapped it up tight and handed it back to him and said, "Let's go show Daddy your blanket, okay?"

I led him out to the living room. Reese was on the couch but had spun around and was facing me, his back now to Ronnie.

"Come here son. It's okay. See? Daddy's right here."

He scooped him up and pressed his body close to his chest. Ronnie turned to me.

"Anything?"

"Nothing."

"What do you mean nothing? There's got to be something. Weed? Pills? Cash? The guys a fucking drug dealer you asshole. There is something, somewhere in this house I can fucking guarantee you that."

He turned from me to Reese. "Just one more time, one more fucking time I'm gonna ask you-"

Reese gently stroked the boys' hair, then turned to Ronnie. "Actually, let me ask you something if you don't mind. What did you think would happen today? I mean, it doesn't seem like you gave this plan of yours much thought. At least that's how I see it anyway."

"I got it covered."

"Yeah, you think? I don't see it that way Ronnie. A robbery? Or what, you're gonna off me? Send 'ol Reese to meet his maker? Please, I know firsthand what a scumbag piece of shit you are, that's a matter of record. But, you are not a killer. That I know for sure." Ronnie raised the gun and said, "You don't think so?"

"Oh, I know that for a fact. And that my friend will be your undoing on this fine day. That, and the fact that you have a gun pointed at my son's head. The offer still stands. Leave my house and this town right now, and never show your face here again, and I will pretend this little scheme of yours was all just a big misunderstanding."

I moved from behind them to near the door and watched two evil men, and one innocent child joined in a situation destined to end poorly. Ronnie said, "What, you think I'm stupid? Think I don't know you'll come for me? Doesn't matter where I go."

Then he spit on the floor and said, "Fuck you asshole."

To me he said," Put your gun on him, I'm gonna go take a look."

"What? No. You heard him, we can go. Let's just go. Right now."

"FUCK THAT! PUT YOUR GUN ON HIM NOW!"

"Listen to the man Ronnie. This is gonna play out real bad for you otherwise."

Ronnie stepped up to him and pressed the gun flush to his temple.

"Yeah? You think so? Well maybe I don't see it that way. How's that sound?"

The loss of control was slipping through in Ronnie's voice. Reese slid his son off his lap, and guided him gently away and toward the bedroom. "Go back to your room and wait for Daddy, okay Kiddo?"

The boy and Reese both looked at me before he did as his father had told. The fact that he was so calm and quiet amidst all that he was seeing, made me wonder how often guns were a common occurrence in his everyday life.

"I'm gonna count to five." Ronnie said.

Reese looked at me and said, "Oh boy, here it comes. Hey, Mister No-one over there, drum roll please."

I said nothing.

"4-3-2."

Reese said, "You're in way over your head man."

I wanted to believe it was just a bluff, that I was not about to see a man's skull scattered about the room. I also didn't want to consider that a young boy would come out and see the mess it would bring.

"1."

"Alright. Alright. It's obvious you mean business. I'll tell you where everything is. You got me. You win cowboy. But first you gotta help me out. You gotta explain something to me. Help me understand."

"Understand what asshole?"

"Well, within this no doubt, well thought out and finely executed plan of yours, did you account for any variables?"

"Fuck you mean by variables? What kind of variables?"

Reese removed the blanket and rested the gun quietly in his lap, smiled, and pointed it directly into Ronnie's stomach.

"Fuck."

It took a minute for him to grasp both the gravity of the situation, and the realization that the gun pointed at him was the same one he gave to me earlier. He turned to face me and said, "You piece of shit! You motherfucker! I'm gonna fucking kill you! Understand me? I'm gonna fucking kill you!"

He took the gun off Reese and started toward me. Maybe it was because we were inside his own house, or because his own son would bear witness, but whatever the reason, Reese didn't shoot. Instead he grabbed him, pinned him down on the couch and wrestled the gun from him.

The animated Reese was back. "Ohhhh boy, things gettin' interesting now."

He tossed both weapons on the couch across from them and punched Ronnie hard in the ribs.

"Hee-haw!!!"

"He turned him on his stomach and fastened his arms behind him. He punched him hard either in the face or side, then waited to gauge the reaction. For all outward appearances, he seemed to be having the time of his life.

Ronnie cried out, "Mark, help me! You fucking piece of shit, you owe me!"

My involvement with him was strictly voluntary with no one but myself to blame, but the truth was, I owed him nothing. What was happening that day way a direct result of how he chose to live his life, and the risks it inherently involved.

"Leave my house."

That's all he said, and all I needed to hear. I backed out to the hall leading outside. The last thing I heard before I pushed open the door was the sound of bone on bone, the cries of a beaten man, and the barbaric laughter of his assailant.

I burst out the door and down the stairs as fast as I could go. I ran through the same streets and past the same houses we saw only an hour earlier. I don't remember finding the subway or deciding which train would lead me home, I just remember sitting down and shaking. My whole body went into some type of uncontrollable spasm. I wanted to cry. To scream out. But nothing would come. I had nothing left inside me.

I spent the next three days in a drunken, smoke filled haze. I didn't eat or sleep. I just laid there in my chair and waited for him to come for me. I didn't know if he would survive that day, but if he did, revenge would be the sole purpose of his existence.

On the third night without rest or food, sleep finally found me. I woke the next morning with an envelope resting on my chest. I began to read it, and as I did, the content brought tears that made reading it to completion a nearly impossible task. It was from Kelly.

Mark,

It's after three in the morning that I'm writing this. I just went to check on you, and as always, I am relieved to find you safe from harm. I am also, saddened to see you in the condition that has become a constant state in your life. The person I met no more than six months ago and the person you have now become, has been a transition that has been both difficult, and painful for me to watch.

I don't know the specifics of what goes on in your life here and I assume that's to protect me, and those around you that love and care for you. I do know this though Mark. If you continue on as you are, you will not survive. Whether it be your body, or you're soul, no human existence is meant to contend with what you're asking of it.

I care for you so much. I miss the guy who could make me laugh and would listen to my mindless nonsense without the slightest sense of disinterest or apathy. Where is that guy? What happened to him? I feel angry but I don't know where or to whom to direct my feelings. I feel like someone has been taken from me, someone I held dear to me is now gone.

I can't bear to watch you live like this anymore. I can't sit back and wait for the inevitable to happen. If you stay here Mark, I believe you will die. Either by the poison you put in your body, or by the hands of someone else, or perhaps even by your own. I hope you take this letter as it was intended. It comes out of both concern and fear for your health and safety, but more importantly, its real message is one of love and compassion for my friend.

84

As your friend, I have no choice but to tell you that you must leave Mark, and don't look back. I have long suspected that your short time here had little to do with your decline, but rather, was just a passage to keep the past burning inside you. Until you face those demons, wherever you are, or wherever you go, you won't be about to escape them, they will always be with you.

I love you and will miss you my good friend. Don't ever look back Mark, only ahead.

Kelly

She was right in every way. I would die if I stayed there. It would be just a matter of odds or circumstance but the result would be the same. So, I did as my friend said. I got up and with the clothes on my back and what little money I had left, I headed back home to face my family. I didn't know what the future would bring but I could only hope it would lead me down the path toward facing the demons she spoke of. I walked through the doors to outside and took one last look up at the building. I knew leaving was the only option I had, and I knew more so how much I would miss her.

Chapter 7

I was awake and sitting up in bed before the guard arrived with my breakfast. The tray found its way through the slot followed by the guard's exhilarating words, "Eat up, you're getting out today."

My initial reaction was one of elation and a misguided sense of optimism. It was now going on my fourth day in seclusion and I was sure one more day would claim the small sliver of sanity I had left.

I could feel my stomach churning at both my anticipation, and the apprehension of the days that lay ahead. I had assumed even before my arrival that I would be seen as a target by the other inmates. I could only hope that if I stayed quiet and kept to myself, perhaps I could become somehow invisible to anyone wishing me harm.

A rustling of keys an hour later let me know it was time. The same guard who led me down to my cell was now cuffing me and leading me back through the same halls we walked just days before. He escorted me in silence until we found the stairs, then he finally spoke.

"Listen son, I don't know what your lawyer told you about this place. It's definitely not your hardcore state institution for sure, but its prison just the same. We have murderers, rapists, drug dealers you name it. But listen up, it's the ones you're bunking with you really gotta watch out for understand? Especially where you're going. They don't know any better. They're fucked up in the head. That's why they're here. Most will never see the light of day in the outside world, they just don't know it yet. They don't know about rules and such. They could look right at you and not see you at all but instead some kinda creature. Somethin' they cooked up in their head. A monster that haunts them, controls their minds. Know what I'm sayin'? Now, most are pretty medicated but still, watch your back son. I don't know why you did what you did and like I said when you first came in, I don't much care. But I hate to see harm brought to anyone that ought not to deserve it."

"Thank you."

"Stay quiet and keep your head down, but don't stay in your cell all the time okay?"

"Why?"

"No place to run."

He removed the cuffs and pointed me in the direction I needed to go. I looked across a large span of grass cut and divided by crossing pathways of concrete. To the right, across a small ridge, sat three buildings. All appeared to be one level and built solid with brick. To look at them, you would liken them to any college or administrative structure. Straight ahead of me were other similar buildings appearing different both from signs of age, and the crowd occupying the space around them.

It was April, and the sun was already high and warm despite the early hour as I walked toward the buildings to my right until I found the one I needed. 'DUKE' is what appeared on the side in big, bold letters. I paused a minute and braced myself before going in. The second I entered, a voice and a hand greeted me.

The hand belonged to a wiry man with a goatee and thin rimmed glasses. His eyes were large and open full in a constant surprised expression. His teeth were yellow and rotted and covered by lips that were cracked and blistered, and his breathe reeked of cigarettes and caffeine. He had a nervous energy about him that was either from some form of medication or a physical disorder of some type, or perhaps both. He pumped my hand and seemed not at all aware that smiling was not something he should enlighten people with upon their first meeting.

"Ben. Name's Ben."

"Hey Ben, I'm Mark. How are you doing today?"

"Not as good as you I bet on a count of you getting out of seclusion on this fine, fair morning. That place sucks hot, sweaty balls huh?"

Before I could form any sort of reply he stepped aside and guided me in saying, "Come on, I'll show you Duke."

"I think I need to check in with someone first."

"Yeah, yeah. I'll show you. Come on, come on. It's on the way."

I followed him down a brightly lit hallway. It was clean, almost immaculate. Wooden doors made up both sides and small, square windows sat in each doors center. The ones that were open showed a set of bunk-beds and a small desk. Most of the cells were empty as I assumed the inmates were using any time available, to be free of their small quarters. Ben carried on ahead of me. He was a mass of hyper energy and nervous twitches, and he was carrying on a very animated conversation about a topic that only he was privy to. That was fortunate for me, because he required no response on the matter. After spending four days underground staring at blank walls, and in the interest of engaging in conversation with someone besides myself, I decided to breach his private conversation and try one of our own. All I could think of was, "Who's Duke?"

"It's not a person. It's a thing. More appropriately, it's a building. All the buildings in the psych ward are named after colleges in the ACC. You know, the Atlantic Coast Conference. The powers that be seem to think that it hides the fact that they're all prison wings. Call them what you want, whistle Dixie while you're doing it, it doesn't change the fact they're all full of whack-jobs and nutcases. Hey, you got a cigarette by chance?"

"I don't smoke."

"Yeah, me neither."

He stopped short at a door marked 'D7' and said, "Ta-da, we're here! Home sweet home."

"You're my cell-mate?"

"Fuck yeah. You think I talk to strangers?"

He turned and stuck out his arm to stop an inmate who did his best to sidestep him. Ben steered him toward the wall and said, "Hey, hey there old buddy, old pal. You got a cigarette you can lend me? Actually, it wouldn't technically be lending such as the aforementioned item could not be returned to your possession in that it would no longer exist in the sense of a materialistic object. But, there is always a but, isn't there? I could, at a date not yet pre-determined but one with which I have a great degree of confidence feel we can set forth as a time for reimbursement. We can book it is what I'm saying."

The inmate's look I was sure even in the few moments I knew him, was a common one in Ben's world. The inmate said, "You're fucking crazy you know that? You're fucking certifiable dude. I'm serious."

Ben ignored his words and said, "Where do we stand on the cigarette request?"

Probably figuring the situation wasn't going away, he said, "If I give you one, would you please, please just leave me be for like, a month?"

"Yes! No! No, uh-huh. I cannot make such a promise. No sir."

"How about a week then?"

"A week, a week. Hmm. Yes, okay I think I can commit to that."

"Well, Jesus H. Christ and thank the Lord."

"That's redundant. What you said. That's redundant."

"What the fuck does that mean? Re-da what?"

"It means you were excessive in your speech. You said Christ and then you said Lord but really, aren't they one in the same?"

"Wow man, are you off your meds? Cause holy shit man, you are one fucked up S.O.B."

"Let's re-visit the task at hand shall we? You asked me a question to which I responded affirmative but we didn't finalize the details of said agreement."

"Christ Almighty. Jesus, man. You are fuckin-"

Ben said, "You're doing it again."

"Doing what?" He did little to mask his exasperation. "Holy shit, what agreement?"

"You said if I let you be for a week right? Or was it leave you be?"

"Whatever, who gives a fuck. Yes, I believe those are the words I just fucking said."

"Let you be, or leave you be?"

"Oh my God."

Ben said, "So, is that a week from today then, or a week from last week?"

The inmate could see I was listening and shook his head in disbelief. He said to me, "Do you believe this fucking guy?" Then he turned back to Ben and said, "What fucking good would it do me if it was last week? That would mean you could ask today."

"That's right and I am. Hence, you see my confusion on the subject."

"No, I don't see your fucking confusion man. I see you're a fucked up mess of a human being who is in strong need of a strait jacket. That's what I see."

The inmate's frustration at both the situation and the person responsible for it was reaching that pivotal moment between men that can either end peacefully, or with extreme aggression. It appeared the inmate's temperament and demeanor lent itself more to the side of finding an amicable solution. He simply said, "Yes or no on the cigarette? And before you say another word, before you even think it, it's one week from today before you can ask again. Today. Got me? Not last week. Not last month. Today. Understood?"

"Understood. Can I have the cigarette now?"

The inmate pulled a cigarette from behind his ear and said, "It's my last one asshole."

Ben said, "Oh, no. Oh, no, no, no. No sir that simply won't do. Uh-huh. No way. I need one from the pack. Gotta be from the pack."

"Well I just got done telling you it's my last one. I ain't got a pack. Take it or leave it."

Ben's eyes expressed the deep concern he had for the situation he was faced with. You could see the wheels spinning and agonizing over the dilemma he was forced to confront. He let out a long breathe and said, "I have a bit of a difficult quandary here do you see it? On the one hand, I need a cigarette real bad. I mean really, really, fucking bad."

"Yeah, no shit." Ben ignored him and continued, "On the other hand, the close proximity of said cigarette to your ear canal is a daunting piece of the equation that may just quell my quenching desire."

Ben leaned in toward his ear, closed one eye, peered inside, and then said, "Do you clean them? Your ears I mean?"

The inmate pushed him away and replied, "I know what you meant you freak. Of course I do."

"With a Q-tip or just your finger?"

"What the fuck? Of course with a Q-tip. What do you use? A god-damned paper clip? I think you nicked your brain while you were at it."

He grabbed Ben's hand and jammed the cigarette into it.

"Take the fucking thing. I'm done here."

He pushed past Ben and started down the hall. He turned back just to say, "A lobotomy should be in your future man."

Ben waved both hands to him enthusiastically, then smiled and said, "Always nice to run into old friends. Chow for now."

I'm sure I would have found the exchange I witnessed quite humorous if it wasn't my own sad reality that I was going to be living with one of its participants, and not the one of choice.

He turned back to me, grinned wildly, and waved me toward our cell. I looked inside before actually entering. It was pretty much identical to all the ones we passed along the way. Bunk beds sat centered and against the wall, and a small desk rested across from them. Ben, ever the escort broke it down for me.

"Here of course is the bed. Bunk beds to be more precise. Do you prefer tops or bottoms? I don't much care but I pee so much so perhaps bottoms would be the obvious choice. Okay, bottoms for Ben it is. Bottoms, bottoms, bottoms!"

He continued. "Over here we have our library which you are at liberty to browse through at your leisure. Just put things back as you found them. Deal?"

"Deal."

The library he was referring to consisted of a few books wedged between a set of makeshift book-ends and several magazines that seemed to all reference religion and the spiritual world. Our literary 'space' was atop a small wooden desk and was littered with a quick count of six instant coffee wrappers, and at least a dozen more rested at the bottom of a nearby garbage can. That solved the mystery of the excessive hyper-active energy. Just to the right was a board supported by two books. On top was a small coffee urn and even more coffee wrappers. I swept my eyes across the whole room and tried to settle both my mind and my nerves and concede to the reality that this was home, and for how long, I was uncertain. I was working that around in my head when Ben broke my train of thought. "I read the classics. Do you? Read the classics I mean?"

Before I could respond he said, "I know what you mean, a bit pretentious for my taste. I mean, a whale and some fucking boat? That's a classic? Or how about the one with the crazy white kid and that half Indian? Or was he a nigger?"

He covered his mouth and giggled through his hands and said, "Better not say that too loud in here, huh?"

"Huck Finn you mean? Or was it Tom Sawyer?"

"Don't know him. Did you meet him in seclusion? I don't know every Harry, Dick, and Tom in this place. Get it?"

He slapped my back and howled with laughter.

"Yeah, I get it." I said. "Very witty guy you are."

"I try you know? I mean in here, it's best to have a sense of humor you know what I mean?"

"Sure. Yeah, I think I do."

"Oh my gosh, I'm so rude. Would you like some coffee? I love coffee."

"Really? I couldn't tell. Thanks but I'll pass."

He fumbled with the process. His nerves were so shot that just pouring water and spooning free some instant coffee was a neural grind.

"How long do you have?" he said.

"I'm not sure. My lawyer thinks thirty days, sixty max but no one knows for sure. I'm open ended."

"Yeah, I'm open-ended too. Supposed to be a one month evaluation they called it."

"Same here. Been much longer than they said?"

"Only by sixty months or so. Should be outta here soon though."

Sixty months. Five years. If there were a scale, or some type of gauge ranging from full to bare, my hope index was already near depleted.

His words put my needle at essentially, empty. Five years. It might as well be five-hundred.

There was no way I could do five years. Or maybe, it would only be two. Or maybe it would be next month. This is what the guard meant down in seclusion. Better to know where you stand than to hang in some unknown limbo. Better to know your fate than wallow in its uncertainty.

I stood back and watched him. He was literate and seemed to speak with some degree of education and intelligence. His mind moved swiftly through dialogue and formulated ideas and concepts like any common man, it was the content of what he expressed, and the way it was conveyed that left little doubt where he state of mental balance laid.

A man approached our cell door. He had a wispy moustache and blotches of sparsely placed facial hair. His scalp was equally inadequate. The fine hairs were parted to the side and strategically placed to cover as much skin as possible. He was short and showed the physical prowess of someone who believed a walk to the kitchen for another beer constituted physical exercise. He flipped open some papers resting on a clipboard and said to me, "You 1161993?"

"Uh-yes, I think so."

He looked down at his sheet again. He showed the same stoic weariness I had seen on every guard's face since I arrived.

"McCullough?"

"Yes, that's me."

"You were supposed to report an hour ago."

"Yes, I'm sorry-"

He stopped me with a raise of his hand and said, "Come with me."

And with that, he turned and proceeded down the hall. I followed alongside him in silence and tried to take in as much of my new surroundings as I could. I was pleased, and much as with the initial walk I took with Ben, I was surprised at how clean everything appeared. The walls and floors were scrubbed free of the grime and residue that one would think to be inevitable in such a surrounding, and the air had the sweet smell of antiseptic no doubt used as some form of disinfectant necessary to mask the smell of too many men sharing the same cramped and stale common ground. The people we encountered on our way were diverse in both age, and ethnic background. Some moved with the same swiftness as a business man hailing a transit bus and even fit its often clichéd description, while others shuffled their feet not seeming to have the energy to simply lift and place one foot in front of the other.

Full on conversations were being achieved without the need of a receiving partner, and the feedback was often animated and full with a spirited energy. At first glance, much like its exterior, the surroundings seemed more to resemble a college corridor and less a prison passageway were it not for the characteristics of its inhabitants.

I was processed and received fresh clothing and my belongings I brought with me when I first arrived. I was informed by the receiving guard that my parents had posted money in the prison commissary and that I could purchase products listed on the days posted in the paperwork he gave me. I smiled and thought of my mother. I thought of the care packages she would send me while at school. They were always filled with treats, both handmade and store bought, and always packed with great care and love. She was doing the same now, at least in her eyes. She was trying to bring comfort and joy from a distance. She was doing her best to boost my mood and build a sense of well-being and peace of mind. Her purpose I had little doubt, was meant to serve the both of us equally.

I made my way back to my cell and found Ben sitting at the desk and drinking yet another cup of coffee. The release of my belongings onto the bottom bunk was met with an instantaneous vocal outcry from Ben.

"Hey! Bunk rights. Bunk rights!"

I quickly grabbed my things and tossed them to the top bunk. "Sorry about that, I forgot."

"No problem. Can't expect you to know all the rules on your first day right?"

"Right. Thank you."

"Of course I'm right. Right as rain. Right as the sky is blue and so are you. Ha!"

He turned his attention back to his coffee and took the pleasure of his witty commentary with him. I tried to change out of my orange jumpsuit as quickly as possible while his back was turned when a knock came. In the doorway stood a black man watching me as I pulled up my pants. He was older, and thin, but wore the wiry type of muscula-ture that some seem to carry more from genetics than any form of physical activity. He had a receding hair line sprinkled gray, and a neatly trimmed goatee shaped to a point on his chin. He carried a disposition that didn't bare any sense of hostility or conflict.

"Hi, how are you?" I asked.

"Well, I'm just fine. How are you doing on such a blessed day as this young man?"

"I'm doing okay, thank you."

If you were to just happen upon the moment, you would believe it was just two regular guys making small talk. Just shooting the breeze. I was new to prison and no doubt ignorant to its ways and practices, but I wasn't so naïve to think that anyone I encountered should be taken at face value. Despite that notion, my first impression of him, justified or not, was that he was not someone to fear or keep at a safe distance. I put my hand out and he reached for it showing a warm and welcome smile.

"Mark."

Before he could answer, Ben jumped from his seat and chimed in. He said, "Shareef!"

Ben took his hand and pumped it with great voracity.

"Hey Ben, you sick crazy fuck, how are you doing my friend? New Cellie here I see."

He had a strong twang in his voice and an almost neighborly way of speaking to you as if maybe he was from a part of the south that con-versing in that manner was both expected and taught from a young age.

"Yes, yes. Ohhh, yes. Shareef, Mark. Mark, Shareef. I call him Shareef the sheriff on a count of he kinda keeps the peace around here for me. Isn't that right?" Shareef turned to me and said, "Around here, we call this man the crazy white boy mother-fucker who done killed some half ass doctor cause he thought the child taken from him during an abortion was the second coming of Christ himself." I said, "That's a long name."

He winked and seemed to appreciate the attempt at humor.

"Far as I can tell Ben, you don't need no tending to round here. Everyone knows you're a few cards short of a full deck. No ill intentions meant by these words, my good man."

Ben seemed not the least bit affected by the stab taken at his sanity.

"So, what brings you to our humble abode, huh? Huh, Mister Ssshareef?"

"Well, it occurred to me that it had been some time since I had visited you and inquired about your current status as it pertains to your cigarette fixation and the actions needed to keep it in check so to speak."

In the few short hours I had known him, Ben's disposition, although juiced from too much caffeine and no doubt an extensive dose of prescribed happiness, was one of an upbeat and enthusiastic nature. At the sound of Shareef's spoken words though, his joyful temperament quickly vanished.

"I'm all out." Ben said.

"Crying shame is what that is."

"You could spot me."

"Now, Mister Ben, you know my apprehensions when it comes to such a practice. Neither a borrower nor a lender be."

"Yes, but a borrowing friend in need, is a borrowing friend indeed."

Shareef laughed and turned to walk away. "That makes about as much sense as tits on a bull, but I'll take it under advisement."

"How much?" I asked Shareef.

"For what?"

"A pack. How much for a pack?"

"Why, you got a roll a dough stuffed in your sock son?"

"No, but I have money in the commissary. I'll take out whatever you need. I'll pay double the asking price."

"Not sure you understand the prison rules and regulations where it pertains to currency and its possession guidelines my good man. You can only purchase and obtain goods at our friendly neighborhood prison supply house. No withdrawals of monetary value can be brought forth."

"Then I'll get you whatever you want. Two for one."

He seemed to process that for a moment then said, "While your proposal is both generous and prosperous for me, I can't help but speculate on the sense and value it holds for you." I nodded toward Ben and said, "Because I can't shop at the commissary until Wednesday, and I will be locked up in here until then."

He read between the lines of my words and smiled. "Yes, I do see the dilemma with which you are truly burdened."

He scanned the halls front and back, then removed a full pack from a coat pocket and tossed them to Ben.

"Thou shalt learn to ration my good friend."

He gave me a glance before turning away and all I could do was quietly say, "Thank you."

"You're quite welcome young man. Remember your word."

Then he was gone. I had hoped his kind was the rule, not the exception during my stay.

"YIPEE!" Ben squealed. He smacked at the bottom of the pack then tore at the wrapping, barely able to contain his excitement.

Fortunately for me, he left to go spend the rest of his afternoon with his new prized possession. I stayed behind still feeling my nerves weren't yet ready to face the idiosyncrasies and characteristics that I knew must derive in a prison yard.

Ben arrived later in the evening bound with the same, perhaps even more, delirious intensity he displayed earlier. It became painfully clear, as I watched him drink yet another cup of coffee and rant on about some misdoing on the yard, that sleep would be hard to achieve, if not impossible, wherever Ben chose to rest his jacked up body.

I laid in bed that first night and listened to him ramble on and on. He passed from one theory or speculation to the next with no obvious transition or attention to subject matter. The only common theme was that regardless of the topic, all his thoughts and reflections came back to the same area of focus. God and religion. I wasn't sure why that was, but I was certain before my time with him ended, he would do his best to make its origin clear.

At some point, I drifted off to sleep and dreamt of the safety and security of my home many miles away. My unconscious mind took me far away from my claustrophobic cell and closer to the constant and unconditional love of my family. Even as I found my consciousness stirring, I tried to remain in my dream and search for the purpose I hoped it would bring me.

When my eyes fully opened, the cell was tranquil. I guess even Ben and his immeasurable energy had its limits. I stayed still, not daring to move and destroy this small stay of peace and quiet. I thought of what my first full day would feel and look like. The day prior began in a fog, and ended much the same. Now I would be forced to go out and see the world around me. Eat meals, interact with other inmates, stand ground when need be, and do my best to be a fast learner of my environment. I had an early morning appointment with my case doctor, and I was eager to move things forward and in hopefully, a positive direction. The fact that my evaluation was meant to determine the true cause and nature of the crime I committed and its outcome would determine whether I left a free man, or spent a minimum of five years behind prison walls, made me both anxious and fearful.

I dressed quietly and stayed in my cell until it was time for my appointment. I walked the path that would lead me to where I was told the doctors resided and I kept my head down, doing my best to avoid eye contact with anyone and everyone.

I found the proper building and an office door marked 'Doctor Sanford.' It was already partially open when I knocked quietly.

"Hello?"

I heard a voice call to me and I stepped forward to follow it. I found a woman sitting at a desk when I entered. She stood to greet me and gestured toward a chair across from her.

"Mark, right?"

"Yes, Ma'am."

"I'm not much older than you so cut the Ma'am crap and call me Diane, okay?"

I liked her immediately. She appeared sincere and perhaps because of her young age, did not seem jaded or worn from many years of what her position and profession would eventually do to even the best intentioned individual. She was also very attractive and possessed a natural beauty that only added to my initial perception.

"Have a seat. How are you holding up so far?"

"I'm fine."

"From what I hear, the first night is always the worst. Are you settled in to your cell?"

"Yes Ma'am. Diane. I mean, yes Diane."

"Wonderful accommodations I'm sure."

"Like the Ritz."

She laughed and said, "I've never stayed at the Ritz, but I'm sure it's a tad bit swankier."

"You don't hear swankier much anymore. I miss it."

She smiled, but it faded quickly. She paused to change the mood and direction of the conversation.

"I read your letter Mark. I was very touched by it. Really, by your whole story. I've reviewed your case history and I saw the articles in the newspaper. I want you to know that I will do everything in my power to help you through this process as quickly as possible. Okay?"

"How long?"

"For what? The evaluation?"

"Until I can get out of here."

"Well, I don't know Mark that depends."

"On what?"

"Mostly on you."

"Someone told me that people have come here for a thirty day study just like me, and are still being evaluated years later. Is that true?"

"Unfortunately, yes that does happen in some cases I'm afraid. Certain circumstances make it unavoidable."

"Like what?"

She was weighing her words carefully now. This was no longer get to know each other chit-chat. We were already into the process that had brought us together.

"Like for instance, if we feel someone who comes to us is either a threat to themselves or to others, we keep them here for both their protection, as well as the well-being of others."

"So, I may never get out of here."

She thought that over for a minute. "That depends Mark. Do you think you're a danger to yourself or to others?"

I knew if I told her the true answer to that question I might as well just put down some roots and settle in because the honest response would put me on the same path as so many of the lost souls who were resolved to live out their lives locked behind the walls that surrounded them. Neither was I going to speak a word of any of the events of the past fifteen years. Although they may have garnered her compassion and empathy, they may have also served to postpone any release date in my future. Beyond that, telling her that contemplating life's end was a daily ritual for me would make ever leaving a senseless fantasy, so I steered the conversation in another direction.

"You want an honest answer right?"

"Of course I do. Can you give me one?"

"You first."

"What do you mean?"

"Can you do it? Answer that question honestly?"

"I believe so, yes. I know that I would never bring any harm to myself or someone else."

"Regardless of the situation? It's just that straightforward for you?"

"Yes, I believe so."

"So, if someone were to harm your child or say, someone in your family, or maybe you're riddled with some hellacious form of cancer that leaves you in constant pain and agony, can you honestly say that without question, you are not capable of ever harming yourself or another human being?"

She didn't answer me for some time and then finally said, "That's not the intent of the question."

"I understand the purpose of the question, I just want you to see that it's not that simple. I'm afraid you are just going to rattle off a series of pre-determined questions some doctor wrote who thinks he understands and can properly assess the true meaning of the responses."

"That's not our process-"

"No? You have it right there in front of you. You ad-libbed the first one I'm sure, but there's a checklist right there on your desk."

She measured my words and then quietly took the pad and slipped it into a side drawer.

"Okay then, how do you think we should continue?"

"See me, see everyone as an individual. Ask them questions specific to what brought them here. If you want truthful answers, be truthful to them. To me. Learn their story, not their I.Q."

"Okay." she said. "Help me with something if you would. My thesis in medical school was on clinical depression. It wasn't something that affected me directly, but I had a sister who struggled with it for years until she finally quit. Gave up the fight. I was only a kid when it happened but I saw the pain and suffering it brought to my family. It destroyed my mother, and with it, much of my childhood. I couldn't understand how someone could make that choice. The will to live, to survive is inherent in all of us so how could it be a conscious decision by someone to feel otherwise? How could she be so selfish? So self-absorbed as to not care how her actions would affect the rest of us? Can you explain that to me, Mark?"

"She wasn't making a conscious decision."

"What was it then? She said she was born that way. That it was a part of her. No different than any aspect of her natural being. Like her eye color or the color of her hair."

"Exactly, that's why it wasn't a conscious decision. I understand her, what she means. When a normal person is depressed it's usually brought on by some circumstance or event in their life. It happens, they experience it, and then it's behind them. They can move on. When it doesn't have a cause or reason for its presence in their life, they have no way to fight back. It can't be rationalized or processed the same way. It's can't be seen, but it's everywhere. It has no form or mass, but it carries such a heavy weight that if you've never felt it, understanding it is not possible. It's tangible but untouchable. You feel like it's right there in front of you and you can reach out for it but it eludes you.

She felt smothered by its existence in her mind, and in her life. She didn't mean to be selfish, and it wasn't a conscious decision so much as the only decision she thought she had. She didn't have the will to live that you have. She said she was born with her depression but she could have also said she was born without the desire for the life you speak of."

Someone knocking broke the energy of the moment. I stood and turned from her, not wanting to match her eyes. To my back she said quietly, "Same time tomorrow."

I left her feeling empty inside and wondering if I had made a mistake, gone too far in the wrong direction with our first meeting. The meeting was so brief and went dark so quickly. I was sure my first impression was both lasting and in no way, a positive one. My ever leaving was predicated on her, and the other doctors' opinion of my mental state. It would serve me well to simply lie, and to speak of how well I felt and the enlightenment I was experiencing with each new day. I had to admit though, a part of me felt good about letting things come through and perhaps that was why I felt so empty, or maybe my notion of why, was simply misguided.

I only took a few steps past the door to the outside when I heard someone say, "Blondie. Hey, over here."

I glanced over at a group of young black men who were gesturing toward me. They were all laughing and posturing in my direction except for one. I should have looked away as soon as I noticed him but I couldn't pull away. His eyes were intense and focused squarely on me. I forced myself to break contact and move past them. I decided to take the direction Ben had told me and find the commissary. I fixed my attention on blocking out the image of the man I just passed and concentrated on my intended location, then finding my way to Shareef when I heard the voice again from behind me. "Duke right? D7?"

Although I assumed it was the one who stared at me, I wasn't sure. Not that it made much difference. All that mattered was the words spoken, and the speculation of what they meant.

I continued on and eventually found the commissary where I bought the cigarettes for Shareef, some coffee for Ben, a Walkman, and as many bags of candy my pockets could hold. Then I headed back to my cell and found my fears of searching for Shareef in the yard were in vain. There he was standing in my doorway, backed turned, as he listened patiently to Ben's ranting about the world and his place in it. He spotted me coming and that drew a big, welcome smile. "There he is. Mister Mark, how are you today my friend?"

"Just fine, now that I have some nutrients to hold me over."

I showed him the bags of candy and he laughed and said, "Hardly constitutes a nutritious diet but it'll do I suppose."

I handed him the packs of cigarettes as I tore open a bag of candy and hopped up onto my bed.

I said, "Gotta be better than today's breakfast." Ben chimed in. "Dysentery is better than today's breakfast."

It wasn't what he said so much as the way he said it, but it struck something in Shareef and I and we both burst out laughing. Ben, realizing it was his words that caused the outburst, joined in on the camaraderie and started slapping the desk and snorting out his own version of happiness. Shareef said, "Ben, you sure are somethin' else my friend. Wish I had known you as a young boy. Sure you must have been somethin' to behold."

I said, "Or to let go of."

We all laughed some more, including Ben, no doubt unaware of my words true meaning.

When the moment passed there was a change in Shareef. His expression seemed strained and reflective. Like a man who had a great cross to bear, and its weight was slowly pulling him down. He turned to me, leaned back to the wall and said, "Stay locked up after supper hear me?"

"Why?"

"There are some folks in here you ought not to be havin' any dealins' with right now. I don't mean to alarm you none, but it would serve you best to stay out of sight for a bit. They apt to lose interest after some time."

Ben seemed neither interested nor concerned about what was spoken. I, on the other hand, had the polar opposite reaction to his words.

He took a few steps then spun back around and said, "A few days usually blows things over with these types in my opinion, but if it takes a different path, you might want to consider goin' back downstairs." Then he was gone.

I didn't bother with dinner that night. Ben offered to sneak me out some bread and milk from the cafeteria, and I gladly accepted.

When he returned, I ate and drank standing up and looking out the small window cut into our door frame.

The hours past slowly as I lay atop my bed. I stared up at the ceiling and thought of all the words of encouragement I got from back home before I left. One well intentioned remark I heard from many was how quickly a month or two goes by in someone's life. "It'll be over before you know it. Thirty days? Piece of cake. No sweat."

Right then, thirty seconds was going by like someone had their finger on the second hand and saw to let it commence only at their leisure.

I started to drift off finally. Fear is like that. It can consume all the energy your body possesses, leaving you with little to fight with should the person or byproduct that brought it to you in the first place actually shows themselves.

I know I hadn't been asleep long when I heard the first faint knock. Ben was still perched at the desk pouring over a magazine and mumbling the words out loud to himself. I had hoped it was a just a guard doing a prisoner count, but I knew it was too early for that. Ben stood and looked out our window and in the same motion turned back to me. He smiled and said, "THEEYY'RREE HHEERREE!"

The fear I felt just a short time ago had little significance now. The fear that this moment brought was completely different. It was the type that starts in your chest and affects your natural breathing cycle. It's easy for us to ignore this action our body provides for us every passing second in our lives. We breathe in, we breathe out, and the cycle continues even when we are at rest. We take it for granted, it's a given factor in our lives. If fear is set in place, and is strong enough, it invades and alters this automatic process we rely on every day. What was once an innate, rhythmic practice is now uneven and awkward. It no longer serves as a common instinct. It becomes forced and irregular, and we have to now work at something that once was just a simple routine we never bothered to give much thought.

That's the type of fear I had that night as I whispered to Ben, "Who is it?"

"It ain't friendlies. That I'm for sure of. Sure, sure, sure."

He twisted his neck back and forth then said, "Yup, yup. Now I see, it's the violators. They've come for you. Such traditional fucks they are. So predictable...so fuckin' predictable they are."

"Don't open the door Ben, please. Whatever you want, it's yours. Name it. Just don't open the fucking door man."

He looked back out the window then stepped away and paced our small cell. A part of me wanted to know, at that moment, what was brewing inside his brain. For whatever was wrong, or maybe more appropriate defective about him, I did not consider him an evil or inhumane man. He was someone who was likely placed into this world with a certain misfortune, or better yet, an imbalance that didn't fit the surroundings he was forced into. It was something he was born with, no different than me, no different than Diane's sister.

"I'm in a pickle here my friend. Hear me?" Ben said." On the one hand, if I don't let them in, I'm gonna hear about it for sure. I'm goddamned sure of it. I know I am. On the other hand, if I do, if I do, if I do... I'm for sure gonna hear about it in spades from you. Sad, but true for you. True, true, true."

I pleaded with him. "Please Ben. Whatever you want. You want cigarettes? Coffee? I can get whatever you want tomorrow. Please Ben."

"I want world peace. I want an end to tyranny. I want equality for all. Except the niggers and the spics, fuck them."

He looked through the window again, and again came another knock at the door. Ben twisted a shirt around the door handle and tied it to the chair then sat down casually and braced to hold the door closed.

"Sounds like three at least, at least three I'd think. Gotta be. Three'd be my guess."

I heard a voice come from outside the door say quietly, "Open the fucking door."

"Were you this popular in high school?" Ben said. "I bet you were. All blonde hair and blue eyed. Varsity jacket type I'd guess."

"Ben, don't let them in, please."

I could see him straining to keep the door from opening. "Yeah but Bunkie, if I don't these assholes just won't let up. Their fucking brains don't fucking work like yours and mine. They're primitive, like monkeys but worse. They can talk and walk, but… fuck it."

He let go and stood up, then he pushed the door open just enough to stick his head out.

"Well, hello gentlemen, how are you on such a fine night as this? Are milk and cookies in our near future?"

"Shut up. Give him up."

Ben smiled, put a finger to his lips and said, "Alas, what fair maiden does thy speak of?"

"Let him out."

"Now, now. Hope to not sound so much as to be full of one's self but, what's in it for me?"

I could hear and feel the effort Ben was spending to stop their entrance as he spoke through the crack in the door.

"Hey now kind sir, doesn't one know how impolite it is to enter one's castle uninvited? Are you an animal of some kind? Is that it? Am I on to something? Are you from a broken, tragic upbringing? Your Mother is a crack whore perhaps?"

"FUCK YOU!"

"Now, now. Pipe down, please. I, we, must think of the neighbors, the neighborhood." A voice from the other side said, "Christ, I forget sometimes how fucking crazy you are."

"Interesting you brought up the world's Divine Being, are you a believer? Do you accept the Almighty Lord as your savior? I think he was just a prophet myself but hey, what do I know? What are your thoughts?"

"Open the fucking door."

"If I do, shall we have some tea and biscuits? Wait, I don't have any tea. Will coffee do? Wait! Hold on! I thought milk and cookies were on the menu. Either way, that does sounds delightful don't you think? A real, old-fashioned bull session with dear friends."

The voice said, "We ain't your fucking friends and I'm gonna say this one last time-"

Ben cut him off and said, "Here's the thing. Here's my dilemma, my problema if you will. If I let you in for what I'm sure would be a night of stimulating, perhaps even inspiring conversation I fear your attention will stray from me and slip unkindly toward my comrade. That would be most upsetting indeed. A man invites you into his home, offers you a bit of nourishment and beverage, the least you could do is entertain his worldly views. Is that too much to ask? I must inquire again, is your mother a crack whore?"

The voice said, "Fuck you just say? Stop fucking asking me that. Now for the last time-"

"I read somewhere about inner city mother's in the ghetto. The percentages were staggering-"

Ben wasn't ready for the weight from the door and it nearly pulled him down but he caught himself and braced hard with his leg and shoulder. Ben was thin and to see him, appeared frail and weak, so entry seemed eminent but I suppose when you're all jacked up on coffee and nicotine, further add in a total lack of fear or apprehension of the current situation, anything is possible. At least I hoped. The voice was clearer now, and appeared to almost be coming from inside the cell. "Last time. Open the fucking door, or it's you I'm coming in to see."

"First, I believe you said last time, last time. That diminishes the quality of your threat, at least as it applies to me. Second, I don't much

107

like the coloreds remember? And, not that it should come as any surprise to you, it's a fact I'm sure you're aware of but nonetheless I shall enlighten you since the need to seems necessary. You, my friend, are a said colored one and as such, actually calling you friend is as much a sordid lie that it borders on the criminal side of this universe but hey, we are in prison so maybe it's suitable after all. So, my third and final testament on the matter is this. If you come near me, if you even look at me with the slightest tone of hostility or ill will, I will bite off your cock and wear it around me like a charm. A big black phallic symbol that just happens to be the real thing."

There was silence for what seemed like a lifetime before the voice spoke up and said, "Some other time."

I knew that was directed only towards me, but since it meant they were leaving, it was the most blissful sentence I could have asked for. I could hear their muffled voices and the shuffling of their shoes beneath them while they walked away. Before he shut the door Ben said, "Thanks for stopping by. I don't need a new vacuum just now but I can appreciate all the hard work you do. Best of luck in your endeavors."

He shut the door and turned to me. "Nice boys. I always enjoy company even if it is a little late to be ringing one's bell wouldn't you agree?"

"Yes, I would, and thank you."

"You're most welcome my good man. You needn't have worried though, I was never going to let them in. I just had my cleaning lady here today. Do you think I would let the likes of them in here? On such an evening as this? Messy mess. No sir. No sir."

He climbed into his bed, stretched out, belched, then yawned and was asleep in minutes, completely unaffected by what just took place. In a way I envied him and his almost childlike view of the events that transpired in his daily life. I admired how unaffected he was by even the most critical, possibly, life threatening of situations. I laid there staring at the ceiling knowing full well sleep would not be on my side that night, and as I listened to him peacefully sleeping without what seemed to be a care in the world, I wished more than anything that I could see the world as he did. Oblivious to all of its misery and torment. I wanted to be free of those things that settled into my mind and refused to leave regardless of how much I pleaded them to do so. Life would be so simple then. Wake up, and your biggest concern, the sole focus of your existence revolved around where, and how to get coffee and cigarettes.

The next morning I had breakfast and then found my way back to the administration building, and back to Diane.

She was seated at her desk and lost in paperwork when I knocked at her door. She pulled down her glasses, smiled, and said, "Come in. Have a seat Mark."

I said, "Thank you. How are you today?"

"I'm fine."

She studied me then said, "Can you say the same?"

"I'm fine."

"You don't look fine. You look like shit. Sorry."

"Long night. And thank you. Love hearing that to start off a session of personal insight and self-reflection."

She laughed. "Sorry. Anything I should know about?"

"No. Everything is fine."

She weighed those words then dove right into the session. "The last time we spoke we talked about your sister."

"It was your sister."

"Excuse me?"

"It was your sister. You said she took her life, remember?"

"I do."

She collected herself.

"Let's move forward. What I meant was tell me about your family. Do you have any brothers or sisters?"

"I have both."

"But you had one that passed away. A sister I believe."

"Where did you hear that? We didn't talk about her yesterday. What's going on?"

I didn't know why she started the session talking about my sister and her passing. Maybe it was just to get me to open up about my family, or perhaps she thought she had done too much of her own on the subject at our last session and wasn't sure why or what to do with how it made her feel. Regardless, a full day later and it was still at the forefront of her thoughts. Still, a small part of me felt this nagging ache that she was headed down that same path of standard psychological practice I had already warned her about and the anger it brought came out in my next reply. I regretted it almost as soon as it passed my lips.

"And what does passed away mean anyway? I've always hated that term. She died. She's dead. End of sentence."

"How?"

"How did she die?"

"Yes."

"My parents went camping. They didn't have much money back then so a cabin at the local park constituted a vacation. My mom was trying to entertain my sister Kathy plus she had a six month old to contend with. My dad was with my brother. I guess one thought the other was watching her. It was just an unfortunate accident. She drowned in the lake by their campsite."

"How old were you?"

"I wasn't even born yet. I am the youngest. She would have been between my two sisters."

"What was her name?"

"Diane."

There was a quiet moment before I said, "Every year, days before her birthday, and leading up to the anniversary of her death, my parents are different."

"How so?"

"They are very Christian people. They hold their faith and its values deep inside. Their faith meant everything to them. Her death, tested their belief in the religion they hold on so strongly to." "How is their faith now?"

"You mean how is it after their son tries to kill himself by robbing a bank, right?"

"Not the words I was looking for. But okay, yeah. How are they after what happened?"

"As good as can be expected I guess. I know it's a long ride back home and I'm sure there will be a lot of praying along the way. That's their way."

"Of?"

"Coping."

"Do you? Pray I mean?"

"No, but if it works for them then so be it. My father is a minister and a marriage counselor. His faith in his God is very much a part of his life. Of both their lives actually."

"You said, his God. What do you mean by that?"

"For him, it's more about a way of life than an individual being or higher power. His family, his work, it all revolves around his church and the way he lives out each day. My father has something that I would guess maybe ninety-nine percent of the population in this world wishes for, but will never have."

"What's that?"

"Well, if you think about it, our days are pretty much split three ways. We work, we have our free time, and then we rest. Most people may have one, maybe two of those things right in their lives but rarely all three. My dad, he wakes up each morning and goes to a job he loves then comes home to the woman of his dreams, his high school sweetheart mind you, and because of one and two being right in his life, he sleeps like a baby every night. That gives him all three. He doesn't need any outside influence to enjoy his life. It's just fine the way it is in his eyes." She thought about that, then said, "Sounds like a fantastic way to go through life."

"Works wonders for him."

"You said outside influences, you mean drugs or alcohol?"

"Yes, he goes through life with no blinders on whatsoever. He sees everything just how it is, perhaps naively at times, but it's not blurred in any way. I envy him for that."

"You don't think that's possible. For you I mean?"

"No. It's not possible."

"So you have outside influences as you call them that help you see the world better."

"No." I said. "But it helps keep the fog in place and you know what I use. I'm sure you've seen the toxicology reports. I thought we agreed no games. First my sister-"

"You're right. I'm sorry. And yes, I have seen the reports. Your marijuana and blood alcohol levels were through the roof the day of the robbery. You had to be still under the influence when it happened."

"I was so wasted, I thought a cop was going to pull me over on Main Street. He slowed when I passed by him and I thought he was turning around but he never came."

"What do you think would have happened?"

"I'm not sure. It might have meant the robbery wouldn't have been necessary after all."

She let that hang there for a minute then I broke the silence. "How many of the three do you have?"

"This is supposed to be about you remember?"

"A very wise man once told me that a good therapist learns as much about themselves as they do about their patients during a session."

"I see. That wise man wouldn't happen to be your father now would it?"

"One in the same. So, let's have it. I'm thinking one out of three for you."

"Yeah? Only one?"

"I think you like your job so getting out of bed isn't a problem but it's after that, that's where it all ends. Two is missing for you and because of that, you don't sleep well at all."

"That's very interesting. You know so little about me yet you surmise so much. Where does this insight come from?"

"I don't need to know anything about you. You didn't have to speak a word. It's in your eyes. It's exhausting isn't it?"

"What's that?"

"Faking it. It's exhausting."

"I'm not sure what you mean."

"And you get good at it after a while too, right? It becomes second nature. A part of you. Like a necessary piece of the puzzle needed just to get through the day."

"Is that what you do?"

"And that's what you do? That's how you get through the day?"

"I'm a master at it. It's who I am. I did what I did because that type of secrecy has a price you are eventually forced to pay off. I reached mine that day."

"And now?"

"Well, I can't say I'm overly enthusiastic about the prospect of living, but I don't want to die if that's what you mean."

"What changed?"

"Seeing my father in court the day after for one thing. He cried in a way that was painful emotionally and even physically to watch. I would sooner go through the rest of my day's pretending to be something or someone I'm not before I would ever be responsible for inflicting that kind of agony on him again. And there's my mother, I let her down even though I promised myself that I wouldn't."

"Anything else?"

"I guess there's enough inside me that wants to see if change is possible or if we just are who we are. Like your eyes are blue or your tall or short. I'm curious enough I guess to see if that's all there is to it."

"What's your gut feeling? Can people change?"

"Let me ask you something first. Would you consider yourself the upbeat type? You know which one I mean. The glass is half full and all that. Is that you? Or are you the one who only sees the negative in things around you?"

"Well, despite your deep insight into my life, I would consider myself the half full type I suppose."

"And do you think it's a conscious decision you make? Do you think it's a decision that can just simply be made? No different than choosing a meal or a movie?"

"I think people can learn to make the best of any given situation if they really want to, yes."

"Then that's where we are different then. I believe people are born into what they are. I think they can overcome obstacles along the way sure, even seemingly insurmountable ones but that's because that's who they are to begin with. You can't change the blueprint of what makes you who you are. Whether you're an optimist or pessimist that's part of you. You said so yourself, people can learn to change but it takes such effort to even attempt to do so. You can't change what's already in place. Not permanently anyway."

"Well, I guess I'm really screwed then because if what you just said is true, then my profession is essentially worthless."

"Not at all. That's not what I'm saying. You will reach some people, and there will be others who want to change. There will be those who are willing and even capable of undoing who they are because the alternative is no longer a choice for them."

"But you just said it wasn't a choice. Didn't you? How can they chose something that according to you, doesn't come with an option button? Your theory either works or it doesn't. I don't see any in between in what you just said. I don't see how there could be a silver lining for some but not for others. The way you spell it out, it seems it only goes one way."

"I didn't mean-"

She cut me off and seemed genuinely upset by what I'm sure she thought was a misguided assumption of her life. "And quite honestly, your hypothesis has a few too many holes in it for me."

"Oh yeah, like what?"

"Going back to your words about choices and who we are and what we are born with, was a hypocritical statement on your part."

"How so?"

"You said we don't have a choice. That our destiny is set in place and not capable of change. Like our eyes are blue or how tall we are. You said that am I right?"

"Yes, I did."

"And you believe in what you said?"

"Well, I said I was curious if it was but yes, I believe that to be true."

"If that's true and we have no choice then you're a liar."

"A liar?"

"Yes, a liar. You said earlier that you no longer wanted to die. That once you did, but now you don't. Weren't you born and if I'm understanding you correctly, programmed to be who you are? That decision to rob a bank according to you, was destiny. Something that was meant to be, and meant to take your life because it was simply part of the plan. Yet, you didn't wait for the police. You left the bank before they arrived because I think you wanted to live."

"You think so, huh?"

"Yes, I do. I think you need to re-evaluate your little theory you've got there because if you really break it down, it doesn't work. People can and do change every day. I see it all the time. Not just here but everywhere. Yes it's true, we are stuck with our height or skin color or our body type, but we are not stuck with who we are inside. That I will never believe and that is where you're fundamentally wrong. That being said, I'll sum it up this way, your theory just plain sucks ass.

I smiled and let the moment and her, have their way.

"Sucks ass?"

"Yes, big time. Now get out of here."

I stood to leave and when I got to the door she said, "Mark, what you said about being one out of three, you were right, but believe me change will come soon for me. And Mark, there is always a choice."

I carried those words with me as I found my way back to my cell. I wasn't so sure any more about my father's theory that a therapist learned as much as they taught in a session. That day it was pretty one sided, and all in favor of Diane.

Chapter 8

More than a week had passed since I left seclusion and settled into my cell and a certain routine, albeit a disturbing one to say the least. Each day the details stayed the same but there timing and sequence changed whenever deemed necessary. I showered at different times, I skipped different meals, and even planned trips to the commissary were strategically plotted out. Only two things remained constant. My sessions with Diane and my time walking the makeshift track on the prison grounds. I had hoped that it was so wide open and clear that no one would consider it a feasible place to bring me harm. I took my Walkman radio and would find my way to the track every day. It felt so good to put on headphones and transport myself to somewhere, anywhere far away from where I was. I hadn't seen or heard from the men who came for me that one night and although it seemed unlikely, maybe Shareef was right, maybe they got bored and just lost interest. Maybe they didn't want to deal with Ben or maybe they just found an easier target.

The days moved along that way for me, and if you would have told me prior to my arrival that the therapy sessions would be what I looked forward to the most, I would have just assumed you were in need of your own psyche evaluation.

Some of the initial fear I felt during the first two weeks had settled and although the meeting coming up involving not just Diane, but a team of doctors was looming in the next few weeks, I could almost say I felt reasonably optimistic. I thought perhaps that after all, I could survive this whole ordeal. That was, until April 29, 1992. On that day, four mostly white Los Angeles police officers were acquitted in a court of law of beating an African American man named Rodney King after a brief car chase. The beating was caught on tape and justice for the attack seemed forthcoming. When the officers were found not guilty, rioting broke out in south Los Angeles. More than fifty people were killed and countless more were wounded. Material losses were thought to reach near one billion dollars on final count. The rioting continued for six days only finally reaching its end when the military was called in.

I had done my best to become as inconspicuous as possible whenever I ventured outside my cell and foolishly felt I was slowly gaining a talent for invisibility. I kept my head down and spoke only when spoken to. On that day though, no trickery or disguise would be of use to me. Fortunately, the prison went on lockdown as a preventive measure should any violence come about. However, it was lifted the next day when no immediate threat seemed imminent and life seemingly went on as before. But not for me. I had lost more weight since seclusion and my hair and skin were getting color from the spring sun. That combination coupled with my baby face and blue eyes, made the type of impression one wishes to avoid when incarcerated.

Everyone in their life inevitably makes decisions that they wish they could go back and undo. It doesn't matter who you are, where you're from, or what you do, it's universal to us all. The day after the lockdown was lifted I made one of those decisions. The fact that I could be so stupid after spending so much time being cautious and alert is still troubling even to this day. Maybe out of boredom, or maybe I was letting my guard down and becoming too comfortable, I'm not sure but that day I chose to seek out the television room in the hopes of finding a game to watch. The NBA playoffs were in full swing and the thought of a few hours wasted away watching basketball seemed to not be a waste at all. I found the room and when I entered, my mood rose. Shareef was sitting with his arms folded watching the game intently. When he saw me, he welcomed me with a big smile then waved me inside.

"Mark my good man, welcome, welcome. Have a seat. Come on, sit, sit."

He pulled out a chair for me and his eyes went quickly back to the screen.

"Just watchin' a little of the game here. This white boy over here just got done tellin' us how much better Bird is than Jordan. Nothin' but nonsense. All you damn white boys are the same. Lame, slow and dumb."

The room, minus the only other white guy there besides me, cheered on his words. Shareef was showing a different side of himself than he had the times he came to my cell. He was more animated and upbeat and less somber and serious than when he came to visit. Ben had that effect on people.

"Just kiddin' man. I'm just messin' with you. Who's your team Mark?"

"The Knicks."

The room erupted with a series of jeers and catcalls.

Shareef said, "Now then, you have come at the most opportune time my friend. They be playin' my Bulls at this very minute. Right there up on the screen is the one and the only Michael Jordan. See him? Can you see?"

"So, you think white people are blind also?"

It took him a second to catch on, then he said, "Most certainly are, least where it pertains to the glorious game of basketball. Look at the man move Mark. Such grace and finesse. He's like a dancer. Like a fuckin' gazelle out there. You gonna tell me Bird's better than him? Please. He's so slow, he runs in a circle and gets lost."

I said, "He's so slow, when he shits, his ass calls timeout."

"Good one, good one. How 'bout this. He's so slow, it takes him two hours to watch sixty minutes."

His words were met with more cheers.

I said back, "He's so slow, he asks what time the eleven o'clock news is on."

The room grew louder with approval.

To see it, you would think we were all old friends hanging at one of our houses, telling stories and just talking trash. Instead, we were strangers with vastly different backgrounds with little in common except a love of basketball and a world of boredom. I knew why I really needed to see this game in particular. I was sure my dad would be at home and glued to the set and I knew he would hope the game would give him the same outcome I was looking for. A temporary reprieve from what was happening in our lives.

Shareef said, "Alright, enough already. I do believe we have adequately established the man is a slow ass motherfucker."

Shareef jumped out of his chair and toward the set. He screamed and howled like some kid on his birthday.

"Did you see that huh? Did you see that Mark?"

"No, I'm white and blind remember?"

"Well then, you best get yourself a fresh pair of glasses cause you be missin' my boy, Michael mother-fuckin' Jordan. He be tearin' up your Knickerbockers. Lay witness my brother and repent. Your team ain't got a chance."

I said, "They took the first game from them."

"Ah, yes my son, this is true but that's why it's called a series. Got me? It's a S-E-R-I-E-S. Anybody can get lucky even against the great Michael Jordan and win one lousy game. They got to win three more. There ain't no way on God's green earth that's gonna happen. Just ain't no way. No sir, nuh-uh."

No sooner had he sat down, then he was right back up shouting and cheering and carrying on like a man without a care in the world. Ben had told me during a brief moment of clarity that Shareef had been found guilty of assault and robbery as well as resisting arrest and striking one the officers. Someone down the line was able to draw him a psych label and he ended up doing time at Butner instead of somewhere more hardcore. Knowing what he now knew about where he was, I always meant to ask him if he thought it was the right decision.

He sat back down and spoke without losing sight nor breaking concentration from the game.

"You play at all Mark?"

"A little yeah."

"Unfortunately, we don't have no courts here, but we do quench our competitive nature with a little handball action. Ever play?"

"A little, years ago."

"You any good?"

"For a white guy, sure."

"Uh-huh, I'll be the judge of that. You know where we play? You know the wall behind the Admin building?"

"Yes, I think so."

"Course you do, I see you walking the track right by there every goddamned day."

"Keeps my head straight."

"Amen Brother. We all need that. Whatever it takes. Anyways, why don't you come down tomorrow afternoon and old Shareef will show you a few moves tucked up under this here sleeve. Sound good?"

"Just don't get mad at me is all I ask."

"Mad, why?"

"Your friends will be watching?"

"Yeah, so?"

"And we'll be playing?"

"And?"

"I don't know much about the ways of prison but I do know getting your ass kicked by a white boy on your home turf is going to be a difficult situation to overcome. But like I said, I don't really know the rules so maybe it won't be that big a deal."

He turned to me, held my gaze hard, and then busted out laughing.

"Oh, so that's how its gonna go down huh? You gonna smack me down in front of all my peeps? Okay, okay. We shall see. The gauntlet has been tossed. I get it now."

"Like I said, just don't get pissed and remember it was your idea. If you-"

The door opened. I didn't have to look myself to know it wasn't someone he was eager to see. His face said it all for him. I heard the voice behind me and without turning I knew who it was. It was the voice I heard the first day I left Diane's office. It was also the voice coming from the other side of my door the night with Ben. The voice said, "Sup fellows. Sup Shareef."

It was only the second time I had seen him that anxious and uneasy. The other time was when he came to warn me about the same individual standing before us right then.

"How are you today Mister Darnell if you please?"

"I'm just fine. Mind if I pull up a chair?"

I could feel him watching me and waiting for me to turn so he could see the fear in my eyes. I couldn't bring myself to do it. In part, because I was so frightened, but more, I didn't want to give him the satisfaction of laying witness to it.

Darnell said, "Y'all watching the game huh? Who's up?"

There was little conversation prior to his arrival. Except for the occasional white guy joke, most were focused on the game, but now it was completely silent.

His presence gave the room a feel of being in church. Don't speak until you're told to and keep your head down and just pray.

"Tie ballgame, but it's still early. We'll pull away." Shareef said.

Darnell shot back. "What's this 'we' shit? I ain't no fan. Bunch a niggers runnin' up and down. White folks in fancy clothes buyin' ten dollar hot dogs and cheerin' 'em on like they was animals. Like some rats in some fuckin' cage. Like we their own private source of motherfuckin' entertainment."

Shareef breathed in and out slowly. "Darnell, those niggers of which you speak get paid a lot of money to run up and down as you say. Some can buy hotdogs for everybody in the stadium and that includes the rich white folk you speak of. You should be proud of your brothers out there."

"Fuck 'em."

I knew it was coming. I knew it was inevitable but I still wasn't ready when it finally came.

"Hey Whitey, what you think about all this? I'd like to have your take on the black man and how you think he fits in with yours. Seems to me, a black man so much as looks down a white man, he gets strapped and slapped into a cell. In the white man's world, you can damn near beat a black man to death and not answer. Even if you on tape. They had it all on a goddamned fuckin' video camera and those mother-fuckers just skipped right on outta that courtroom. That seem fair to you white boy? Huh? Mister skinny ass white trash. Hey, I like that, I'm gonna have to remember that one. Skinny ass white trash."

"Filthy ignorant ghetto shitstain."

Shareef stepped in with an attempt to turn the course of my words and said, "Gentlemen please, enough already-"

Darnell ignored him.

"Fuck you just say to me?"

"You heard me."

I stood to leave.

"Sit your scrawny ass down."

I said, "I'm not a part of this. Just let me go."

I was shaking almost uncontrollably now, and I wondered how much it showed.

"No, see that's where you're wrong. You are a part of this, you are very much a part of this. Matter fact, you're the main event."

Shareef was trying to slow down a situation that was gaining momentum fast.

"Come on Darnell, look at the kid. You better than this man."

"Don't go preachin' to me alright? You ain't so fuckin' innocent up in this place."

"I am not a perfect man by any means," Shareef said." but what you are proposing, it's bull-shit and you know it."

"I ain't proposin' nothing. You think I want his bony ass? Shit, I'd come out his front. He gonna do somethin' else for me though."

He started to rub his groin and stare me down. His smile was hideous. He ran his tongue over his lips and said, "Gonna do somethin' real nice for me with those pouty lips, for sure."

He was between me and the exit and seemed to be hoping, almost daring me to step closer. His size and the lifestyle I'm sure that brought him to prison meant any attempt to pass him would likely be futile.

Shareef said, "Darnell, come on man. Let it be. He's not the one responsible for what those cops did. Ain't nothin' to be gained by what you're proposing-"

Darnell laughed. "What you say? Ain't nothin' to be gained? Look at this bitch. He finer than some of the whores I fucked in the real world. In here, he's Miss Fuckin' America."

He laughed as if it was the funniest thing he had ever said, maybe even ever heard in his life. I knew I couldn't just scream for help. Doing so inside prison was thought to be much the same as being a snitch. Win or lose, you had to fight. The decision to charge forward and hope for the best was made just as the door pushed open and a guard stepped in.

"Everything okay in here? Someone reported shouting."

Shareef perked up. "No, sorry. Uh, that was just me yelling at the television. I get a little too excited sometimes. I do apologize."

I walked past him and out the door to the outside world. I could no longer entertain the guarded optimism I had just a few days earlier. Then, I entertained the thought that perhaps this would all eventually be over. Maybe even, in some twisted way, it could be a learning experience. Maybe some good could find its way out of all this mess. I no longer felt that to be a plausible, or even a possible outcome.

Chapter 9

Two weeks passed and I hadn't seen Darnell. There was enough of his type to go around though, so I pretty much subsisted on candy and whatever Ben could sneak out of the cafeteria. I rarely left my cell and no longer showered. I would remove my shirt and wash with a towel, then put it right back on. I would then do the same from the waist down. I washed my hair in the sink, and only when fully dressed. I spoke to few people and when I did, it was always in the open and always afforded an escape route should it be necessary. I lived for mail call and word from the outside world. Letters arrived daily from my family and their love and concern were overwhelming and drove me to at least try to survive my situation, and not just give up as I had done so many times before in my life. To this day, over twenty years after l left that horrible place, I still have every one of those letters. I even kept the receipts showing all the candy I bought to live on, and how much coffee and cigarettes I purchased to keep Ben happy. The Walkman radio with my inmate number etched into it sits in my drawer beside my bed as a reminder of my time there.

On the night before I was to meet with Diane for the last time prior to my final evaluation with the prison board of doctors, I was in my cell when Ben came in like a nicotine charged, caffeine soaked tornado. His eyes were bulging and he was profusely sweating through his shirt. He paced back and forth and kept mumbling in some incoherent, nonsensical language only he understood.

Although I was always weary around him, and did whatever was necessary to keep the peace, as the days went by I no longer feared him. Until that night. He was a whirlwind of pent-up rage and aggression. Ben's hair was severely receding with just a few wisps still lingering on top so you could see the vain running right along his temple bulging and pounding and ready it seemed, to explode at any moment. Leaving the cell was not an option, so I was going to do the best I could to appease and soothe a bi-polar, severely agitated murderer.

"Hey Ben. Buddy, what's going on?"

It didn't seem that my words were heard by him or if he could have even understood them if they were.

He said to no one in particular, "Who the fuck are they to tell me?"

For the first time since he stormed in he noticed me.

"Huh? Who the fuck are they to tell me? Who the fuck are they? Can you answer me that?"

He grabbed all the contents on the desk and slammed them into the wall then kicked and stomped them repeatedly, cursing and accusing someone of some grave injustice.

"Ben listen, slow down okay? Who's they? What happened? Did you see someone?"

He continued, increasing the intensity of his madness. He tore through his sheeting and ripped his mattress from the bed frame.

His actions were now beginning to draw attention from outside the cell. Inmates were starting to gather around and watch the spectacle Ben was making of himself. I thought about jumping off my bed and shutting the door, but who locks themselves inside a room forming essentially, a caged animal?

Spittle was now forming and crusting at the corner of his mouth. He again seemed to tune me out and continued swearing and ranting through a chorus of dialogue that made no sense to me. I could understand the words, but they did little to form a literate word structure.

"Today was supposed to be my day. Who the fuck are they to tell me, huh? They think they can control me with fucking medication? I don't need medication. They promised."

He seemed to be speaking to me now, not through me. I still had no idea what was going on but had hoped engaging him would further defuse the moment, so I said, "Hey Ben, why don't you have a seat?"

I climbed down from my bed and righted the chair then offered it to him with a guiding hand.

"Want some coffee? I got some for you today. I got donuts too. Coffee and donuts. Your favorite, right?"

He took the seat and let out a deep sigh, as did I.

"What kind of donuts? Make mine black please."

"I got chocolate donuts. Just what you need right now."

"And stimulating conversation."

"That's right Ben. And stimulating conversation."

He said, "I've got bread too. Bread doesn't go much with our menu for this evening, but it'll have to do."

"I love bread Ben. Ask me, it goes with everything."

I took out the donuts and poured a cup of coffee for him.

Ben said, "I have a pastry dish too but that seems inappropriate, right? Can't have donuts and a pastry. That's like having a steak and a hamburger together. Who does that? If we did indulge though, which one do you think would be the steak? For me, it would be the pastry dish."

"No way my friend, chocolate in a landslide."

"You are a bit of a chocoholic."

"It does a body good."

"Not really…"

I was hoping, even planning to get him off on one of his senseless, irrational tirades and keep his mind away from whatever occurred earlier and upset him to the point of smashing our cell to pieces. He was breathing easy now and carrying on about the pros and cons of chocolate and empty calories and their role in our digestive system when a knock came at the door. A guard entered and directly behind him stood a full bearded and thinly framed man wearing a tie supported by a crisp white shirt and large, round glasses too big for his narrow jawline. He looked nervous and weary of his surroundings. I had seen him on several occasions and knew right off he was one of the prison doctors. Ben's I assumed. The guard said, "The doc is here to see you Ben. You gonna act up? I don't want no funny business, got me?" Ben said, "Of course sir. No funny business coming from me. To be honest with you my good friend, anything and everything related to what I am pondering is anything but funny. You can be rest assured of that. Would you like a chocolate donut?"

He turned to me.

"Is it okay if we share? We have guests."

I looked at the guard, then the doctor, then back at Ben.

"Sure Ben, we have plenty." The guard held up a hand and said, "No thank you. Ben, the doc here wants you to come back with us okay? It's better if he can talk to you in private." Ben folded his arms and turned out a face of mock confusion. "But I just had a long discussion with the good doctor. I don't know what else needs saying at this time."

The doctor spoke for the first time.

"We didn't finish Ben."

"Oh, yes we did. You told me all you needed to. I can respect that. I do not however, choose to accept its content or validity. I choose not kind sir."

The guard reached for Ben's arm but he recoiled away and wagged his finger and gave a look that made clear that would be a bad decision. The guard assessed Ben, his demeanor, his expression, and backed off and said over his shoulder to the doctor, "Get back-up."

The doctor hurried out and left the guard and Ben locked eye to eye. The guard said, "Don't make this any harder than it's gotta be Ben."

"Today was my day. They promised."

"No one promised you anything Ben. You need to take your meds-"

Before he could finish the words Ben was on him. It happened fast. Ben didn't strike him, instead, he used both arms to grab his shirt and pull him close to his face.

"You're lying. You don't know what they promised. Do you know? Huh? They promised me! They promised me!"

I learned on several occasions in my life that the worst people to have any type of physical confrontation with, the ones to fear most weren't necessarily the biggest or the brawniest, but rather, the ones who show no fear. No fear of the pain they will inflict, no fear of the pain they themselves may actually endure, and no apprehension for its eventual consequence either way.

I always believed Ben fit in that category, and what little doubt I may have had faded quickly as I watched him struggle with the guard. He was attempting, and with little success, to gain control of Ben while looking over his shoulder for help to come. I had always found it to be a tremendous disadvantage to fight someone who displayed great anger and malice toward you, but you did not share an equal temperament to match their energy and ferocity. That's the circumstance the guard was faced with at that moment. He simply wanted to finish out his shift and go home to a hot meal, a cold beer, and his family. Fighting a crazed prison inmate may have been a potential job requirement, but not one high on his list to carry out that day. Ben started pushing and spitting out words that were garbled and incoherent again. Fatigue should have been a factor for a man who existed only on coffee and nicotine but I guess absolute rage knows no limits. Ben took the moment where I had hoped he wouldn't and attempted to strike the guard. He partially deflected the blow and managed to turn him around and force him down to one knee. Ben continued screaming out when the second guard made his presence felt by lowering a shoulder into Ben's side driving him to the ground and pulling his arms back behind him. Ben continued screaming out at full volume, his blurred words ringing in my ears.

I watched them first subdue Ben, then restrain him with cuffs the whole while he continued with his maniacal verbal assault. They pulled him up and dragged him out all in one motion as the doctor stood nervously watching from outside the cell. I listened to them carry him down the hall. I could still hear his cries as they passed through the set of doors and out to his resting place for the night. His new home would almost surely be in seclusion. I don't know what set him off, if it was something real or just an imaginary injustice dreamed up inside his twisted, diseased mind. One thing I was fairly certain of was I wouldn't be seeing him any time in the near future.

The next morning I followed my daily routine of doing everything at a different time and location as the day before, then headed for the track. I spotted Shareef and a group of inmates playing their style of makeshift handball against a building wall and walked over to join them. He watched me coming towards him and extended a hand for me to grab hold of.

"Glad you finally decided to grace us with your presence."

"Sorry, I've been busy."

He slapped at the ball and said, "Yeah, I know how it is. Should be stayin' low anyways."

I let that go and watched him focus on the ball as it hit the wall. He tracked it into his palm and sent it back with the same momentum it brought to him.

"Not too bad for an old guy."

"Yeah, I still got a few moves. And I ain't old neither. Just cause I ain't a young buck like you don't mean I can't still have game."

"I didn't say all that."

"It's what you meant to say is how I read it."

I laughed. "Yeah, yeah."

I would never openly give him the credit, but he was good. While the others were reacting to his play, and trying simply to keep up, he was responding to theirs with confidence and a determined aggression.

"How have you been my friend? Haven't seen you since-"

He grabbed the ball and wrapped it up tight in his palm, then stroked his goatee to appear reflective and to portray a sense of confusion and uncertainty. He finally came out with,

"Oh yeah, I remember now. The TV room, right? Yeah, that's it. What I can't remember is who won that game. Actually, I've been kinda outta the loop a tad bit. Who won the Bulls- Knicks series do you know? Cause I don't recall hearing, did you?"

"It was close. Four to three. You got lucky."

"No such thing as luck with the man Michael Jordan on your team. No such thing as luck period. Remember that."

He smacked the ball and it echoed off his hand and found the wall with a hard thud.

"Thanks by the way."

He cursed his shot selection and said without turning to me, "No thanks necessary. He's not the only one to keep an eye on in here. I suppose that's not news to you anymore."

"No, it's not."

"These walls can fool some folks. Seem harmless when you first lay eyes on 'em but they holdin' a heap full of degenerate low life's just the same. Just looks more pleasin' is all."

He patted his own back in approval of his play, then continued. "Any more word on your time?"

"No. My team meeting is this week sometime. I'm heading to see my counselor later."

"Do yourself a favor and tell 'em only what they want to hear, not what you want to say. No good ever comes from a man speaking his truthful self to a bunch of prison issue quacks. Understand?"

I nodded. "I understand, but I think the truth will work best for me this time."

He stopped his play and turned to face me. "Work best for you huh? Is that what you think? You tell them motherfuckin' head docs what you really think and believe me when I tell you, there will always be an excuse, some fucked up, made up justification to keep you here. Ain't nobody gonna sign off on somebody they think ain't right and let 'em just walk out them gates. Too much at stake. Nuh-uh. No sir."

He cocked his arm back and continued, "Listen to what I'm preachin' friend. You tell that room full of white coats everything they want to hear, hear me?"

The ball came my way and I hit it hard and low. It smacked off the wall, then bounced twice before it reached him. It was followed quickly with taunts and jeers from the crowd around us.

Shareef said, "I stand corrected. There is such thing as luck in this place."

As he hit one high off the wall that chased me backward I said, "Luck is the residue of design my good man."

He repeated it back to himself.

"Luck is the residue of design. I like that."

He countered my shot and said, "Don't have the slightest god-damned idea what it means, but I like the sound of it anyways."

We both laughed and carried on playing and bantering back and forth for hours. For the second time in weeks, he made the time spent feel as any pleasant afternoon in the free world would, with laughter, and filled with good spirit and better company.

I was actually no match for him, but the time away from my cell and outside the troubles imminent in both my present and near future, were well worth the ridicule and mockery he hurled my way.

"You know why you suck?" he said. "Cause you're a goddamned left-handed freak, that's why. Nothin' and nobody worthwhile ever comes from being a southpaw."

"Yeah? Chris Mullin?"

"White boy. All shot nothing more."

"Dave Cowens?"

"Pasty white brute. No skills."

"Bill Russell?"

He paused and seemed to think about it. "You got me on that one. I guess there are exceptions to every rule my friend. Besides, he's black. That makes it okay."

"How about Michelangelo or Da Vinci? Or Einstein or Benjamin Franklin?"

"Unless they playin' on the present or future Chicago Bulls they just a bunch of ill-skilled peons in my eyes."

The ball hit low and away.

"That is the game, the set, and the match." He said with an obvious satisfaction he had no intention of concealing.

He grabbed two water bottles from his bag and tossed me one.

"How come you know so much about all kinda book shit but you ain't smart enough to keep outta this place?"

I tapped my skull and he smiled. "Can't let on though, right?"

"Now you talking, remember that when speakin' to the docs and you got a chance of leavin' this place someday."

"Someday sounds like a lot of forever."

"Not lookin' to knock the wind outta your sails none but you gotta prepare yourself for that being a possible outcome in your future, son."

"I'll die first."

"Nah, maybe at first you'd feel that way. Everyone does. You get used to it."

"Not me." I said. "First thing I hear my lawyer talk about an extension, that's it for me."

"Yeah well, you best keep that piece of information to yourself, or it'll be for certain."

We stood in silence and watched the sun high in the sky. It was the month of May now and the cool nights were leading to hot and humid afternoons. I knew I had to leave and meet Diane soon. I also knew I would have to wash up somewhere, and the thought itself made my stomach turn.

"I have to get going. Thanks for the game and the water."

"Anytime." he said. "Lessons always free from Shareef the sheriff."

I had turned from him and headed towards my cell when I heard him call out. "Hey, I heard about Ben. Is he back yet?"

I yelled back. "No, I won't be looking for him around any time soon."

"Yeah, heard it was somethin' else alright. If I can, I'll stop by later on after supper. It's roast beef and some potato bull-shit on the side. Maybe I'll steal ya some. I know all you corn fed white motherfuckers like that kinda shit."

I laughed and said, "Yes, we do."

The cell area was quiet, with most of the prisoners enjoying the warmth of the day, and the break from their claustrophobic living quarters. Because of this, and the fact that it had been over two weeks since my last one, I risked a full shower.

I was relieved when it came and went without incident, and I was even more pleased with how good it felt. My face was scrubbed clean and my hair smelled fresh. I felt human again. I put on clean clothes and started on my way down to Diane's office. The sun hit my face hard as I walked the concrete path that led to her. I watched some inmates passing their time with cigarettes and idle conversation, while others were tossing balls or racing one another. Anything to move the clock forward.

I thought about what Shareef had said and I agreed. Our surroundings looked good on the surface, but its interior revealed nothing neither worthy, nor capable of any true value. "Prison is prison." he said. "Paint it nice and put a smile on its face, it's still filled with a bunch of incarcerated degenerates bangin' their heads against a wall."

Despite that, I was feeling at least a twinge of something I would loosely call optimism once again. Maybe it was just the warmth of the sun, maybe it was the prospect of a few nights without Ben's constant chatter, or maybe it was Diane. She had been able to help me try to see things from a different angle. She had also pretty much blown up all the philosophies and principals I felt constituted life and how inconsequential its meaning really was. I still had failed to tell her any of the actual events that contributed to those theories and wondered what her rebuttal would be had I shared them with her.

I arrived at her office only to be informed that she had to cancel and I was to return the next day at the same time. I was upset because I enjoyed our sessions, but also, it meant I would now have to figure out a way to pass the time normally spent with her. I took the wise and prudent choice of heading back to my cell and staying out of sight. I shut the door behind me and opened up and re-read all the letters I got from home. I heard from everyone, but my one sister Mary Jo wrote most often. I spent a lot of time with her since coming back from Boston and I think somewhere inside, she felt some blame for not stopping the robbery, and not seeing its true cause. There was never blame to be assessed toward anyone, least of all her. My sister and her boyfriend had given me some of the few moments of humor and happiness I was able to experience in spite of myself. I loved her dearly for that and those times we shared. Everyone's unconditional love and concern shone through the pages, and even the ones I had read many times before brought tears of joy and appreciation.

A knock at my door shook me from a state of nostalgia and sentiment and into one of apprehension and fear. I was relived to look

133

through the glass and see Shareef smiling and holding up a folded napkin and a small container of milk. My feeling of comfort quickly faded when I opened the door. Instead of entering, he stepped aside and let three men enter.

Just before they covered my mouth and pulled me down, and before he shut the door, our eyes met and I thought of something else he once told me. "Don't trust no one in here. Ain't no one who they seem." No truer statement was ever said to me. The shock of what I knew was about to happen paled in comparison to the grief I felt at the realization that someone I trusted, a brief reprieve from the daily struggle of prison life, someone I valued as a friend, had simply traded me for favor and gain. I was no different than cigarettes or candy.

They forced me into the far corner. One kept me from screaming while the other pinned me on my stomach. The third man I had seen around the yard and knew him to be called Snowman. I had always assumed the nickname was inspired by the shape and size of his body. He was older and always seemed harmless and good natured. He wore his beard long with little care for its appearance or cleanliness, and he gave the impression of a backwoods country hick.

He said, "Well, hello there son. Mark I believe. Am I right? Just nod son."

I did as I was told.

"That's a good boy. Now, my friend here is gonna remove his hand from your mouth. If you should start hootin' and hollerin', he's gonna cover you back up, then this won't go nearly as nice as I planned. Are we clear?"

The man removed his hand slowly but kept it inches from my face.

"What do you want?"

He laughed and said, "Now that's kinda like askin' the fox whatcha doing in the chicken coop."

He peeked out the window then said to the men, "Get his pants down. Go on now, hurry it up."

He loosened his belt and lowered his pants, then began to pleasure himself. The man shifted his weight from me to gain access to my belt and I flung my elbow hard into his face. The other attempted to mount me and hold me down but I was already half on my feet and headed to the door. Snowman punched me hard in the chest and held me where I stood.

I spit in his face before being dragged back down by the two men. Snowman wiped the spit from his face and said, "Now that was not nice, not nice at all. I'm known 'round here as a gentle man. Doesn't mean I have to be."

"You're a fucking pig old man. Fuck you!"

They covered my mouth again and I kept fighting to get free. I could feel the weight of both of them on me and a knee being driven into my back.

"I have a proposition for you that I feel will serve us both very well. Listen to what I have to say, before you judge okay? I am not an animal, or a pig as you say. I would not come here simply to take without an offering to put forth. That is not how my Mama raised me."

He continued to slowly masturbate.

I stopped struggling and for the first time since I arrived there, I no longer felt fear. In the absence of fear, which was the emotion that most dominated my thoughts and drove my actions, I simply felt nothing. Like a switch had been turned off inside me. Whatever fuels the process we encounter when we experience the tier of emotions all human beings are capable of was no longer with me.

He continued on. "Now, I've seen you on the yard and I know for a fact that this place has not been kind to you and it doesn't suit you none neither. When is the last time you ate proper? Or slept through the night? Today was the first time you showered full bore since you came up if I'm not mistaken." He increased his arousal pace. "That's right, I know you was in there today. See, that's what I mean. This place ain't for you. It's like puttin' a monkey in a lion's cage. He can run and hide, but sooner or later, he becomes breakfast. See where this is goin'? I can make that all go away, just like that. No more fear, no more hidin'. No more lion's cage."

He rose from the chair, and knelt down next to me. "I'm too old for all this fussin' and fightin'. You just do as I say, whenever I say it, and things will be a whole lot better for you. Whattaya say to that?"

I spit in his face again and fought to get up. I felt something again. Not fear, not disregard, I felt anger. Anger and hatred toward him, against others in my life like him, and mostly, anger toward myself.

He wiped the spit from his face and said, "So, that's how we gonna play this, huh? Can't say I'm not just a tad bit disappointed but I don't mind it rough once in a while."

I pushed to get up. The men slapped at my face and buttocks all the while laughing and taunting me. They were enjoying every second, like they were having the time of their lives.

"I said get his pants down didn't I?" Snowman said. "I ain't got all day now."

He intensified his stroking.

"Would you two hurry the fuck up please? I can't keep my wood up all night no more. This ain't like the old days, but he sure is prettier than some of them two bit skanks from back in the day. Come on, come on."

He was watching me struggle with the two men. I'm not sure what was more exciting for him, the anticipation of what was soon to come, or seeing another human being struggle and fight for their life. To him, it was probably much like hunting and capturing an animal in the woods except in his eyes, watching it slowly die instead of putting it out of its misery likely presented far more pleasure and satisfaction.

A knock came from the door. He turned to hear it and realized its meaning.

"For fuck's sake, you two are worthless. Turn him around, let me see his face."

I got my hands free and pushed one man up and partially off me. The other drove his knee back into me and turned my head towards Snowman who was now standing over me, and thrusting himself toward me.

"Let me see his fuckin' face asshole. Goddamn it. Okay, okay. Steady. Right there. Hold on, hold on."

I kept fighting and struggling against their will to force me toward him. Then I felt his discharge hit my face, neck and hair. The men jumped back and released me. He kicked me hard in the stomach

136

and side, not bothering to pull up his pants in the process. The men started to kick and punch my back and head repeatedly.

I'm not sure how long it was before they left, or how long I laid there but when I woke up, it was quiet and dark in the cell. The two emotions I felt earlier, one void of fear, the other, the process of feeling total and complete anger were working together inside me. The rage I felt was beginning to overwhelm me, and with nothing to balance its power, or slow its steam, I was a complete train-wreck.

I stood up and felt the pain in my sides and stomach but moved forward. I walked from my cell to the showers and stripped out of my clothes. I showered and washed all of him from my face and hair, but never would I be able to cleanse him from my mind. I left the clothes where they lay and walked back to my cell naked.

I dressed myself, and headed from cell to cell in search of him. I no longer felt the pain from the beating they gave me. All my thoughts were consumed with revenge and the anger inside me. I wanted to suppress it and let it build until the last minute then release it into a flow of retribution and punishment. It was in the final place I looked that I finally found him. He was seated with his back to me, his arm draped over a chair, watching television. Like a man without a care in the world. He turned to see me watching him. He smiled and said, "Well, lookey who's here. Hey skinny ass white trash. How you doin' today?"

I don't know why I went to him first instead of Snowman or Shareef. I suppose it was because they had already done their damage. What they did, both physically and emotionally, could not be undone. Their actions were set into my psyche and would forever have their place in me. Darnell however, represented something not yet established, but its eminence was clear, and would always be, a threat to me.

"What you want Mr. White Trash?"

"I want you."

"Well, alright then."

I walked up to him and slapped him hard in the face. The others in the room got up and left quickly. I slapped him again and pushed him back when he tried to rise.

"I'm supposed to do something for you right?"

I struck him once more. I could feel the tears on my face, and the rage flowing out of me. He no longer fought to stand. Perhaps seeing my emotional state made him think better of it.

"I'm the big attraction right, Darnell? No, the main event is what you said, right?"

I smacked him again harder. "You want me to suck your dick is that it? Huh? Is that what you like?"

I slapped him again.

"Big fucking tough guy. Wants some white boy on his knees for him."

I was face to face with him now. "If you ever come near me, I won't be able to stop what you do, but I will come for you after. I will stab and cut you. I will leave some mark, some reminder that you will carry with you for the rest of your life. Do you understand me?"

He didn't answer. I hit him hard again and screamed out, "DO YOU UNDERSTAND ME?"

I started striking and beating him repeatedly and saying over and over, "DO YOU UNDERSTAND ME? DO YOU UNDERSTAND ME?"

He finally grabbed both my arms and pushed me back to stand up.

"You're a fuckin' whack job motherfucker you know that? You right at home up in here."

I slid down the wall as he left me there and screamed out over and over, "DO YOU UNDERSTAND ME? DO YOU UNDERSTAND ME?"

Chapter 10

I knocked on Diane's door the next morning and watched for her reaction. She looked up from her desk and pulled off her glasses.

"What the hell happened to you?" She stood and sized me up some more. "Mark?"

I walked in and tried to sound casual. "I tripped on the track yesterday. No big deal."

She didn't sit right away but instead watched me as I sat down, no doubt to gauge whether there was even a hint of truth in my answer.

"What's going on with you?"

"Nothing is going on. I'm fine."

"You know, they should put that on your tombstone. Here's lies Mark McCullough. He was always fine."

"Because I am. Can we move on please?"

She still kept her eyes set on me. "Somewhere to go?"

"No." I said, trying to sound annoyed. "Everyone is always asking me if I'm okay. I'm-"

She cut me off. "I know, you're fine."

"What happened to Ben?"

She sipped her coffee and looked over the brim at me. "I'm not at liberty to discuss other patients with you, but I can assure you that he is getting the best possible care available. If he cooperates and agrees to take his medication-"

"Medication?" I said. "There is no medication for what he has and you know it. You're just pumping him and every other nutcase in this place full of whatever you think will knock out their lights just so you can justify your job and sleep at night. Ben called you on it so that gets him yanked from his cell and tossed into some underground cage like an animal. That's the best treatment available? Who are you kidding? Not me, and certainly not Ben."

She was quiet for a moment before responding. "How are your medications? I mean, how are you feeling?"

"What? You're going to start on me now? Is that it? You want to make me into some walking zombie who just shuffles up and down the halls drooling and mumbling to himself?"

"Mark, what the hell is wrong with you? What happened? You came in here a confused and troubled young man who was in need of help. Now, I hardly recognize you. Please... tell me what's going on so I can help you." I ignored her.

"What kind of questions are they going to ask?"

"Who? Who's they?"

"At the final meeting. You said at our last session we could go over what to expect from the other doctors. What are they going to ask?"

She seemed either to lose her train of thought, or just not know in which direction to go with me.

"Um-well, they are going to want to go over the specifics of the robbery with you. They're going to ask you about your state of mind at the time. Maybe they'll ask what you did the weeks and days leading up to it. Do you feel remorse-"

"Of course I feel remorse, it landed me in this shithole didn't it? What else?"

"They're going to ask about the gun, any medications you might have been taking, were you under the influence at the time-"

"They already know all of that."

I stood up and started pacing the room. I refused to look at her because I knew she was watching me closely.

"This is a waste of time. They're never going to believe me. Why should they? I'm going to be stuck here."

"They are going to believe you. Everyone has been on your side from the beginning Mark. The judge, the prosecutor, the F.B.I. You

were released on your own recognizance after committing armed robbery of a federal bank. They let your parents transport you down here
instead of riding in some Marshall's backseat. Are you kidding me?
The way I see it, the only person not on your side is you. I don't know
what's going on inside that head of yours, but you better get yourself together because if you go in there tomorrow and act like this in
front of a panel of trained clinical psychiatrists, you're right, you will
be stuck here, and you will only have yourself to blame. So my advice to
you is, get yourself together. Get your shit together. Pull it in somehow,
from somewhere, whatever you have to do but figure it out, and do it
before you walk in that room tomorrow."

"It wasn't supposed to happen this way."

"What wasn't? The robbery?"

"I made a tape the night before. I left it for my parents. I told them how
sorry I was and how much I loved them but I just couldn't do it anymore."

She asked, "Do what?"

"Live inside my head. Live with my thoughts. Live with the past."

"What happened to you Mark? What happened in your life that was
so terrible? Tell me."

"I told them I was going to miss them and that they were amazing
parents. I said that ever since I was a kid, I thought this would eventually happen. It was just a question of time and place."

"There's a reason why you're still here Mark. There has to be. You
just need to find it."

"No one ever asked me why I did it."

"What? The robbery? You said-"

"Not why I did it, why I didn't stay. Why did I leave the bank
before the police came. Maybe it was like you said, maybe I did want
to live, but there was something else. No one ever asked me why I
left."

"Why did you?"

"What do you believe happens to us after we die? Do we just cease
to exist? Just fade to black and drift off into nowhere? Is that all this life
is worth? Just a random one shot deal?"

"I don't like to think so." she said. "There's more to it I believe."

"Do you think we come back as something or someone else? This time you're you, what you are right now, next time around maybe you're a cat or a tree, or someone else."

"There's an argument for reincarnation, sure."

"Or maybe it's what most people believe. Maybe there is these two individuals, two entities running the whole show. One guy has long white beard and a cane and if you're good, you go to see him. He will guide you into his arms for all eternity. If you're bad, you go see the other guy. The one who breathes fire and carries a poker. He will see to it that you suffer great pain and torment for all your past sins and press down on your soul forever in the hereafter."

"There are many who feel that's the way of the universe. Good versus evil."

"I don't believe it's any of those things. I believe that when we die, what happens is based solely on how we lived our lives here, as we are now. I do believe in an afterlife, I just struggle with it being so easily explained or controlled by a single individual, especially one we can't see or fully understand its origin. I think it's important to pay attention to what we do here and now, and after will take care of itself. That's why I didn't wait for the police. Making someone else take my life could not possibly lead to a better place after this. That came to me that day. That's why I left."

"Would it have been okay if you had just done it yourself?"

"I can't answer that. I've thought about it many times but I just don't know. I'd like to believe it's acceptable. That if life is so unpleasant and so full of pain and darkness that you have that choice. If life is a gift, can't you return it if it's defective?"

"Maybe the gift of life can never be defective as you say. Maybe it was always meant to be flawed but can also be mended, if we see it that way."

"I saw the women's faces. They were terrified."

"The tellers you mean?"

"They thought that day was their time to find out what happens next. I had no right."

"Mark, you had an extreme adverse reaction to a medication you were using for a very serious illness. Depression has always been for

142

me, the most difficult and elusive affliction to treat. And you were under the influence of-"

"If I stay here, I'll die."

"That's what I'm talking about Mark. You keep saying that. If you talk like that tomorrow you will be staying here. You can't-"

"But you told me to tell the truth."

I walked out before she could respond and made my way back to my cell and found Ben sprawled out on his bed, reading. He looked up at me. "I must say, you look like shit."

"Please Ben, don't hold back. So nice to have you back."

"I'm not kidding. You look fucking atrocious man, holy shit."

I jumped up on my bunk and laid back. I could feel the effects of yesterday's beating. All the muscles in my side were screaming now and any movement brought pain and with the pain, came more anger. Ben stood and stared at me. "I mean, I've seen road-kill that-"

I leaned into him and got inches from his face.

"Ben, shut the fuck up, right now."

He studied me for a moment, then without word, laid back down.

I jumped off the bed and grabbed my Walkman. I walked the track for hours that day. Each new time around, I would see Shareef by the wall. Just yesterday, we stood there as friends. We shared sport and laughter. He carried on about the ways of prison life and expressed concern for my safety and well-being. I took his word as gospel and was grateful for his experience and guidance. As I made another lap around toward him, he was watching me, no doubt concerned as any inmate would be, that retribution was the sole inhabitant of my thoughts. Strangely though, despite my anger towards him, it wasn't. Although I did have a desire to make him answer for what he did, if I could, I would trade violence for words. I wanted to understand why and how it could seem so simple. I needed to know how he could so easily look someone in the eye with compassion, but only have malice in his heart. I knew if we did share words, they would not be legitimate in nature, nor would they reveal any genuine truth or meaning for his actions. He would probably flash a big smile and ramble on in his senseless, mindless way but all the while preaching a lesson of real value, that is that people aren't who they seem. I circled him over and over, each time searching for the truth, and every time finding nothing. I would never know the reasoning behind what he did, maybe it was a debt repaid, or simply to have an edge to strike a deal in the future. I didn't know why and didn't much care to. Its purpose was irrelevant, its consequences and the indelible impression it left were all that concerned me.

I walked until near dark and then finally found my way back to my cell where I stayed all night, and found little sleep. I considered the following day and how the outcome of the rest of my life rested in its wake. As I laid and listened to Ben's senseless babble even while he slept, I wondered if I would be listening to him, or someone much the same, for the months, or perhaps years to follow. The individual was insignificant to me, it was the dwelling, and its surroundings that kept my thoughts in a twisting downward spiral.

I woke the next morning and watched the clock until it was time to meet the team of prison doctors. I made it to the administration building and waited inside until Diane came to get me.

"Are you ready?"

"No."

"You'll be fine. Come on. It's time."

She looked at me for a moment, I assumed to assess my mental state. Then she turned and nodded for me to follow. I guessed she was satisfied with whatever she thought she saw. The time had come and we were going with whatever I had left in me, for better or worse.

I followed her into a large conference room and she instructed me to sit at the head of a long wooden table. All the seats were filled with men and women of various ages and ethnic backgrounds, but they all had two things in common. A very serious demeanor, and all their eyes focused squarely on me.

Diane sat to my right and introduced me. "This is inmate 1161993. His name is Mark McCullough. Case number 64114. Mark was brought to us after committing a crime that brought into question his mental capacity during the course of the incident. Mark was taking medication at the time to treat his depression. He was arrested and charged with armed robbery of a federal bank. At the discretion of both the prosecutors and the corresponding judge in this case, he has been ordered here for evaluation prior to his case reaching any further litigation on the matter. Mark has completed all necessary testing set forth in accordance with the terms presented by the prosecution. Today he is here for his final case study which upon completion, and in accordance with the judge's mandate will be forwarded to him for further study and clarification within this case.

She looked up and addressed a clean cut, well-kept man with reading glasses hanging down on his nose. His appearance, much like the doctor who came for Ben the night he broke down, seemed more the college professor type than a prison psychiatrist. He flipped through some papers in front of him, then held on a particular page. He addressed me without looking up from the table.

"Hello Mark, how are you today?" I could feel myself shaking and wanting more than I had since I arrived there, more than any other time in my life, to just be home, and with my family.

"I'm fine sir. Thank you."

"My name is Doctor Morgan. I will be the one heading up your assessment today."

He looked up at me briefly, then went back down to his files.

"You have been under the supervision of Doctor Sanford during your stay here, correct?"

I had to think back to our first meeting and introduction. She was always just Diane after that first day.

"Yes, sir."

"How has that been for you?"

"Fine sir. She's made me feel very comfortable."

"Did you understand what she was saying earlier? About why you're here?"

"Yes sir. Yes I did."

So, why do you think you're here Mark?"

"To see why I did it. To see why I robbed the bank."

"It's not so much the why we are looking for from you Mark." he said. "But more the cause. We hope to learn today the factors that lead up to your crime and determine your accountability concerning its occurrence. Can you help us with that?"

"I'll try."

"Okay good. Let's get started then. This is a copy of the statement you gave to the F.B.I on February 27th, 1992. Do you remember giving them a statement?"

"Yes, I do."

"It says you confessed to walking in to a bank at 9:04 a.m. It further states you then brandished a gun and pointed it at the women behind the teller line and stated "This is a robbery." Are we still on track?"

"That's what I remember sir, yes."

"It then goes on to say that you told them that they shouldn't worry, and that everything would be over soon. What does that mean?"

"It means I could see how scared they were and I didn't want them to be afraid. I wasn't going to hurt them. I couldn't. The gun was fake."

He said, "I meant the last part. When you said it would all be over soon. What would be over?"

I dreaded answering the question. I knew he was aware of the meaning, but to hear me say it out loud I felt would do far greater harm than reading it off some piece of paper. I didn't answer right away, so he decided to take a different approach.

"Here's what I don't understand Mark. Here is where things get a little odd to me. Correct me if I'm wrong but, you have never been in trouble before as far as I can tell. You never even had a speeding ticket. You have no history of violence of any kind yet you suddenly decide to commit a crime as serious as bank robbery? I'm not getting the connection here Mark. Is there something I'm missing?"

"Did you read my file?"

"Yes, I did. It's right here in front of me."

"So then, why are you asking me that question?"

"Because I want you to tell me."

His tone and demeanor were becoming increasingly condescending and I could feel the anger rising up inside me. For everything Diane was, he wasn't. I can understand now, and appreciate what his job and intentions were, but right then it felt like just another person attempting to maneuver and manipulate me to best suit their needs.

"Why? You already know the answer to the question."

"Because it's important we hear it from you."

"Important to who? To you?"

"It's not so much who but-"

"Because I wanted them to shoot me. There, I said it. Happy now? Is that what you wanted?"

The room was quiet. I could see Diane pleading to me with her eyes. He broke the silence and said, "Who Mark? Who did you want to shoot you?"

"The police."

"So," he said. "the plan was for you to rob the bank and have the police show up, see what was happening, assume you were actually really robbing the bank and then shoot you. Is that correct?"

"There you go. You're on board now."

"So why didn't you wait for them? Cold feet?"

I didn't answer him. I just stared at the floor and put all my effort into not shouting out and not jumping up from the table.

"What I don't get is why bother with all you did, then not follow through. It just doesn't make any sense. It really doesn't."

"You work with people who have mental and psychological problems every day, yet you are mystified that someone started but didn't finish a suicide attempt? That's something new to you? Now I'm the one who is baffled. Enlighten me on your confusion."

He ignored my response. "Did you regret not staying?"

"Part of me did, yes. It surprised me. I was ready."

He straightened up his glasses and flipped forward a few pages. "It states here you had two opportunities for the police to shoot you that day. Is that correct?"

I didn't answer. Not because I didn't want to, I just knew what he was leading into, and I wasn't sure how to properly respond.

He continued. "It says right here that after the robbery you were pulled over by a police officer and asked to step out of your vehicle. Why not just get out and have him shoot you right there?"

"Because I recognized him. I knew him when we were kids. We played little league together."

"So, let me see if I get this. You wanted someone to shoot you, just not a childhood friend yet you were okay with a total stranger doing it?"

"That's not it." I said. "I saw his eyes. His hands were shaking. He looked terrified. And I did get out and step toward him and he was pointing his gun at me. He could have shot me right then, and I assumed if he knew what I had done he would."

"His gun was pointed at you? Then what happened?"

"He saw who it was and started laughing. He was relieved I think."

"I'm sure he was. He's out looking for an armed and dangerous robbery suspect and he happens along an old childhood buddy. I'd be relieved too."

I wanted to scream, to yell out. I wanted to tell him he was off track. That he didn't know or understand anything about me, yet seemed so ready to patronize me with his arrogant opinion, and to pass judgment so freely.

"What happened next?"

"He shook my hand and told me to be careful."

"He shook your hand? Wow, that's got unpaid leave written all over it."

He went back to his papers and creased them back, holding one in place.

"Let's back up a little bit. After you walked out of the bank, what did you do?"

"I walked to my car and drove home."

"How long were you there?"

"I'm not sure. Not long."

"Ten minutes? An hour?"

"Maybe fifteen to twenty minutes."

"What did you do in that time?"

"The reality of what I did and what didn't happen hit me."

"Then what? What did you do next?"

148

"I heard the fire sirens coming from town and I knew they were for me. For what I did. I got back in my car and left the money somewhere where I knew they could find it."

"Suppose someone else did first?"

"I put it in an old abandoned guard station near my house. No one ever goes in there."

"So, then what?" He put a finger on his paper and read aloud. "Actually, I'll answer that. It says here that you left the money then you went to the nearest payphone and called the F.B.I. Is that correct?"

"Yes."

"Who did you ask for?"

"I asked for whoever was in charge. I said I was the one who robbed the bank and needed to speak to someone right away. A man came on the other end shortly after and I told him who I was."

"You told him your name?"

"No, I told him I was the one who robbed the bank in town. I told him my name was Kevin."

"Then what?"

"I told him that I didn't want to do it. For money I mean. That it wasn't my true intention. I told him where he could find the money and I told him I was sorry. I said to please tell the women I was sorry for what I did and to please forgive me."

"What did he say?"

"He said he understood and that I should turn myself in. I said I couldn't. That I had hurt my family enough and didn't want to add anymore to it."

"Yet killing yourself would have been okay with them? What you're saying is you just didn't want to have to see things play out."

"You've got things all figured out don't you? Why even bother asking the questions? Why not just fill in the answers for me."

He ignored me and said, "That was just after ten. What did you do next?"

"I drove to another phone and called him back."

"Why? You gave back the money and said you wouldn't turn yourself in. Why risk another call?"

"Because I wanted to make him understand. I wanted to explain myself and why it happened."

"After that call, did you speak to him again?"

"Yes, I did. I spoke to him one more time after that. He pleaded with me again to turn myself in. He said they were out looking for me and he was afraid I would get hurt if they found me. I told him I could see all the police cars out on the road and that I knew it was because of me."

"So there were more opportunities for you that day?"

I knew what he meant by that, and I felt silence was the best recourse I could take. Not because I didn't want to answer, or didn't have one, but instead because its context may have ended the meeting right then.

"What happened next?"

"I went home and waited."

"Waited? For what?"

"For them to come for me."

"But they didn't. They couldn't. You had no record. Your prints weren't on file. You were home free. Did you count the money before you left it?"

Diane quickly stepped in.

"Johnathan, really? Is that relevant?"

"Nine thousand eight hundred and ninety three dollars."

"Why did you count it?"

"Because I wanted to know what my life was worth."

That brought him pause, but again he ignored me and pushed forward.

"Did you leave the house after that?"

"Yes, but not until later that afternoon. My mother came home and told me she heard about the robbery when she was at the grocery store. The bank was in the same lot where she did her shopping. She joked with me and said she knew it wasn't me because they said the suspect had on a trench coat and she knew I didn't own one."

"She said that? What do you think that meant?"

"It meant she knew. Or at least, suspected. She came into my room the night before, right after I made the tape and she saw how fucked up I was. I guess she put it together."

"Weird don't you think? A mother hears of a bank robbery and automatically assumes it's her own son?"

It was clear that no response was better than asserting what was in my own thoughts.

"Continue. What happened after your mother accused you-"

"She didn't accuse me. She knew her son, and she could tell when things weren't right with me. She knew I was taking medication and drinking heavily."

"But she didn't stop you?"

"My mind keeps coming back to the same thought. You do this for a living right? You listen to people all day long talk about how fucked up they are. They discuss their worst and darkest thoughts and fears with you. You help them examine who they are and why they are what they are, yet you can still ask me that question? My mother didn't stop me because I did what all people do when they are fucked in the head but don't want you to know it. They convince those around them that they're okay. They know its bull-shit. But they also know the alternative is worse. My mother, although her instincts were correct, and she knew what a mess I was, convinced herself that everything was alright because I convinced her that everything was alright. That everything was okay and she shouldn't worry. If you would just listen, you could learn more, and you would judge less."

"After you and your mother spoke, what happened next?"

"After a while I couldn't handle the guilt anymore. I called the doctor who prescribed my medication and told him what happened. What I did."

"What did he say?"

"He was blown away. He said to come to his office right away."

"And did you?"

"Yes I did. I hung up and went to see him. We went to the hospital soon after."

"Why?"

"I don't know. I assume he was concerned about me and wanted me someplace safe."

"Then what happened?"

"I told the nurse who examined me who I was and what I had done. She called the police and I was placed under arrest."

"Did they take you in?"

"No. My doctor and the hospital staff convinced the authorities to let me stay in the psychiatric ward under police surveillance. The next morning I was taken to the federal courthouse and formally charged."

"Where did they take you next?"

"Nowhere. The judge released me on my own recognizance under the condition that I was to go back to the hospital and remain there for treatment and evaluation. After a week, I was placed under out-patient care as well as house arrest until a cell opened up down here."

"How long was that? I mean, how long were you at home before you came here?"

"About two months."

Diane interjected again. "You said you went to the doctor who pre-scribed your medication. What led to you taking it in the first place?"

"I went to church one Sunday morning to hear my dad preach. He's a minister and he was going to be speaking that day. He was a friend of my doctor and he happened to be there that morning. When he saw me… I'm not sure what he saw, or what I looked like to him but he asked me to come and see him in his office the next day. So I did."

"And he prescribed your medication then?"

"Yes."

"Did you feel it helped? That it was working for you?"

"At first, yes. But as the weeks wore on, it was having a negative effect on me."

"How so?"

"I started having blackouts. And I started to feel angry and vio-lent more often. I wasn't in control of myself. My thoughts weren't my own."

"Did you contact your doctor? Let him know how you were feeling?"

"No, I didn't. I should have and if I could have thought things out clearly, I would have, but I didn't."

"What were you taking? Let me re-phrase that, what were you using when you were prescribed your medication?"

"I was smoking marijuana and drinking alcohol."

"Nothing else?"

"That was more than enough."

"Did you use anything during your time under house arrest?"

"No, I was clean. I was afraid to use anything."

"Why?"

"Because I was afraid of what I might do. What I was capable of."

"You said you made a tape the night before. Why?"

"So they would understand."

"Who is they?"

"My parents."

"Did the authorities hear it?"

"I believe so, yes. I made it in my car a few hours before the robbery. They confiscated it I think."

"Did you think about keeping the money? Just saying what the hell, what's done is done, who is it going to hurt anyway?"

I knew what he was doing. He was jumping back and forth, from one topic to another, testing me. Seeing if what I said matched what was in his papers.

"I didn't want the money. Have you listened to a word I've said?"

"How would you describe how you are feeling now? I mean in regards to your depression?"

I looked to Diane. Her eyes again pleaded with me.

"I feel like I'm heading in the direction I need to be."

"Do you think you will continue with counseling in the future?"

"It's done wonders for me so far."

Diane looked away when I spoke those words, but a small smile was clear on her face.

"What else?" he said.

"There is nothing else. That's it. That's all there is. That's all I have."

He pulled his papers together, tapped them neatly in place and said, "Okay, I think we're done here. Thanks for coming."

Thanks for coming. Just like that. Dismissed. I stood up and turned to leave. I watched Diane's expression and again I could see her eyes appealing to me to just go. Walk out and don't say a word. Unfortunately, I couldn't accommodate her wishes. "I envy you. I really do. You were able to assess me and examine me, what I did, why I did it, who I am and what I am in what, an hour? You sit there and seem so sure you have the answers. You know all about me, right? Well, you don't. You don't know shit about me. You know why I'm here and what brought me here but not the cause. That's why I'm here you said right? To find the cause. You act so smug with your arms crossed and your nose in the air but you know nothing about what goes on in my mind, or the minds of any of these people here. You spend so much time focusing just on the facts, the words written on some fucking piece of paper. Maybe it's time you forgot about what you learned in some classroom and started paying attention to what really matters. That, will never be found on any paper or in any file. You said this was an evaluation to find out about what I did, and why I did it. Maybe you should have your own evaluation. Maybe you need to ask yourself what you do, and why you do it. I think I could give you the answers just as easily as you presume to know mine."

With that, I walked out and found my way back to my cell. I was so angry with how the meeting went, and the assumptions that were made. I knew he was simply doing what he was paid to do, but I also knew he was working with incomplete information, and I still felt judged by an action, not by its motivation.

Ben was on his bed reading when I came in. I looked at him and the space around him and tried to face the reality that I was likely no longer open ended. I would be there for as much time as the assessment team, and Doctor Morgan felt necessary. It was at their discretion now as to how long it would be, how many days and nights and countless sessions lay before me until I would be re-evaluated. I had no idea how I would handle that truth, or what I would do with it. The prospect of years or even months inside were not something I would be able, nor willing to accept.

The next few days I walked through the time in a state of nothingness. I simply went through all the motions. I ate and slept. I walked the track, and I read my letters. But I was numb to everything and everyone around me. There were no more sessions with Diane to look forward to and to help pass the time. I went on as all the other inmates did, in a mindless sense of existence. Just passing the minutes and hours in a futile attempt to feel like a human being worthy of life, to be someone living a life of purpose, of promise, all the while knowing it was bullshit. There was no plan or objective for me now, and the only direction I was headed it seemed, would be down. My thoughts now were constantly consumed with the proper method for escaping my situation and the ramifications it brought. I knew I would find a way, I wasn't the only one who ever chose leaving their life behind instead of living it without meaning or significance.

On the fourth day after my meeting a guard came to my cell.

"Doc wants to see you right away. Head down there pronto."

I found Diane at her desk when I arrived. She looked up at me and smiled wearily. I knew this conversation was inevitable but still felt unprepared for its passing.

"Have a seat."

She pulled off her glasses and studied me.

"How have you been?"

"Peachy."

"How did you think the meeting went?"

"I think I aced it."

She laughed.

"He has a job to do you know. It's not easy hearing people every day talk about what a mess their lives are, and how fucked up they feel."

"I know." I said. "It doesn't mean he should stop listening."

"You're right it doesn't. I don't think you're giving him enough credit though. I think he heard you loud and clear. Way more than you think."

"You are far more confident than I am concerning his methods."

I tried to read her but couldn't.

"What happens now?"

"What happens now is you need to go gather up all your things. You're leaving today."

I was both confused and overwhelmed by her words. I wasn't even sure I heard them right or if this was some sort of twisted and malicious joke at my expense.

"What? I'm leaving? For where?"

"For home." she said. "Your dad and brother are waiting outside. I called them yesterday."

I didn't have words that would properly convey my emotions to what she said. I just sat and stared at her, waiting for the punchline I knew had to be coming.

"Your evaluation is over. Your lawyer will be contacted when the report is complete."

"I don't know what to say."

"Don't say anything. Just go get your stuff and meet me out front. I'll walk you down. Oh and Mark, careful what you say to Ben. He did not get the same news you just did."

I knew then what caused Ben's outrage and I understood. I'm sure I would have reacted the same way if put in that situation. I don't know if my feet ever hit the ground on my way back to my cell. My head was spinning with both joy and bewilderment. I gathered my belongings as quickly as I could, fearing this was all just some big misunderstanding and that I wouldn't be leaving after all.

Ben came in as I stuffed a paper bag full of my clothing and other essentials.

"What are you doing?"

"I'm being moved to another cell."

I was touched by the sad expression that followed my words. He seemed genuine in his objection to my departure.

"Why?"

I inspected the room one last time for anything left behind and consciously avoided any eye contact with him. The truth of the matter was, I didn't want anything I had brought there with me or anything I purchased while inside except for my trusty Walkman radio. The only other material possession I wanted and would hold onto for life were the letters sent to me from loved ones back home. Those I knew, would have a special meaning for all the years to follow.

"I'm not sure. They didn't really give me a reason."

"I don't understand. Did you say something? Did I say something? Wrong I mean? I thought we were friends."

"We are friends Ben. It's nothing you did, I promise."

He sat on his bed and stared at the floor. Although I always did my best to appease him and keep him happy, he never showed even a hint of kinship towards me, or that he even cared about me at all. But as I watched him absorbing the news I just gave him, it was obvious to me that I meant more to him than coffee and nicotine.

"Can we still hang out? And break bread? Nothing says we can't still enjoy one of our friendly bull sessions together right?"

"Of course we can."

I felt sorry for lying to him but I knew there was no other option. His reception to my leaving could and likely would, produce a reaction of catastrophic proportions.

"Take care of yourself, Ben."

"Wait." He caught my arm as I turned to leave. Then he hugged me.

"I'll see you tonight? Dinner? Then some stimulating conversation?"

"Sure Buddy. See you then."

I knew little of his life outside of prison. I suspected that for all his rambling, he kept his life and its experiences close to him and chose not to share them most likely because they were of a dark, and no doubt sad nature. In some strange way, I knew I would miss him.

I threw open the main doors to bright sunshine, and to Diane waiting to lead me down to the processing room.

"What happens now?" I asked as we made our way.

"As I said, as soon as the report is complete it will be forwarded to your lawyer."

"And then?"

157

"Based on what it states, your lawyer and the prosecution will make their case either way."

"So, it's possible I could be coming right back here. I mean, if the report isn't favorable which I can't imagine it would be, leaving could just be temporary. Right?"

"I suppose that's true Mark. But like I said earlier, Doctor Morgan heard more than you realize and he is a good man. He wants what's best for you, even if you don't believe it."

We arrived at the doors that would lead me away from prison and to the outside world. Temporary or not, I would soon see my family. I would know freedom again and sleep in my own bed absent of fear and uncertainty, if only for a while.

I looked back and let out a deep sigh toward the place I called home for five weeks. The time spent there would leave an indelible mark on me and had produced memories I knew were stamped on my psyche and would remain so for all my days.

"Mark, if I were you I wouldn't concentrate all my energy on if you might be back, but instead on what brought you here and how to cope with it. You need to focus on you and what goes on in that head of yours. Okay?"

"Okay."

She smiled and turned away from me. I would miss her. She was a bright light in a dark place and I knew she had done her best to guide me through the time I had there and had also done what she could to match its horrid qualities with her comforting nature. I also knew what she was telling me without actually forming the words. She was telling me she knew what was in my report and that I wouldn't be coming back.

My father and brother greeted me as I stepped through the main doors and outside into freedom. I hugged them both and cried. I thanked them for all their love and support and for their letters, then I quickly hustled them to the car wanting nothing more than to see the prison walls and barbed wire fences fade far from my view.

Chapter 11

That was a Friday morning, by the following Monday afternoon, just days after leaving the prison my lawyer called me. He was a close friend of my father's and someone I no doubt, owed a great deal of gratitude and appreciation to.

He said, "Mark, Will Patmore calling. How are you today son?"

I could hear the emotion and enthusiasm in his voice.

"I'm fine sir, how are you?"

"I'm just fine. I was just going over the report I got from the doctors down at Butner and I have great news. It's a home run son."

"What does that mean?"

"It means we got what we asked for. The report states that the robbery was caused by a psychotic episode attributed to your medication and depression."

"I don't know what to say-"

"Now, I still have to talk this over with the prosecution but with this report coming from their own people, there isn't much to say. I'm going to shoot for that pre-trial intervention program I told you about. As long as you stay out of trouble, this whole thing goes away."

"No more jail time?"

"No more jail time, no. How do you feel?"

"I feel great sir. Thank you. Thank you for all that you've done for me."

"Listen Mark, I know I don't have to tell you that this thing could have gone a whole different direction. Somehow, it went our way which means you are getting a second chance. Do something with it, okay?"

"Yes, sir." I said. "I will."

"I've known your dad a long time and this really took a lot out of him. Make him proud okay?"

"I will. Thank you again."

"Take care of yourself." Then he was gone.

I would like to be able to say I changed after that conversation. I wish I had taken the news and used that second chance he spoke of and turned it into something positive. I wish my sole intention that day was to aspire to do something meaningful, to have a purpose that I could aspire to, but I didn't. I was no longer confined inside prison walls but I was still trapped inside my own head, and with the past. That, is its own type of confinement and one which has no release date, and needs no walls to keep you trapped and at its mercy.

Chapter 12

(THE LOST YEARS)

25-32 years old. It saddens me a great deal to realize that those years were filled with nothing of any real consequence, certainly nothing of a favorable nature anyway. I was placed in a pre-trial intervention program and I kept myself free from trouble for the three years that were mandated as part of the agreement between Mister Patmore and the prosecution. I faithfully saw my case supervisor monthly and kept myself drug free during that timeframe. It seemed foolish to me that they diligently tested me for drugs, but didn't care at all when they regularly found alcohol in my system.

Aside from the drinking I was doing, which was substantial by any standard, I was trying to put together the pieces of my life. I attended therapy and I even tried going back to church and finding religion. I had seen it work for so many others, I thought perhaps I could seek out and take joy in its benefits as well. To the outside world, even the ones closest to me, I'm sure it appeared as if things were looking better for me. That I did have some handle on my life and what it had become. In truth I was doing what I always did. I fell back on what I did best and what had always worked the most for me. I pretended. I was so skilled at showing only what I wanted people to see, and giving only what I wanted them to take. That was all I knew.

During the three years in the program I did little, if any socializing. The few friends I had prior to the robbery slowly drifted off, taking their friendship with them. If I did happen to meet someone I always kept them at a safe distance because my trust level was essentially, non-existent. I felt like the three years set me in some type of holding pattern, for what, I didn't know. I just knew the days and nights went by in a blur, a dismal haze of isolation and loneliness.

Inevitably, and despite my skepticism of it ever becoming a reality, the day ultimately arrived and I was released from the program. I was now free to go and do whatever I wished without restriction. I did what I think most people who shared my outlook on life would do, I slowly started drifting back to what I knew and was familiar with. I went back to the comfort zone I knew all too well. I also knew it would come with a price.

The first day after my release, I bought and smoked marijuana for the first time since I was arrested. I also drove to field five and parked under the trees overlooking the field. I'm not sure why I went there on that particular day. I used drugs as an escape from life's most regrettable encounters and yet there I sat staring right into the middle of the biggest one. Maybe I was there to try to make sense of it, perhaps if I focused hard enough somehow it would become more logical and belay some insight to its meaning, and more importantly, its effect on me.

I believed that I was where I was in my life because of what happened in that dugout. I knew that's where it all began, and where it ended for me. I would never know who or what I truly was because it was taken from me that day. I know that most abuse of children is done by someone they know. I also know I can speak for myself and would venture to say I can speak for most who have encountered the same fate that the actual act is not what scars you, it's what it does. It takes away your ability, your capacity to trust. We are so vulnerable and impressionable when we are young, and so trusting of our faith in others. This trust is not just an emotion, it's a necessity. When that bond is broken, it cannot simply be repaired nor can the damage it inflicts be forgotten. I wanted to travel back in time to that day. I wanted it to be raining or that I just never went to the field at all. I thought of all the scenarios that would have changed the events of that afternoon, but that was senseless I knew. Nothing would change the outcome, it would always be there with me, and it would always be real. I drove away seeing the dugout through my rearview mirror and as I watched it become smaller and out of focus with distance, I knew its memory would never do the same.

The four years after being released from the program found me drifting further and further from what minimal steps I had taken towards a positive lifestyle and closer to a dangerous direction I was bound, conscious or not, to follow. I bounced from job to job with little concern with the future or its prospects. I would smoke and drink alone and let my mind wander into dark places that were better left uninhabited. I knew I was slipping away, and I knew why. What I didn't know was what to do about it, or if there even was something to be done.

Each day was lived purely for someone else. I had hurt my parents and my family so deeply by what had happened that I was going to do whatever was necessary to never cause that same type of pain again. They did not know what was brewing inside me and they would never know. The love I felt for my parents and my desire to keep them from ever feeling pain or guilt again because of my actions, was the only thing that got me out of bed each morning. I held no illusions or expectations about my future, nor did I have any real aspirations for what to do with the rest of my life. It simply existed to protect someone else, and was void of any real dreams or ambitions.

I wandered aimlessly through those four years and each day I could feel myself slipping deeper and deeper into a hole that I knew once entered, there would be no way out. I felt the walls slowly closing in on me and I began to wonder if even the strong love and respect I had for my parents and my family was any match for what was growing inside of me.

Chapter 13

At the age of thirty two I was out of work so my father found me a job at a high end grocery store through a friend he knew at his church. It was only temporary and would end once the Christmas holiday season was over but at least it was something. I actually enjoyed it because the hours were long and tiring and the work kept me occupied.

After the holidays were over, the company offered me a spot at their main store and I accepted. Much like the other location, the hours were long and the work was exhausting which was just the combination I needed.

The store was located in my home town and was only a mile or so from my father's church so most of the employees knew who I was and what had happened years earlier concerning the bank. Most were friendly but also weary and unsure of how to approach me, so they kept their distance. During the first week I noticed a woman who worked in the section next to mine and I found myself walking past her as much as possible in hopes of drawing her attention. She had the biggest blue eyes I had ever seen and the few times she actually noticed me she would smile and I would feel like a teenager struck with his first crush. I don't know why I was bothering to entertain any notion of her. I assumed it would end much the same way it had with any woman I met in the years following the robbery. They would either elicit some type of misguided sympathy and want to take care of me and just be friends or they would barely hide their disdain for what I had done, and why I did it. Still, I kept finding excuses to cross paths with her and kept hoping she would show the same interest. After weeks without so much as a simple conversation, I finally gave up. I concluded by that time someone would have told her about my past and she wouldn't be interested anyway, so I let my hopes pass.

One afternoon a few days later I heard a voice behind me.

"Where's the basil?"

I turned to answer and when I realized it was her, no words would come out. I was flustered and no doubt, beet red. Finally I managed to spit out one single word. "What?"

"Basil." she said. "You know, green leafy plant used in cooking. Do you need me to spell it for you?"

I just kept looking at her and praying I would say something witty or amusing. Actually, I would have settled for just a complete sentence.

"It's not a trick question."

"It's a-it's right over there. End of this row here."

"He speaks."

"Come on, I'll show you."

I walked ahead of her down the aisle and again hoped in vain for some humorous narrative or an amusing anecdote to come to mind but all I could say was, "So, you're going to cook with it?"

"No, I'm going to smoke it. Of course I'm going to cook with it. Swift one you are."

I liked her right away and if she knew who I was, she wasn't showing it. She caught me studying her and said, "Didn't your mother ever tell you it's impolite to stare?"

"I'm sorry it's just-I think- Do I know you?"

"Interesting you would ask a question only you can answer."

"No, I mean from somewhere. Do I know you from somewhere?"

"Again, see how this works is-"

"High school." I said. "That's it. You went to Marlboro right? Class of '84?"

"What's your name?"

"Mark, Mark McCullough."

"Oh, Jesus Christ. Yes, we do know each other. Or of one another I should say. You were infamous to everyone in my third period English class senior year."

"Why was that?"

"Because you were the one always making out with that girl-"

"Katie Finnegan."

"That's the one. We all thought you were trying to suck her face clean off."

"It was a project for my science class. I was shooting for an A."

"A for effort anyway."

She was sifting through and inspecting the different fruits and vegetables laid out in bins up and down the aisle. I was hoping she would stay forever.

"New here huh?"

"Yeah, I came over from the packing house after the holidays."

"Moving up in the world huh?"

She must have read something in my face because she immediately touched my arm and said, "I was only kidding."

"No problem."

"Hit a nerve huh?"

I didn't answer her as she spun away from me, then turned back, her arms full with all they could carry. "It was nice to meet you Mark. I'm glad I could finally put a voice to all the face sucking. See you around. My name is Ursula by the way."

"Nice to meet you too, Ursula."

I smiled and watched her walk away. It took me another week to work up the nerve to ask her out. I kept trying to catch her alone, but it never seemed to materialize until I ran into her by the time clock one afternoon.

"Hey."

"Hey back."

"How was your basil? Did you know it's one of the main ingredients in pesto?"

"Yeah? Is that right? What is pesto?"

I could feel my face get red and hot.

"I'm sorry I keep doing that. I'm just teasing you. How are things going? Getting the hang of things over there in fruits and vegetables?"

"I'm finding my way. How are things in meats and cheese?"

"Just wonderful." She said without hiding the sarcasm. "Something new and different every day."

People were cutting in between us and trying to get to the clock. I could feel how anxious and nervous I was, and I wondered if she noticed. Probably not or no doubt, some caustic commentary surely would have been shot my way.

"Listen," I said. "I wanted to ask you something."

I believe if it were not for my jacket covering me, seeing my heart pounding through my shirt would have been a certain reality.

"What's that?"

"What?"

"You just said you wanted to ask me something, that's what."

"Oh, yeah right." Panic crept into every inch of my body.

"Are you okay? You're sweating."

"I don't feel well. Coming down with something I think."

"Great. I'm glad we're not standing in a stuffy hallway, face to face, with you breathing right on top of me."

"No, I think it's something I ate."

"You're coming down with something you ate?"

I blurted out. "No-um- what I meant was-what I wanted to ask was- do you have room for someone new in your life?"

She answered without the slightest hint of hesitation.

"Not really."

She must have realized how harsh her response was so she tried to soften it.

"Besides, I have a kid. A four year old."

I guess this revelation was meant to scare me off, but instead I smiled and said, "I love kids. I have a ton of nieces and nephews. Irish catholic, you know how that works."

Now she was the one wearing her thoughts on her face.

I said, "Boy or girl?"

"What? Oh, a girl."

"What's her name?"

"Vienna."

"Vienna. That's different. I like it."

"I got it from a James Michener book. He described the city in such detail that I fell in love with it."

"Did you ever go?"

"No, but I'd love to... someday."

"Well, I hope you can. Maybe take your daughter along. Let her see what you read. See where she came from. So to speak."

I punched my card and left her standing there. I felt deflated and humiliated that she turned me down, and I was already dreading having to see her now during work hours. I also knew I would do my best to avoid her and let the whole situation fade from memory.

The next morning I got in early, hoping to get to my station before she came in. I grabbed my time card and found a note folded neatly and pinned to it. I opened it and it read: 'It seems, I do have room after all, if you're still interested.'

I looked around to see if it was some kind of joke. Maybe someone heard us talking and this was their attempt at humor at my expense. My doubts were quickly erased when I saw her later and she greeted me with a wave and warm smile from across the room.

We had our first date, if you can call meeting in a public park a date, later that week. It was a beautiful, warm spring day. I got there before she did and sat down on a bench and watched a family of ducks swimming and enjoying the scraps a young boy was tossing to them. I squinted up at the bright blue sky and considered how to approach her. I wasn't sure if she was aware of my past, so I weighed my options. I could tell her what happened right away and likely scare her off, or I could wait and give it time. Let her get to know me. I quickly dispelled that idea though, how could her getting to know me be the better choice? I didn't even know myself, and what I did know, wasn't something a single mother of a young child would be drawn to.

I saw her pull up and was surprised to see her back passenger door open as well as her own. She scanned the area for me as she tended to the occupant in her backseat. I watched a young girl with a round face and short brown hair emerge and plop down on the pavement. Her mother dusted her off and checked her appearance before turning and searching the area for me again. I waved to her and she grabbed the little girl by the hand and headed toward me. As they grew closer, I could see the girls' eyes. They were big and brown and full of all the expectancy a young child would be anticipating from a day at the park. They both approached me.

"Hey, how are you two?"

"We're fine." she said. "Been here long?"

"No, I just got here."

The little girl was pinned to her mom's side and watching me closely. Not seeming shy so much as wondering who I was and if I was going to be a participant or a detriment to the fun she was hoping to experience at the park.

"This is Vienna. My daughter."

"Hi Vienna. How are you today?"

"I'm fine."

"I love your name. It's very unique."

"Yeah, I know. My mom says it fits me because I'm kinda unique too."

"She said that? I don't believe it. How so?"

Before she could answer, her mother answered for her. "Don't worry, you'll see."

"What's your name again? My mom told me but I forgot."

"Mark."

"Do you want to come see the ducks with me Mark? We can't feed them though, it's against the law. Those people over there are criminals. Hey you-"

"Ssshh-" Her mother said.

I started to laugh then said to her, "Sure, I'd love to see the ducks. And I promise not to feed them."

"Okay, come on."

Without the slightest hint of reluctance or hesitation, she took my hand and smiled up at me. I have never been able to accurately explain that moment to anyone, regardless of the countless times I have tried. To anyone watching, it would have seemed to be an ordinary, everyday action. To those around us we would have appeared to simply be a father and daughter taking full advantage of a gorgeous spring day. To me, it was so much more. It was something that has frustrated me for years because of my lack of proficiency in clarifying its importance. Most of the defining moments in my life have become cloudy and vague in my mind. Some, just from the passing of time and others by way of my own denial. But seeing the trust and confidence that showed in her smile, and her tiny little hand guiding me down to the water is still, to this day, a feeling that warms my heart and brings tears to my eyes whenever I re-live it in my mind.

We got to the water's edge and she said, "Be very quiet or you'll scare them away."

I whispered, "Okay."

She pointed and said, "That one is a Canada goose over there."

"I knew that one."

"That one is a mallard."

"Got it. With you so far."

She lowered her voice more and jabbed her finger toward one standing alone near the waterline. "What's that one over there?"

I whispered quietly back. "I have no idea."

"It's a loon."

"Oh, right. I knew that."

She quickly shot out, "Ha! It's not a loon. It's a wood duck."

"I know, that's what I said."

"No you didn't. Liar. You-"

She cut herself off in mid-sentence and pointed to the other side of the lake, unable to suppress her enthusiasm.

"Look at that! See it!?"

I did see the cause of her extreme enthusiasm. A tall thin bird was standing motionless directly across from us.

"It's a heron! It's trying to eat all the fish just like in our pond at home!"

She took off down the path that lead to the other side. I shouted to her but she was off. Determined to save all the fish from the certain death that in her eyes, they were facing that day.

I heard Ursula behind me say, "Let her go. She knows this park better than the ones who built it."

I walked back to her and we sat and watched Vienna fearlessly, and with great focus, tearing after the ghastly winged fish assassin. Unfortunately, as she made the shoreline on the far side her eagerness and determination were squashed as she splashed into the shallow water, and the mud that surrounded it. The bird spread its wings, rose up, and was off. She looked to us quickly and yelled out with a bright smile, "I'm okay. I scared him off did you see? Did you see Mark?"

"I did. Are you okay?"

Ursula said casually, "Trust me, she's fine. That's a daily occurrence at home."

"What is? Chasing herons?"

"No, falling in the mud. I'm telling you, if she ever gets married I'm going to wrap her in cellophane right up to the ceremony just so she stays through it clean. Even then, there's no guarantees."

We looked over at her and she smiled and waved while she attempted to clean off the mud but only spread it further and deeper into her clothes.

"You never had any kids?"

"No."

"You want mine?"

I laughed and said, "Sure."

I toed the dirt below me and we sat in silence for a while.

"I left her father when she was just a baby."

"Is he involved in her life at all?"

"Not really. He picks her up every once in a while. Drives her around. Gets her a happy meal. That's about it. It's better this way."

"Is she okay with it?"

She shrugged and said, "She asks about him. She wants to know why we don't live with him anymore but she loves where we live now."

"Where's that?"

"With my parents. They have a farmhouse nearby. It's full of all sorts of critters and animals to keep her occupied. I grew up in that house." She paused a moment then said, "Where do you live?"

I squirmed and tried hard to figure the best approach to the question.

"I live in Colt Neck with my folks."

"Relax. You think I don't know that already? Our occupations hardly qualify us for rent in any part of town, least of all around here."

"I love the house. It's surrounded by water and sits way back in the woods."

"Yet you still can't identify your basic, garden variety wood duck? I don't know about you Mark."

I knew right then that any notion of waiting to disclose anything about my past could not wait any longer. I liked her, and more importantly, I was comfortable around her so I knew it was best to speak up right away. The thought of spending more time with her, then losing her, was not an emotion I wished to experience. She listened as I spoke and whatever her perception of my words were, she didn't give it away with any facial expression or body language. When I finished stumbling through it she said, "Christ, what's next? Knocking over a liquor store with a machete?"

She called out to Vienna to come to her.

"You're leaving?"

"We have to get home. My parents are waiting for me."

Vienna came bounding toward us, a whirling dervish of energy caked in mud.

Ursula said, "Is that duck shit on your face?"

"It's dirt Mama, not duck shit. I swear."

"Watch your mouth young lady."

"You said it, I just said it isn't. Duck shit I mean."

I laughed at her response. Ursula waved her hand and said, "Don't encourage her."

"What? The kid knows the difference between mud and duck crap-"

Vienna cut me off and whispered, "I think the word you meant was shit."

I laughed again. "I stand corrected. Your daughter knows the difference between mud and duck shit. That's a good thing right?"

"Yeah, she's a regular whiz kid."

She grabbed her belongings and took Vienna's hand. "Say good-bye Vienna."

"But, we just got here."

"Omi and Opa are waiting for us, remember? We have to get back now. I told you we couldn't stay long."

"But Mama, we didn't show Mark the pigs they have. Or the goats."

"I'm sure he knows what they look like. Come on, say good-bye."

She stuck out her hand and smiled at me and said, "Bye Mark. It was nice to meet you. Maybe you could come to our house some time so I can show you my dog and my cats and my guinea hens and my chickens. One's named Chocolate Chip."

I smiled at her and said, "I'd like that a whole lot."

She smiled back and seemed satisfied by my response and started off with her mother.

Ursula, likely gauging my perception of them leaving so quickly to be the result of what I had revealed to her, turned and said, "I don't care what you did Mark, and I don't care why. It's part of your past and that's all it is. We all have one. None of us can change what has already happened. What's done is done, but we can learn from it, and move on. You should try it sometime."

With those words, she turned and walked away. Vienna looked back and smiled and waved again. I knew what she meant, and I knew she was right. I was aware trying to erase the past was not a viable option, but living with it, and living in spite of it, was perhaps, a possibility.

We spoke every night on the phone after that day in the park and we saw each other every weekend. They both became a vital part of not just my life, but also, my well-being. Every day, I could feel my focus shift away from myself, and toward them. I took a job which presented greater earning potential that could support both myself, and a family, and I started exercising regularly. Although I was still drinking, the frequency and quantity had greatly diminished and any drug use was out of the question.

I would dream up different ways for the three of us to spend our time together. The first summer we dated, I emptied what little savings I had by taking them to literally every single town fair in the entire county. It was worth every penny and more, to see Vienna's face light up at the prospect of ferris wheels, roller coasters, and ice cream. She would hold my hand while we walked the fairgrounds, and she would hug me as we passed the time and waited our turn for one of the rides. That entire first summer we were together was without question, the best time of my life. I worked hard all week and could hardly wait for the weekend to arrive. Life had never held that type of anticipation or excitement for me. It was completely new, and something even I was aware was an emotion to be cherished and valued.

One particular weekend, we took Vienna shopping to get her ready for the new school year and I had a plan that her mother wasn't nearly as excited about as I was, but she humored me nonetheless.

"Want to bet me?" I said.

"I'm not betting you."

"Why not?"

"Because I believe buying my daughter ice cream to see the probability of her managing to get some in her hair borders on child abuse."

"No it's not, it'll be funny. Come on."

She looked at Vienna at the exact time that she managed to collide face first with a support beam, then said, "How much?"

"I say she does it."

"No, I'm betting with my little girl. I say she stays clean."

"Movies next week?"

"You're on."

She turned to Vienna who was now rubbing her head and smiling. I assumed she was trying to figure out how the beam got there in the first place.

"Hey Kiddo, want some ice cream?"

She smiled and of course said, "Sure!"

We found a booth at the ice cream parlor and sat side by side watching her. She didn't get more than five mouthfuls in before inexplicably, her spoon and the ice cream it held wound up in her hair.

"How is that possible? We're sitting right here. I was looking right at her."

"I'd like popcorn please. A large plus a drink would be nice as well."

Vienna smiled, pulled the ice cream from her hair, and started to eat it.

Things went on like that for nearly two more years. My parents loved Ursula and adopted Vienna as one of their own grandchildren.

When the time had come for me to ask for Ursula's hand in marriage, Vienna would play a strong hand in altering the course of my proposal. I decided to ask her at a park with a surrounding lake near my parents' house. I thought it was a romantic and fitting location because Vienna could also bring along her bike and hopefully give us the privacy we needed when the right moment arrived. It never occurred to me to ask her without Vienna nearby. She was a part of our relationship, a part of the bond we had formed, and a part of the future we would all share. We walked the trail that circled the lake and I waited for Vienna to get ahead of us. The day was beautiful. The sun was strong and warm with a cool breeze at our faces. A wonderful day to ask for a hand in marriage. When Vienna was a safe distance away, I grabbed Ursula's arm and turned to face her. Before I could say a single word, she turned bright red. I assumed she now knew what was coming and I didn't know what to make of her expression. But it wasn't for me or about me. She was looking over my shoulder at Vienna. I turned just in time to see her slowly losing control of her bike and catapulting head first over her handlebars. So much for my romantic proposal.

Vienna was fine, but the moment was lost. I still ended up proposing that day, although she called it more like a wrangling. I was so nervous when I popped the question that my intention of putting my arm around her and asking her sweetly to marry me, felt to her, more like a strategic wrestling move. Regardless, she said yes and we settled on a wedding date the following June.

The changes in me never dawned on me more, than when I was sifting through the newspaper and searching for a place for us to live. I had always been simply a son or a brother. Soon, I would be a husband and a father. The day had long ago passed where I started to view Vienna as my own child. Though not in the biological sense, she was in every other way, my daughter. She had, without any conscious effort, changed my life. There are no pills, no doctor, nor any therapy session that possesses the power of love one feels for their children. One simple touch from her hand on that first day started a relationship both with her, and as important, maybe even more so, with myself. I knew for all my days going forward I would reward her for that trust in me, and be forever grateful that she was able to at least in part, heal some of the mistrust I already had in people when I was just a few years older than her.

The months and weeks leading up to the wedding were joyful and full of anticipation. They were also taut with stress and anxiety. The wedding was a little more than five weeks off and the strain had become unbearable so I decided a phone call for some fatherly advice was in order.

"Hey Pops."

"Hey there son, how are you?"

"I'm fine."

"Yeah?" he said. "You don't sound fine. What's going on?"

"Actually Dad, nothing's wrong. I'm just trying to get everything all squared away for the wedding is all."

"I know, it's coming up fast. I have my part all written out."

"You're not going to try to speak any German are you? Please say no."

He laughed. "No, I'm not. I wouldn't embarrass you like that now would I?"

"Yes, you would so I'm holding you to your word that you won't."

He laughed again. My father had this loud, booming laugh that you could hear from down the street if you were locked in your basement with the radio blaring and headphones on.

I could hear the happiness in his voice and it warmed me to know that I was at least in part responsible for it. For all the pain and suffering I caused him his only thoughts now were of my happiness, and the optimism my future now held.

He grew quiet, and his usual resounding tone turned soft and light. "It occurred to me son as I was writing my part in your wedding, how proud I am of the man you have become and continue to be. I am so glad, as is your mother that you found someone to share your life with. I could never pretend to know or understand the path your life has taken, I can only say that I know it's been a long, and difficult one. Seeing the changes in you has brought us a measure of joy no words could possibly convey. Don't worry too much about these next few weeks son. Things will work themselves out. With things like this, they always do. You have the love of your new family to look forward to and that's all that matters. Your mother and I can't wait to see the two of you exchange your vows and start your new life together, although I doubt she'll see much through all the tears."

It took all the force I held inside me to keep from crying as he spoke. He was right, things would work themselves out and more importantly, I now knew and understood through Vienna how he could love me through and in spite of all that happened. It didn't alter or diminish its energy or strength. The love for our children is after all, unconditional and knows no boundaries.

"Thanks Pop. That's all I needed to hear. I better run. Love you guys."

"We love you too son. Bye now."

I hung up the phone and cried. My father, if you really put it to him would be hard pressed to find anything in my now over thirty years of life that he could be proud of where it pertained to me. Maybe a good game on the hardwood or a strong outing on the mound may stir something up, but I'm sure, nothing of any real relevance would come to mind. But just then, right after that call I could not only hear it in his voice, I could feel it shoot straight through my body and into my heart. He truly was proud of me. The start of a different relationship with him was now developing in my life, and was yet another outcome to which I felt forever grateful for, and couldn't help but contribute to little Vienna. I fell asleep that night without the usual thoughts or demons clouding my sleep. I dreamt of only the future, and all the possibilities it held.

Chapter 14

At 4:30 the following morning, just hours after the conversation with my father, a frantic phone call came from my mother. I could hardly understand her. All I could determine was that an ambulance was at their house.

"Mom, is someone there I can talk to?"

She dropped the phone without saying a word and then a female voice came on.

I said, "Could you please tell me what's happening?"

"Who are you?"

"I'm their son. What's going on?"

"We got a 911 call from your parents' residence and we're here right now with your father."

"What happened?"

"I'm not sure."

"Is he conscious?"

"He is. We're taking him to Memorial Hospital right now. You should come right away."

"You said you don't know what happened but do you think it's a heart attack? Did he fall?"

"They will know more once we get him to the hospital and they can examine him, but I believe he's had a stroke."

Those words rang loudly through my head. Just the night before, really just hours earlier, he sounded so strong, so energetic and full of life that what she was saying couldn't possibly be true. She was wrong

178

or simply mistaken. She wasn't a doctor after all, and couldn't possibly diagnose such a serious ailment. I hung up the phone and called my sister to tell her the news.

Forty-five minutes later I was at the hospital. When I saw him, I knew that no medical background of any kind was necessary to reach the same conclusion as the voice on the phone. He was conscious and attempting to speak, but the words were not words at all. Instead they were a steady stream of odd noises and jumbled sounds. He kept rubbing his head and trying to get off the gurney. Through his muddled speech you could see the effort being made to focus his eyes and read his watch. I found out later the he had passed out on the bathroom floor and dragged himself to the door. He alarmed my mother of his condition by pulling on the oxygen cord she had run through their house. She herself had only been released from the hospital the day before. I approached him and tried to settle him down. His arms were swinging wildly now, but he actually managed a coherent sentence.

"What time is it?" he said.

"It's five-thirty in the morning Pops."

I only understood one more word he said that day. "Late."

Work and family were his life, and disappointing or failing either one, was not an acceptable outcome to him. He was in the bathroom getting dressed to exercise before he was due at his office for counseling sessions. Even in his condition, he was only thinking of others who needed him that day.

Three men pushed back the curtain that surrounded us. Two stood on either side, and one leaned in to examine him.

"Where are you taking him? What's going to happen to him?"

The examiner spoke without turning to me. "We are taking him upstairs for a series of tests. We need to find out what's happening inside his brain."

"Is he going to be alright?"

"You are his son?"

"Yes, I am."

"What's your name?"

179

Mark, my name is Mark."

"Mark, we won't know that until we get our test results back. Has the rest of your family been notified?"

"Yes. They are on their way."

"Do you know if your father has a living will?"

"A will? Why?"

"Listen to me. I need to know if he has one. Who in your family would know?"

My thoughts and emotions were all over the place. I couldn't understand how this could be happening. Why was he asking for my father's will? Why did he need to know his last wishes? He was right there, alive. Just treat him and make him better.

"Uh-my mother would. So would my sister I think. She should be here soon."

They began wheeling him away and as they did, the doctor said to me, "Have me paged when your sister gets here, okay?"

I nodded numbly and watched them take him away. My father kept trying to speak, but all that came out were the same incoherent, unnatural sounds.

Hours later, the doctor came to meet us in the waiting room. From his face, it was obvious this was a speech he had made many times before, but one he would never be comfortable with. He saw my sister first.

"Hi. How are you? I'm Doctor Stevens. You're here for Ralph, is that correct?"

My sister Kathy said, "Yes, I'm his oldest daughter and this is his youngest son, Mark."

"Yes, we met earlier."

Kathy said, "Did you get all the information you needed? I think that was everything."

"Enough for now yes. I still have a few questions though. Did he-"

I cut him off. "How is he?"

He let out a short breath and weighed his words carefully. "Your father suffered what is called a hemorrhagic stroke. We're still unsure whether it's intracerebral or subarachnoid in nature."

"Sorry but, what does that mean?" Kathy asked.

"I'm sorry. Forgive me. Both mean essentially the same thing in that a blood vessel breaks or leaks within the brain and causes bleeding. We are giving him a series of corticosteroids to help reduce the swelling as well as various types of IV fluids which should help control it as well."

"Is he going to be okay?" I asked.

"It's still too early to tell the extent of the damage. We won't know that for sure until the swelling goes down and we can stabilize his condition as well as do further testing. To be straight with you, your father is very sick. This type of stroke is the worst kind someone can experience and usually causes the most amount of lasting symptoms. If your question is, will he live I would say yes, most likely. If the question is, will he be the same as he was, the answer unfortunately, would be no."

By the following morning everyone had arrived to see him. Even my mother, who we all knew to be too sick to even leave her own house had to come to see her husband of over fifty years. The entire experience was, of course, overwhelming to her. She had battled her own set of illnesses over the years, and now she faced the prospect of dealing with them alone, and without the man she had loved since high school.

Four weeks passed by in a blur since my father's stroke. His condition improved to the extent that an attempt with rehab was looming. I was sitting on our couch at the home I now shared with Ursula and Vienna trying to absorb all that had occurred during the last month. I knew of course, that not only would my dad not be speaking at our wedding, he wouldn't be attending at all. I was considering if we should postpone the day, in hopes that by some miracle he would be able to attend at a future date. I could hear Vienna hard at work in her room in the home we purchased, making it her own. She was eight now, and had become so much a part of my life, that delaying the time frame of her officially becoming my daughter was not a concept I wished to entertain. She trampled out of her room, and found a spot next to me on the couch.

"Whatcha doing?" she asked.

"I'm thinking about your Pop-Pop."

"What are you thinking about?"

"Well, I'm wondering if we should hold off you know? Maybe just wait a little before your Mama and I get married. What do you think?"

"It makes me sad."

She put her head on my chest, and I kissed it gently.

"I'm not set on it, I'm just kicking it around is all."

"Mama would be upset."

"I know. Like I said, I'm not set on anything."

"What do you think Pop-Pop would want you to do?"

I had to think about that. I knew my father, and if there was any way possible to come back from what had happened, he would be the one to do it. And if that were the case, he would want me to wait. But I had done some research on his condition and the type of stroke he had, and any real recovery was unlikely. That being known, I believed he would want us to continue forward with our plans and more importantly, with our lives. Everything he had ever done, he did for the sake of his family, so being the motivation for us to delay our future would be something he would have never wanted to be a part of, or agree to.

"I think he would want us to go on with our plans."

"I think so too."

"You do, huh?"

"Yup. Plus, Mama would be really upset if you didn't."

"I know." I said. "You mentioned that. How about you? How would you feel?"

She hugged me. "I said, I'd be sad."

"Why?"

"Because I want to be a family. I mean, I have a family but I want my own."

I knew what she meant, or at least I thought I did. She loved where she lived and she adored her grandparents but there was one thing lacking in her life. A full time father. We were always very close and when we were together she was in my eyes, my daughter, my own flesh and blood. I believe she felt that bond as well, but the inevitable moment would always come where we would go our separate ways until the next weekend rolled around. I thought this was her way of saying she wanted that to end, that our time as family should begin now, and that postpone-ment was not an option she would take to lightly. I so loved her for that.

"No change of plans it is. We can't have both you and Mama being sad now can we?"

"So it's still going to happen? The wedding? You and Mama?"

"Me and Mama, and you."

A week later, our wedding went off as planned. Vienna was our flower girl and from all outward appearances, was the most excited to see the day finally come.

We had a quiet wedding followed by a simple reception in the base-ment of Ursula's church. Despite the excitement of the day, and the joy that came with it, there was a darkness, a black cloud that hung over all of my family members that afternoon. No one could help but notice how beautiful, and yet how sad our mother looked. She was dressed in all white with a pair of long elegant gloves to match. Her face though, showed what was in her heart. She was supposed to share this day with the man she loved. They were supposed to dance and dine, and soak in all the day's rapture. Instead, she sat alone. Not in the sense of being alone by herself, we all surrounded her and did our best to see her through the day. But rather, alone in a way that she could be seated with many, but still feel only the emptiness and torn heart of a woman who was without her true companion, the one who shared the same joy she did that the day had finally arrived.

She was strong for us, just as I knew she would be. Her pain though, will always be among the many memories forever fixed in my mind on the days that my thoughts travel back to our wedding day.

During the moments of mixed nostalgia I often feel for that day, there is one memory in particular, one very special moment that never ceases to bring a smile to my face. Despite the close bond Vienna and I had developed over the years, she always called me by my proper name, Mark. But literally minutes after the ceremony was over she came to me and said, "I can call you Daddy now right?"

"Of course you can."

She smiled and walked away. I didn't think much of it. She had called me by my name for three years and I couldn't imagine that changing anytime in the near future. Children are creatures of habit, much like adults are, and breaking any form of repetition is a challenging task despite one's focus and determination. But from that day forward, and without a single slip of my formal name, she always addressed me as 'Daddy.' The first time she referred to me in that manner was downstairs at the reception. Her inflection as the words passed were of something she had just recently acquired, and would hold onto tightly, never letting go. To someone who invested little in their self-worth or purpose, the concept of being so important and so significant in another's eyes brought on an emotion of pure euphoria and elation.

That night they both moved full-time into our tiny, yet comfortable condominium. The size would never be an issue for any of us despite our close proximity to each other. In some ways, I believed it to be a true blessing. Constant interaction and insight into one another's lives was not only a daily event, it lead to a closeness that would serve us well as the years to follow would cause that bond to be tested over and over again.

We settled into our life as a family. I felt truly blessed and so fortunate for what my life had become. This unforeseen turn for me was something I sometimes felt was accidental, a mistake in fate almost for my worthiness in this endowment seemed neither logical, nor deserved. Nonetheless, I did my best to nurture its growth and hold onto the strength it had blessed me with.

We passed our days as most families did. My wife and I worked hard to provide a comfortable and warm existence for us to live our lives, and Vienna attended grade school and would enlighten us nightly, often while we settled around our small kitchen table, about the trials and tribulations one encounters in the third grade.

Despite the comfortable routine we had settled into, and the contented nature our lives were now accustomed to, the intrusion of grief and sorrow were always forcing their way into our thoughts and lurking in our background. My father's condition and my mother's declining health hovered over us daily, and served as the example of what the following years would represent.

Much to the surprise of most in my family, my father managed to make it through his rehab assignment and ultimately back home.

Watching him struggle to do simple chores, or just trying to get around from room to room couldn't help but bring on the sad reality that his survival while initially bringing a sense of euphoria and promise, slowly turned us to the realization that the spirit of the man had survived, but the body had taken a toll that even the strongest willed could not overcome.

It pained me greatly to sit in the living room of his home, and remember how he would walk into a room, more like burst onto the scene. A man, a presence really, of so much undeniable energy and enthusiasm, you couldn't help but get pulled into its embrace. To see him as he was after the stroke, moving a mere few feet, or formulating a complete sentence, seemed then to be far more strenuous and difficult than any marathon he had ever run. If I could, I would have spent endless nights alone in seclusion, or even face more time with Ben, locked up in our little cell if it meant wiping away the image of my father shuffling with a cane and mumbling helplessly to himself while he strained just to reach his living room couch. The strongest man I knew, the strongest I would ever know, was now a helpless and tragic shell of what he had been just months before. To watch them both sitting there, my father in his state, and seeing my mother's deteriorating health, I felt as if I was witnessing my own personal hell on earth.

During the next year, I could feel my old demons creeping into me. Finding their way through the cracks I had done my best to seal up and leave behind. I knew once they gained momentum, once they set up again inside me, withstanding their charge would take an energy I wasn't sure I possessed anymore.

I kept Vienna close to me and although I didn't realize it then, I was using her as a sort of shield, a stance against the last twenty five years of my life. The past, and all the weight it carried, was being held back by an eight year old and her unconditional love.

Chapter 15

A year passed before the phone call came. It was inevitable I suppose, but no less painful in its meaning. My father had suffered a second stroke and this time, although he would survive again, coming home was no longer an option. He would be admitted to a nursing home, separated from his love, my mother, and the life they shared together.

I knew that would be the end for her. Although he was nothing of the man he once was, he was still there with her. They could sit on the couch, hold hands, and watch television or just enjoy their quiet time together. That was perhaps, what was most special about their relationship. There needn't be any action or words spoken for them to be in a complete state of happiness. Both were after all, just exactly where they wanted to be.

Now that was gone for her. The man she loved literally her whole adult life and much of her teen years was now absent, and the sad reality was it wasn't short term. There would be no more rehab, no more counting the days until he left the hospital and set off for home. He wasn't coming back to her. Their separation was permanent and without recourse.

The times we would get them together at the nursing home were some of the most painful and gut wrenching moments of my life. To see the two people who raised you, who loved you the most and who loved each other through more than fifty years of life crying and clutching each other and mourning the loss of their life together was a sadness not to be wished upon anyone.

The following year passed much as it started. My mother's health continued to decline as did my father's. Most weekends were split between either seeing him at the nursing home, or visiting her in the hospital. During that twelve month period, I doubt she spent half of it sleeping in her own bed.

The Sundays spent visiting my father took a toll I was aware of but didn't want to face up to. Every time I came home from seeing him, I did as I always did afterward, I shut down. Seeing him in such a place and in that condition was more than I could bear. My sister Kathy was far better with him than I could ever be. She could sit and talk with him, hold his hand, and spend hours by his bedside. Whenever I saw him, I wanted to run, to get out as soon as possible. Not because I didn't want to see him or bring him comfort, but rather because his condition brought on such a deep sense of grief and sorrow that quite honestly, was dangerous for me to be experiencing. I would leave there every week angry at his God, the one he dedicated his life to, the one he prayed to and worshipped for letting this happen to him. This life he now had, or lack thereof, was really no life at all. He was trapped between two worlds. He was no longer living, at least not to any standard you would call a thriving, positive existence, yet despite the catastrophic failure his body had experienced, he was still alive if only in the sense that his heart was still beating and his body while critically damaged, just didn't know it was time to quit.

I would also leave him with the conviction that I would never live out my life in a place where strangers are forced to feed and bathe me. Where it's someone's job to change my diaper or shuffle me to the toilet. My father had lived a life of dignity, grace, and commitment to both his family, and to his religion. There is no justice, no reasoning why such a man could end up this way. Living out his final days in isolation, sadness, and fear. I knew that I could never live that way, and I knew more so, that I never would. I didn't know it then, but that conviction would loom large in my life just a few years later.

On one particular Sunday after arriving home from a visit to see him, I barely made it to the top step into our living room when my wife said, "You can't keep doing this."

I knew what she meant, but I had done my best to put off the conversation that I knew was coming for weeks.

"Doing what?"

"You know what I mean Mark. Don't try to pretend you don't."

I tried to walk past her but she grabbed me by the arm.

"Every Sunday you come home from seeing your dad and you
don't speak for days. The only words spoken are to our daughter and
even then it is only when spoken to."

"I don't know what you want me to say."

"I want you to tell me how you feel. I want to know what's going on
in that head of yours."

I looked at her square in the eye and said, "No you don't."

"Yes Mark, I do want to know. I am your wife and I love you but this
can't go on. We can't live like this, I can't live like this. You are so lost.
You seem so far away from us that I don't know if you can ever find
your way back. Or if you even want to."

"Don't say that-"

"Why? Do you disagree?"

"You don't understand."

"So help me. Make me understand Mark."

She pulled me close and was crying freely now. "I love you so much
Mark, but this is affecting us, it's hurting our marriage. If you don't
find some way, something inside you to pull yourself through...I don't
know if you, if we, can survive much longer."

Those words stung, and they went deep. The thought of not having the two of them in my life, of not having Vienna as part of my every
day existence, was too much to bear.

I hugged her back and said the only two things that I could say.
"I'm sorry. I'll try."

And I did try. Unfortunately, that meant I spent less time visiting
him. I wondered what he thought when I didn't show. I hoped in some
way he understood. I wanted to believe he knew his son, and accepted
what I was doing as a form of survival. If things continued as they were,
I feared more than my marriage would be lost. Still, the guilt of my

own selfish demands forsaking my father's needs is something I carry with me every waking day.

The year came and went and was lived in a blur of emotional exhaustion. By early 2004, my mother's health turned to the point of us all knowing, that the end was near. Spending more time in than out of the hospital was the norm for her now. She no longer possessed the strength to perform the simplest of tasks, and perhaps more importantly, she seemed to no longer have much will to live. I couldn't blame her. In her eyes, she had lost everything she lived for. Yes, she still had her children and their love, but that could not replace nor compensate for the loss of her one true love. Her husband and her best friend. Every week consisted of a few days in the hospital, the days at home were just a temporary delay until she finally made her way back.

In late February of 2004, she was admitted again. This time though, there would be no reprieve. She would not be going home anymore. Three days passed from the time she was admitted until she left us, although none us would believe the time had finally come. She had so many moments where the end seemed certain only to see her bounce back just enough to put off the inevitable. If that happens enough, you assume the pattern will continue. On the third day, I went to see her in the morning and it seemed much like all the mornings she had spent lying in a hospital bed. Although she was quite ill, I didn't believe that the end of her life was coming later that evening until my brother-in-law called me at home and said the nurses thought I should come back. I didn't have to see his face to know what he meant. His tone said all I needed to hear.

She was still conscious when I arrived but was no longer speaking. All her energy was focused on warding off the oxygen mask the nurses were set on applying to her face. It was when she stopped the fighting that we knew the end was near. Two things I will forever be grateful for happened that evening. One is that as she slowly slipped away from us she had the most serene smile on her face. She seemed at peace and comfortable with whatever she was experiencing. One could argue that this expression was merely a natural occurrence, an arbitrary display common when life leaves the body, but I disagree. I don't believe the smile was random or part of the customary course of death. In my heart, I know she was met by the loved ones who had passed on before her, particularly her Sister Alice and her daughter Diane. She was at peace with them now and the last few years of pain and suffering were no longer haunting her. The second thing I will always remember and hold dear to me is she had both my sister and I holding her hands and watching this blissful reunion, as she took her last breathe. I was never more aware than in that moment that not everyone experiences the love and unconditional loyalty I was blessed with where it came to my mother.

For the unfortunate, a mother's love can be sporadic and inconsistent, or even worse, not felt at all. I have compassion for those who do not know, nor have ever experienced the same fondness and appreciation I share with my siblings when we think of our childhood, and the bond we shared with our mother. The idea of no longer hearing her voice, or sharing in her laughter and silly nature was a void I knew could never be filled in any of our lives, and the absence of her love would leave a wound that will never truly heal until we meet again.

The sense of closure, and the warmth I felt being beside her as she left us was something that despite the immense sense of loss, also brought a feeling of relief that her pain and suffering were now over.

That appreciation for the moment was short lived though. The following morning brought us into the nursing facility my father now called home. They brought him into a separate room away from the other residents so we could share with him the news we all believed would mimic a bulls-eye shot to his heart. We had to tell a man who had lost his ability to walk, to talk, to eat without assistance or to relieve himself without aid, that his true love, the only lover he had ever known, had left this world. Until that day, I believed the emotion my father showed during my arraignment in court the day after the robbery was the most painful sight I had ever seen, but seeing his tears and the intense anguish on his face after hearing he had lost his wife, his soul-mate, proved to me how wrong I truly was. He was without question, the very definition of a broken hearted man.

Chapter 16

The years of our lives moved on and continued to pass much like the others. I worked and I tried to keep all my focus on my family and our time together.

In what seemed like just a blink of the eye, Vienna was approaching graduation from grade school. I had continued to center my energy and attention on our relationship and viewed it no differently than I did almost ten years earlier. She was my saving grace. She unwittingly, kept me fixed on what was most important, and more to the point, what wasn't. Simply through the act of unconditional love, she left me with no choice but to concentrate and abide by the promises I made to her, and to myself about her.

I can dare to say that by that time in my life, although depression and the past were never far away, keeping their importance and influence on me at bay wasn't a monumental task in the least. Often, it was blissfully obvious to me how much influence she had on my life and my outlook toward it. Time spent at the beach or the movies or at play of any kind, was a consistent remedy for any of the dark thoughts that tried to entertain themselves within my daily thought process.

Life I learned though, has a way of intruding on those moments when you feel most at peace both with yourself, and your place in it.

I was walking toward my car after a day at work when my sister Kathy called me. Her tone was much the same as I heard from her husband the night of my mother's passing so its meaning once again was not hard to decipher.

"Mark, its Kathy."

Although I almost knew the words verbatim that were to follow I simply said, "Hey Sis, what's up?"

"Unfortunately, it's not a good call little brother. It's Dad. You should probably come as soon as you can."

That call went out to all my father's children and started a week long vigil surrounding his bedside. He was no longer conscious starting with the first night. His breathing was labored and although we were told differently, it appeared painful and to be a tremendous strain to his body with every gasp he took.

It had been nearly six years since his first stroke and our conversation about my looming wedding nuptials. It was hard to comprehend that the person I spoke to that night was the same as the man who was lying in front of me. His powerful two hundred plus frame was whittled to now likely no more than a hundred, if even that much. The round full face, flush with color and health, was now gaunt and gray. Although I knew it to be true, it was difficult to believe it was actually the same person. His decline through the years was obvious to the eye, but paled in comparison to the individual lying before me.

We passed the time holding his hand and talking to him, telling him it was okay to let go. He didn't need to fight any more. Not for us, and certainly not for himself. He had done more than enough, and it was now time to let go and finally see his beautiful bride once again.

There is no more an agnostic person than I, for just as the meaning of the word states, I simply do not know how a man or woman can claim to have certain knowledge for or against the existence of God. I am also by no means atheist, I just can't stake a claim for or against its existence. That being said, through the years I grew to believe in a reality or maybe more so a continuation of some kind once we leave our natural body here on earth. How that occurs or the nature of its characteristics are likewise a mystery to which I hold no answers. What I believe is that we are reconciled once again with the loved ones we have lost in our lives much like I witnessed the night my mother passed. That concept, and the sweet prospect of a reunion between my mother and father is a vision I not only wished to become reality for them, but also hope to share in when my time here in this world comes to its conclusion.

My father's pattern remained steady each day. He would decline more each morning, and then reach a point in the afternoon where his body seemed to come to an impasse. It wasn't going to get any better obviously, but it no longer, at least for that day, would continue its downward turn. As I had done each day during that week, I went to see him early in the morning, then left after he reached his plateau later that afternoon.

One the evening of the fourth day I came home and did something I hadn't done since my wife and Vienna entered my life. I stood in our kitchen with both of them seated on our couch just a few feet in front of me and without their knowledge, I started drinking vodka straight from the bottle. I'm not sure how much was actually left in the bottle when I started, but within the three hours I had been home, it was empty. Up until that night, I had been drinking sporadically since my marriage began, and even that consisted of only a few light beers watching a ballgame on a Saturday afternoon so to say the liquor hit me hard, would be a considerable understatement. I'm not sure why I did it. Maybe it was the strain of watching my father's disturbing, even frightful breathing pattern, or perhaps the realization of now losing both of my parents was too much to absorb. I'm not sure, but whatever brought it on, I was too drunk to analyze the reasoning. Perhaps, that was the whole point to begin with. I gathered myself together enough to formulate an excuse as to why I was going to bed so early and was in the process of fumbling through a quick goodnight when the phone rang. It was my sister Mary Jo. Yet again, the inflection in her tone told me all I needed to know.

"You need to come back. It's not going to be too much longer."

"What do you mean? I was just there."

"I know. I don't know what happened but he took a turn for the worse. How long till you get here?"

My wife was already gathering her things and heading toward the door.

"Forty minutes."

My head was spinning beyond control now. The amount of alcohol I consumed coupled with the news I just received made me nauseous and extremely unsteady on my feet.

"Are you alright?" My wife said.

"I'm fine. Let's go."

We didn't make it out of our complex before I vomited all over myself and the car's interior. I was too drunk and groggy to even make an attempt at opening the door. I threw up three more times before we got there.

When we finally arrived, I was soaked through to my underwear with projected alcohol and whatever else I consumed that day. It even managed to find its way into my hair. Mary Jo met me at the door and her first words, and the only ones that mattered were, "He's gone."

I managed some incoherent sentence, then pushed past her and found the nearest restroom where I again started another violent puking session. After all that was left were painful dry heaves and a pounding head, I did what I could to clean up and went out to face the reality of what my sister had said.

When I think back to that night, I feel so much shame and embarrassment for my actions. Not just my drunken behavior, but also my reaction to seeing my father's lifeless body. I went to his side and just kept saying over and over, "No, no. I was just here. I was just here."

Not poor words of choice, but the vision I must have been to everyone and the blurred structure to my sentences was something I wish to bury somewhere and lose track of its location forever. I wanted to mourn properly the reality of losing my father, but I was too drunk to even focus my eyes on him. I threw up all that was left in my system earlier, but the room was still spinning too fast and my head felt ready to explode.

I was kneeling next to the man who raised me, and who loved me so completely and without judgment through all my years both good and bad, yet I couldn't even properly say good bye because I was too shit faced. Even for me, that was a new low. If there was any comfort to be found in his death, it was that much like my mother's passing, his suffering was now finally over. The following day was Easter Sunday and the week leading up to the holiday was always a favorite of his each year. I knew for me, it would now be a week I would simply close my eyes and wait for it to pass.

Chapter 17

In the summer of 2010 we left our small residence to live with my wife's ailing parents. They were both in poor health and needed our help to sustain their daily lives, and avoid entering into an assisted living facility. I was comfortable in our little space and enjoyed both the years we spent there, and the relatively low cost associated with its size. Nevertheless, that's where my family was headed so I followed along. My wife had grown up in the house and Vienna had lived there until we married so their comfort zone was much different than mine when we finally moved in.

Almost from the beginning, weekly calls for an ambulance were part of our routine. On the nights where emergency services weren't needed, we listened to any signs of distress through a baby monitor we set up in their room downstairs. Sleep came in increments of minutes not hours, and even when it came, it was fitful and without satisfaction.

I spent the whole summer working whatever hours I could and tried hard to fit into our new living arrangement. I respected my in-laws and admired their courage to forge a life in a country that was foreign to them. They came here with three children to provide for, and little else. I could not imagine myself ever having the will or fortitude to succeed in such an endeavor. That being said, and all due recognition being realized, I wasn't comfortable living in someone else's home.

The decision to move and the action of making it a reality, made clear to me the love I had for my family. It was not where I wanted to be, but it was where I had to be, and where I was most needed.

I found a routine that made daily life if not pleasant, at least manageable. The extra hours at work served to both keep me away from the awkwardness of our living situation, and help provide money for a family vacation we had planned for later that year. The summer went on much that way until fall finally arrived.

One morning in mid- October I awoke with a pain in my head, the likes of which I had never felt in my lifetime. A simple step forward, or even the slightest movement, caused excruciating pain and nausea. I brushed it off with some aspirin and a hot shower, and proceeded to go about the day. This attempt lasted only a few hours before I found myself at a walk-in clinic seeking an answer to the severe throbbing in my head. I had never been, even in my days of heavy drinking and little sleep, prone to headaches or migraines of any kind. This was unlike anything I had ever experienced. The pain started on my forehead and ran a straight line across my skull and to the back of my neck. My right ear was pulsating and I could actually hear a 'popping' sound from within it. The clinic doctor found nothing and assumed it to be some type of infection. He prescribed antibiotics and a strong pain medication and sent me on my way. I spent the rest of the day feeling as if my head and neck might actually blow off and separate from my shoulders. I slept fitfully that night both from the pain I was feeling and from the doubt I had that whatever it was, whatever the cause of the headache, was not from some generic infection.

The following day I woke to the same type of headache but was glad to find it had diminished some in its strength. My temporary sense of relief faded when my wife entered the room and gave a look that said more than words could ever accomplish. "What happened to your eye?"

"Nothing, why?"

"Did you just wake up?"

"Yes. What are talking about?"

She grabbed my arm and pulled me to the mirror hanging on our bedroom wall. "Look."

My right eye seemed to recede far back into my skull and the lid drooped and appeared hooded. I leaned closer and could see the pupil was nothing more than a small black circle and no bigger than a pinhole.

"Holy shit. What the hell happened?"

She ignored the question and instead asked one of her own.

"How is your headache?"

"It's a little better. Not like yesterday."

"I'm calling your doctor. Something's not right."

"What do you mean, not right? The clinic doc said I have an infection, maybe that's causing it. Or maybe it's an insect bite or something. Maybe a spider or whatever. We are out in the middle of the boonies here."

She walked away and as she did she called out. "I'm calling the eye doctor too."

I turned back to the mirror and it was hard to argue with her. My eye looked hideous.

Monday morning I saw the eye doctor first. He took one look at me and said it was an infection. Nothing more, and not much to worry about. He prescribed some more antibiotics and didn't seem the least bit concerned.

That afternoon I saw my regular doctor and in describing my symptoms he came back with a response that nearly knocked me off my feet.

"I want to do a cat scan."

"I don't understand, why?"

"To rule out a few things."

"Like?"

"Well, for starters, a stroke."

"A stroke? I have a headache is all."

Just the word itself made my blood rise.

"A stroke?" I said again. "That's a big jump isn't it?"

"The type of pain you're describing and its location is often unique to certain types of brain related injuries, namely strokes. I'm not saying you had one, I'm saying its best to be sure."

He told me to look up then turn my eyes down.

"What's with your eye?"

"It's an infection. I just came from my eye doctor."

The answer didn't seem to satisfy him.

"How long have you had it?"

"A couple of days."

"Same day the headache started?"

"No, the next day. Why?"

He didn't answer but instead handed me a prescription and said, "Take this over to the hospital next door. I want that cat scan done today."

"I'm getting on a plane in a few days. Will you know anything by then?"

"I will if you go now."

With that, he left me alone in the room. A cat scan to check if I had a stroke. Was this some sick joke? A bad dream maybe? Was he just being cautious or maybe too thorough? It didn't matter, I could not and would not even entertain the possibility he was presenting.

I made my way to the hospital and hours later the scan was performed. Days had passed and I hadn't heard from anyone. We were leaving the following morning to fly across the country to enjoy the vacation hopefully, of a lifetime. So out of frustration and perhaps more so, fear, I finally called the doctor's office to vent my dissatisfaction at the lack of professionalism and courtesy his office was showing in not updating me on the status of my cat scan. Before I could get through my list of transgressions, a voice cut me off and said, "I'm so sorry. We just got the results back today. You're clear."

"I'm clear? What does that mean?"

"Your scan came back normal. No signs of trauma. You're fine."

"So, everything is okay? I can get on a plane tomorrow?"

"Where are you going?"

"San Diego."

"Very nice. I'm so jealous."

"It's okay to fly? I can go?"

"Yes you can. Enjoy."

I was stopped at a street light with a co-worker close behind me when I got the news. I always meant to ask him how I looked dancing and hollering in the middle of a busy intersection on that fine day.

199

Our vacation was everything we hoped for and more, but the headache and the supposed infection in my eye hadn't changed since my last visit to the doctor. That gnawed at me and stayed on my mind throughout the entire trip. I was starting to slowly acknowledge the fact that I knew something more was wrong. I didn't care what the scan said or what the diagnosis of my eye was, there was something they were missing and I knew it.

We arrived back home and I tried hard to push that thought from my mind. I was told after all that things were okay so I needn't worry right? That's what I tried to sell myself each morning, and each morning that passed it held less and less value. My eye was no better, and had drawn enough attention that my boss had me where sunglasses inside if a meeting was scheduled. Finally, my wife spoke the words I knew needed to be said, but didn't myself have the courage to voice. "I'm calling a specialist."

I didn't fight her or offer any resistance. I knew she was right and I knew I needed answers. What they would be I didn't know, but I did know they would confirm what I had known for weeks just as I did that morning. There was something going on inside my body that no antibiotic was going to cure.

The day before Thanksgiving I went to see a neurologic ophthalmologist. She performed a test called a cocaine evaluation to help determine the cause of my eye irritation. The test consisted of drops being administered into both eyes with the concept being that ideally both pupils should dilate. If my 'bad eye' didn't react, then the cause was likely something neurological in origin, but would not reveal the exact location of the condition, nor its cause. She showed no sign of surprise when my right eye did not cooperate as it should. It stayed small and unresponsive, yet my left eye reacted normally.

"What does it mean?"

"I can't answer that until we do more testing."

"I just had a cat scan done a few weeks ago. It came back clean they said."

"Was it done with contrast? Do you know what they scanned? Was it the brain only?"

"I have no idea? What's contrast?"

"It's a dye they inject into your bloodstream so they can see things clearer. Did they use a needle?"

"No."

"Then it wasn't with contrast. I prefer an MRI over cat-scans anyway. I'm going to schedule one of the entire neck and head region. It's important we see the neck as well as the brain. Sit tight."

She came back a few minutes later and handed me prescription and a piece of paper with an address scribbled on it.

"Do you know where the Avery Center is?"

"Today? It's scheduled for today? It's the day before Thanksgiving."

"Yes I know, and if you leave right now they will fit you in before they close for the holiday."

"I don't understand. Why-"

She didn't really give me a straight answer, she just said calmly, "We need to find the cause of your Horner's."

"My what?"

"The issue with your eye is called Horner's Syndrome. It's indicates a problem within the sympathetic nervous system."

"What causes it?"

"There are many causes. Most are benign."

"But not all?" I said.

"No, not all. Listen, just get down to the center and I'll call you when I get the report back."

I left her with my mind in a tailspin. Most are benign but not all? On the drive I tried to rationalize all that I knew. My headache while not gone, was better than it had been in weeks. That was good. The pulsating sensation in my ear was also not as noticeable or as consistent as before. That was also good. My eye though, that had remained the same, and that was what she seemed most focused on. She didn't ask about my other symptoms or even how I was feeling over all. Her attention was centered squarely on what was the cause of my eye injury, and its origin. A myriad of dark possibilities crossed my mind, but I pushed myself to concentrate on what I knew, and what I didn't. It is human nature to assume the worst possible outcome.

All of us do it. It's just part of some warped defense mechanism we all have. If we assume the worst, make it real in our minds, somehow we believe it won't actually happen. It's a game we play. We convince ourselves we are doomed and that a hopeless course is inevitable, only to find the outcome in most cases to be neither dire, nor as catastrophic as we made it out to be. I'm not sure why we are not programmed to think positive and to only focus our minds in that direction. If we could only realize the truth will come regardless of how we focus our minds, then being positive should be just as easy as seeing only the negative.

I decided as I parked my car and stared up at the sign stating that I had arrived at the testing center, that I would choose the positive route of thinking and even if that failed me, I would at least take the 'wait and see' approach.

The testing went by quickly, and I stayed committed to my mantra of at least staying neutral to the situation. I turned out of the complex and tried to look forward to the following day. Thanksgiving had always been my favorite holiday as a child. The memories of my mother and sister's cooking and carrying on in our kitchen always has, and always will bring a smile to my face. I tried to put aside my anxiety and accept that I wouldn't get any news until after the holiday. It was after lunch on Thanksgiving eve after all. I was surprised the Center was even open never mind taking new customers.

I hadn't made it more than a few miles when my phone rang and I recognized it to be the number of the doctor's office who ordered the MRI. In the seconds before answering my stomach turned sour and suddenly ached. I hoped for an insurance glitch or a signature missed, but once again, the tone in the voice on the other end told me different.

"Hello?"

"Mark?"

"Yes."

"Mark, its Doctor Burns. Are you driving?"

"Yes, why?"

"Could you pull over please? I need to speak with you."

I pulled into the first lot I could find and parked. She sounded as if she was doing her best to sound calm and professional, but she wasn't pulling it off.

"Are you parked?"

"Yes."

She let out a quiet sigh, then said, "Mark, the problem is in your neck. It's your carotid artery."

I never had much interest in human anatomy when I was younger but I knew the function the arteries carried out, and having any issue with them certainly would not fall under the category of benign.

"What does that mean?"

"It means we think your internal carotid artery on your right side has dissected. Your eye has been affected because the artery nourishes the nerves surrounding the eye. The supply was cut off when the dissection took place. That's what is causing the Horner's Syndrome."

I tried to slow myself, and her down. "What do you mean dissected? It split apart?"

"Not exactly."

I could feel the panic start to build up inside me.

"How serious is it?"

"It's very serious. Do you have a pen?"

"I think so, yes."

"Right this address down."

I numbly did as I was told then tried hard to contain the fear I knew came across in my voice.

"How did this happen?"

"I have no idea. It could be from a tumor or some type of trauma. There is no way to know at this point. We need more testing to be sure, and even then the origin may not be clear. The address I gave you is for a doctor in Middletown off highway 35. Do you know the area?"

"Yes, I do. Who is he?"

"He's a vascular surgeon. He has some experience with this type of condition. He should be able to give you more answers than I can."

"Wait, a vascular surgeon? Did you say a tumor?"

"I don't know that for sure. Just go see him, okay? I made an appointment for you at four o'clock. His name is Doctor Dixon. He's agreed to see you after his shift at the hospital is over as a favor to me."

I watched the cars speed by me and searched for the proper words to express what I was feeling but all that came out was, "Thank you."

"You're welcome Mark. Good luck."

I hung up but couldn't figure out what to do after that. Should I call my brothers and sisters first? What about Vienna? Do I call my wife and scare her half to death when I really didn't know anything yet? Actually, that wasn't true. I did know something. I knew that a doctor, a surgeon, was willing to see me late in the afternoon the day before a major holiday and after his shift was over and he was free to start his holiday with friends and family. I also knew of the thinly veiled panic that was evident in Doctor Burns' phone call. What I was aware of the most was how scared and alone I felt at that moment.

The doctors' office was in the next county, and was situated right across the street from a shopping center that housed a major bookstore chain. I had gathered myself during the ride and was testing my mental limits and hung on to the 'wait and see' methodology.

When I found the bookstore, I found every piece I could on carotid artery dissections and was disappointed to find little insight into its cause. I found all the information I needed on its meaning, but little to tell me why it happens, and even less was written on the proper method to correct it. Or, if that was even an option. I had noticed people's reaction and diversion to eye contact with me since everything started, but it was never more evident than that day. I knew the reason, but I didn't understand why on that particular day it seemed more pronounced and apparent until I found the restroom and looked in the mirror. My right eye was blood red and appeared even more sunken into my skull. The lid was more hooded than it had been since everything began, and my pupil, while small and shrunken from the start, now seemed almost invisible.

I washed up and avoided all eye contact until I found my car in the parking lot. I intended on spending the rest of my time prior to my appointment free of any human contact. I knew I had to call my wife and tell her everything but I just couldn't bring myself to do so.

My hesitation proved fruitless as the phone buzzed quietly in my hand, and I answered in as casual a manner as I could.

"Hey, Sweetheart."

"Hey, yourself."

I didn't wait long to blurt out what needed to be said. I did my best to down play the possibilities and hung up with her as quickly as possible in the hope that my fear and anxiety wouldn't make its way to her.

After what seemed like an eternity I finally met with the doctor. He was a short man with glasses pressed upon a round face and hair slicked back in an attempt to hide the receding process. He stretched out his hand and smiled warmly. I didn't exactly know what to expect of him given the time of day and its close proximity to the following days' festivities.

"Hi, I'm Doctor Dixon. You're Mark right?"

"I am. Thank you for seeing me so quickly. I really appreciate it with the holiday coming and all."

"Don't worry about it, this will go quick."

He turned and waved a hand to me. "Back here."

He fumbled with some type of machine set upon a cart with wheels and when he turned it on it reminded me of a tiny, buzzing television set.

"So, Doctor Burns is thinking dissection."

"That's what she says."

"Based on the MRI?"

"That, and she did the cocaine test on my eye. I guess my right one isn't cooperating."

He came over to me and examined my eye closely.

"Well, you have Horner's for sure, I can see that. But jumping right to the cause being a dissection, I'm not so sure about that one."

"Can the MRI be wrong? Is that possible?"

"Yes they can. I'm not a huge fan of MRI's. They serve you well in certain circumstances but I favor cat scans myself."

"I had one already, but not with contrast."

"And probably of the head only right?"

"I believe so, yes."

"Alright well, we're getting ahead of ourselves here. And I should correct myself. It's not so much that the MRI could be wrong but rather the individual reading it could get it wrong."

My hopes were rising, and I could see and feel the possibility of this all being a bad dream and going home to my wife and daughter with just a close call and nothing more to speak of.

"Human error?"

"Not error so much as simple misinterpretation. It doesn't happen often, but I have seen it especially as it pertains to images of the carotids."

A device that resembled a microphone slipped into his machine and the screen lit up and displayed a series of waves. He ran the device up and across my neck while he spoke.

"I'm getting nothing."

He kept prodding and searching with his device.

"When did things start? Your symptoms I mean."

"I don't know, I guess about a month ago now I think."

"What happened?"

"I woke up with a headache that felt like my head was going to explode."

As he continued with his machine, he said, "Any history of headaches, migraines, that sort of thing?"

"Never. I hardly ever get headaches period."

"Any other symptoms other than the Horner's? Nausea? Lightheaded? Anything like that?"

"Not really, no. Why?"

"Any trauma of any kind? Did you fall or injure your head or neck area in any way?"

"No, nothing like that."

He said yet again the words I was so closely holding onto. "I'm still not getting anything."

He stopped and pulled up a stool next to me.

"As I said, I'm having a hard time buying into the dissection aspect. Especially given the fact that there's no obvious outward cause. It can happen, but for a carotid to simply dissect without provocation is rare. Usually they are brought on from say, a car accident or a blunt force trauma to the neck area, that sort of thing. For them to be spontaneous like this, well, it happens, but not often, not very often at all."

"So, what do we do?"

"Well, we need to determine what caused the nerve damage to your eye. That does not just happen on its own."

"What do you think it could be?"

"Could be a lot of things. A tumor comes to mind first. Then possibly a stroke of some degree."

There was that word again. I could feel the hope fading fast.

"A tumor? Where? A stroke?"

"We're doing it again, we're getting ahead of ourselves."

I could feel the shaking start at my hands and quickly travel throughout my entire body.

"What now?"

"I'm going to order a cat scan with contrast of the brain and neck area. Are you familiar with Monmouth Hospital?"

"Yes I am, but now? Right now I'm going for the test?"

"Yes, right now. Would you enjoy your holiday with this hanging over you all weekend? We need answers."

He was right. I needed to know what was wrong with me. The waiting and not knowing is what kills most of us. I was no exception.

"Besides," he said, "I really don't think there is that much to be concerned about."

"I think a tumor would concern me."

"I just said it was a possibility. Even at that, it doesn't mean it's not treatable. The stroke aspect is more of an issue to me."

"My dad had one. Two actually."

"Really, how come you didn't mention that?"

I don't know why I didn't tell him earlier. Maybe saying it out loud would somehow confirm it was a possibility for me as well.

"I didn't think it was important. He was much older than I am now."

His casual manner was gone.

"Was he sick or overweight? Any blood pressure issues?"

"He was being treated for high blood pressure but otherwise he was very healthy."

"Did he drink or smoke at all?"

"Not a drop, and not at all."

"How about you?"

"Well, if drinking or smoking could in any way have caused or contributed to whatever is going on, then I'm screwed."

"Any drugs?"

"Not in recent years, but when I was younger, more than enough for ten people combined. Is that an issue?"

He seemed unsure how to respond. "It can contribute, yes. Here's a script. Head down there now before the afternoon shift leaves otherwise you'll be there all night."

Just like that, he shook my hand and off I went. It was a short drive to the hospital but no matter, I wasn't going to remember it anyway. I was numb. The only feeling I had was in my mind and it was racing faster than I could possibly keep up with. I had never been afraid to die. As a matter of fact, most of my life, prior to my wife and Vienna, I actually welcomed it, looked forward to it almost. But not in this manner. The possibility of something long and drawn out was not what I had in mind, and something I knew I wouldn't tolerate.

I couldn't get Vienna out of my thoughts. I kept picturing how she would take the news, and how quickly the results of the test could drastically change the direction of our lives. I knew how sensitive and emotional she was, and I knew she would not take it well. Should things go poorly, I knew I would be strong for her of that I was sure. But for how long, I did not know.

I'm not really certain how all the essential aspects of me getting to the hospital and through the maze of corridors and finally, my ultimate destination actually occurred. I found where I was going but I was completely lost. The simple process of putting one foot in front of the other must truly be an automatic progression, for if any actual intellectual input was necessary, I would surely have fallen flat on my face.

When my brain finally began to adjust itself to my reality, I found myself alone in a room with only a hospital gown to cover me and an IV dangling from my arm. The television set hanging on the wall was broadcasting commercials showcasing the upcoming holiday season. The weeks between the Thanksgiving and Christmas season were always a period where I could find it within myself to put aside the dark thoughts that filled my head. I'm not sure why that was. Maybe it was the memories of how wonderful my parents made our holidays as children, or maybe even I was simply able to get caught up in the spirit of the season.

The test came and went without much drama. I was confused to say the least when the radiologist came to find me as I dressed back in my own clothes and said, "Just sit tight okay? Don't leave the hospital just yet."

"Why?"

But he already had his back to me and was gone. I found a bench in the lobby and waited. For what I did not know. Surely the test wouldn't be read so soon, would it? And if it was what would that mean? Nothing I would assume, to be of a positive nature. It was now early evening and I watched the energy of the room around me. The walls were decorated with reindeer and snowmen and drawings of pilgrims and turkeys I guessed were made by some of the young children forced to spend their holiday away from family, and within the halls of the hospital. The anticipation and excitement of the following day showed clearly on all the faces before me, both young and old.

I wanted to feel what they felt and share in their promise of a beautiful day to come. I craved the wonderful sight and sound of my mother standing before our stove in my childhood kitchen cooking turkey and potatoes as her chocolate pies cooled next to her on the counter. I wanted to watch my nieces playing in the fall leaves my father gathered for them. Most of all, I wanted my reality to just simply be a bad dream.

My phone rang and I immediately recognized the number.

"Mark, its Doctor Dixon. I just got the results back from your cat scan. I'm afraid it's not quite what I had hoped for. Unfortunately, the scan confirmed the original thought process concerning what is causing the issue with your eye. To be more precise, it's called a right internal carotid artery dissection with a pseudo aneurysm."

I had already, in a few short hours earlier that afternoon learned what I could about the causes and complications of a dissection, but I didn't read or see anything about an aneurism. Just the word itself brought my father and his struggles to the immediate forefront of my mind.

"Did you say pseudo? As in fake?"

"Yes I did, but it's not fake at all. In some ways, it worries me more than the dissection itself."

"Why?"

"Because our first course of action will be to thin your blood to allow flow past the collapsed section of your artery. With the blood thinned out and the artery weakened from the dissection, the aneurism... well, it stretches out the outer wall...that can be a problem."

I knew what he meant and seeing what my father experienced, I was aware it could cause much more than just a 'problem'.

"So, what do we do?"

"Well, the best and least invasive course of action is to get you on a blood thinner right away to avoid any build up near the affected area. We need to do that immediately to avoid a clot. That could be catastrophic. Then we hope for the best that the artery corrects itself."

"And if it doesn't?"

"Then we will have to weigh other options, like if surgery is a possibility."

"Does this all mean I actually had a stroke?"

"It means you started to. If the artery hadn't opened back partially then yes, you would have likely suffered an ischemic stroke. It's what is commonly referred to as a blockage stroke. The dissected flap would have shut down all circulation. The severity after that typically depends on how quickly someone gets treatment.

I heard his words, but all I could think of was my father.

"I see you live near Baystate Hospital. I have residence there. What I need you to do is get there right away and go directly to the ER. I'll call ahead to let them know you're coming."

I asked the question I knew I had to but was also sure the answer wouldn't bring me much hope.

"What are the chances with this? I mean, in your experience-"

He cut me off quickly. "The problem is there isn't much experience with this condition to begin with so the answers I'm sure you need, I'm afraid I just don't have. I can tell you I have heard of complete recoveries. Unfortunately, I've seen things take a turn for the worse as well. As I said, we'll get you the treatment you need and we'll hope for the best. Now get over to the hospital right away."

With that, he signed off.

I sat for a while on the bench and once again found myself watching the world go by around me inside the hospital. The day prior to any major holiday always seems to have a certain buzz about it and this day, was no different. I watched a woman walk past me holding her new born child. Her face glowed with both fatigue and the anticipation of showing off her new gift to friends and family over the weekend. Other faces were not so cheery or opportunistic. Perhaps they too received some verdict on their health whose outcome was unknown and meant to cast a shadow on their holiday plans. Still others, seemed rushed to finish their business and take comfort in their home surroundings and wait happily for the following days' merriment to begin.

I can't consciously remember finding my car and heading to the hospital. I felt I knew why he was sending me to a different facility instead of keeping me in the one I was currently at, but I guess I just didn't want to admit it to myself. He was sending me close to my house and near my family so that should anything dire occur, they would be nearby.

The ride crossed through several towns and took me past shopping malls and restaurants along the way. I watched, just as I did in the hospital, the excitement and enthusiasm that was abundant in every direction. Billboards and highway signs gleamed with the expectation and joy to be shared during the coming days. A cold, light rain was blowing across my windshield which fit perfectly with the mood I carried with me as I moved closer to my destination. I called my wife and Vienna on the way and did my best to explain what was happening. I doubt I was able to effectively hide the fear from my voice and was sure that my explanation was as confusing and muddled as the thoughts in my head.

They met me in the parking lot and I hugged them both without words being exchanged between us. The rain was heavy now, but none of us seemed to notice. When we entered the emergency room the woman behind the reception desk said, "Can I help you?"

"Yes, my husband was told to come and check in by his doctor."

"Name?"

"Mark McCullough."

"Yes, Doctor Dixon called ahead. Do you have his insurance information?"

If I were in the proper mindset, I would have been alarmed at how quickly I was being processed and would have noticed the urgency of those treating me. Within minutes, I had an IV in my arm and was laid out on a bed with Vienna and my wife each holding a hand.

It wasn't fear so much that I felt then, but rather a desire to reach the end of wherever this was all leading me.

I was placed in a room and was now coming to realize the pace at which everything was moving. I knew from past experience with both of my parents that nothing happens quickly inside hospital walls yet I had a room within an hour of being admitted.

The nurse smiled down at me and said, "The doctor will be with you shortly."

The three of us sat together in silence. My thoughts were suddenly filled with anger. I felt cheated and tricked by my fate. I had finally found some peace, some type of purpose and direction for my life, and now it would seem that its presence would be abbreviated and soon to pass.

I said to my wife, "I want to see it again."

She knew what I meant, she also seemed to feel that acknowledging its presence only made it more real. Regardless, she unfolded the paper given to me by the radiologist and handed it to me.

'Findings are reported for a right internal carotid artery dissection with a pseudo aneurysm involving the distal right cervical internal carotid artery at the level of c1. Intramural thrombus extends superiorly and surrounds the distant cervical ICA, as well as the petrous portion of the internal carotid artery.

I read the content over and over, hoping to find some silver lining hidden between its words but I could find none.

Doctor Dixon never showed, no doubt finishing his day and setting out to enjoy the holiday with friends and family. I couldn't blame him, nor did I really care to see him. His final passage of 'we'll wait and hope for the best' was all I really needed to hear anyway.

After hours of the three of us doing our best with mindless conversation, I feigned exhaustion and asked my wife and Vienna to leave me with the promise they would return first thing the following day.

"I love you Daddy."

"I love you too sweetheart. I'll see you tomorrow okay?"

I knew no sleep would come for me that night, and I was also sure my thoughts would not be my friend while the hours passed. I watched the IV drip over and over with the same slow and constant pace as I thought of Vienna. I wondered how much she understood about what was happening and if she sufficiently grasped the possible ramifications. I let my mind travel back through the years that were shared with both her, and my wife until the sun rose into the room and they both stood over me by the foot of the bed.

My wife asked, "Did you get much sleep?"

Before I could formulate a response the nurse interrupted us. "I need to take some blood Hon. I'll just be a sec."

"Blood for what?"

"To check your Coumadin levels. See if we're getting close."

"To what?"

"I'll let your doctor explain all that when he comes in."

My wife asked, "Do you know when that will be?"

"Probably not until this afternoon sometime. He has rounds this morning. We have turkey and potatoes for lunch. How does that sound?"

I knew her words were meant to cheer me up, but the idea of the holiday meal spent in a hospital bed with a needle in my arm could in no possible way, bring merriment.

"That sounds great, thank you."

The morning passed with the two of them sitting bed side and all of us doing our best to keep the conversation light and away from the reality that brought us there so early on what should have been a wonderful morning.

I thought again of holidays past, when the entire house would smell of our intended meal and the table would be set and extended to hold the mass of people who would occupy it later that day. I'm not sure why, but the lesson of living in the moment, and truly appreciating all that we have was never more meaningful to me than at that moment. I still believe that to be the hardest, and most elusive lesson for all of us to learn. We get it, but we can't grasp it. We understand its value, but not its importance. If one can actually embrace its significance in their lives, they are truly blessed with the real understanding of the meaning of life.

I reminded them both of their obligation to attend the holiday meal with relatives, and shooed them out the door.

As much as I knew I needed their love and support, I wanted simply to be alone with my thoughts. I knew what was beginning to creep in to my mind and I wanted the time to assess how serious and real its content was to me. I also wanted to be sure that a clear mind was entertaining the possibilities and that rationalization wasn't its only cause.

The morning passed and I was no further along with my inner deliberations when Vienna and my wife came back with tales of gossip and drama from their holiday afternoon with family.

"How was your meal Daddy?"

"It was awesome. Never better."

She was seventeen now, a young woman, but she still understood the power a hug from your child possessed.

"You're lying Daddy."

She rested her head gently on my chest.

"No, honest. It was just like Mamma makes. Maybe better."

The words 'Happy Thanksgiving' filled the room before the speaker was known to me. It was Doctor Dixon. He entered with a smile and an expression that showed his professionalism, but did little to mask his irritation of being at work instead of with his loved ones.

"How are you feeling today?"

"I feel okay. The headache seems better."

"That's a good sign."

He flipped through my chart and studied its content.

"Your levels aren't quite where they need to be yet, but it's still early. I'm not surprised by that."

"How much longer do I have to stay here?"

"Why?" he said. "You didn't enjoy your holiday meal?"

I smiled. "It's not that-"

He cut me off. "I'm just teasing you." He drew in a deep breath, then let it out slowly. "We can do this two ways and I'm comfortable with both as long as you follow my direction. You can stay here for another few days, maybe a week, until we reach the proper thinner level by way of IV, or you can leave today and I can prescribe it orally in addition to doses of Lovenox until you reach the right level."

"Lovenox? What is that?"

"It's another blood thinner we often use in conjunction with the Coumadin to speed up the thinning process."

He barely got the words out before I quickly responded.

"Yes, let's do that. I think I can handle another pill."

"Unfortunately, it doesn't come in pill form."

"How do you take it?"

"You have to inject yourself with a needle. Usually in the stomach, twice a day."

My optimism and the joy at the prospect of sleeping in my own bed quickly faded.

"Inject yourself? In the stomach?"

"Twice a day."

Vienna said, "Just come home Daddy. You can do it."

"No, I can't."

"Can I do it?" My wife asked. "Can I give him the shots I mean?"

"Absolutely. The nurse will instruct you at discharge if you choose to go that way."

She gave me a confident shrug and said, "It'll be fun. I've always felt like stabbing you anyway, now I can do it in the name of your health and well-being."

"You look entirely too comfortable with this situation."

She smiled and ignored the comment then turned to the doctor.

"How long will he need the shots?"

"It depends. We'll test him every few days until we achieve consistent levels then the Coumadin alone should suffice."

"Can I do it wrong? I mean, can I hurt him in any way or make things worse?"

"Not really, no. It's pretty basic really. You just have to make sure it's all completely disbursed before you remove the needle. Besides that, it's pretty cut and dry."

I looked at her. "What do you think?"

"I think you will go crazy in here. And I think you should be home."

I knew she was right, and I was also sure that a needle to the stomach twice a day, while not a pleasant thought, was far better than one stuck in my arm for the duration of the next few days, or possibly a week.

I said, "Let's get out of here."

"Okay, I'll start your paperwork. A few guidelines though first. Actually, they are not guidelines so much as rules to live by and if not, you probably won't."

He let those words hang there, no doubt in hopes that there severity would find a home inside all of us.

"No heavy lifting of any kind. Don't even lift grocery bags if they're over five pounds. No exercise at all. You can take a walk if you feel the need to, but never alone. No alcohol or smoking. Also, your blood pressure is very important so try to keep your stress level down if possible. And yes, I know how silly that sounds right now, but just do it. Your life depends on it. Lastly, if you notice any changes at all, if you get a headache, or if you start to feel lightheaded or your speech is off in any way, come to the ER right away. Do not wait."

"My speech?"

"Mark, as I said you essentially had a stroke, or started to anyway. The fact that the artery opened up enough to let some blood through is the only reason things aren't much worse. The artery is still very unstable, and until the blood is thin enough to pass through easily a clot is a real possibility."

My wife asked, "So should he not be leaving then?"

"I didn't say that. If I thought it was a bad idea, I wouldn't even have mentioned it. As long as you keep to the rules and stay aware of any changes, I'm sure he will be fine. What we are hoping for here is that the dissection in a sense, re-sets itself. That would likely eliminate the aneurism as well but you have to take it easy and let your body heal itself. Can you do that?"

Vienna said, "We'll make sure he's a good boy."

He smiled. "Good. Let me get things started then."

A short time later, after reviewing the directions concerning the shots and what to look for, my wife seemed confident and relieved as she wheeled me through the hospital corridors.

For the next two weeks, our routine became well, routine. Each morning when we woke up and every night before bed, she injected me.

My stomach came to look like some twisted, black and blue road map filled with bumps and misdirection. It was with great relief when the call came letting us know that I had reached the appropriate thinner level and that the shots would no longer be needed after the final dosage was finished.

"Last one."

My wife stood above me in bed and waved the needle over my stomach with a menacing grin planted on her face.

"This bears repeating, I think you have enjoyed this way too much."

She sank the needle in deep and smiled at me.

"It has been fun."

"Yeah, I can see that."

Her smile faded and she laid down next to me, and rested her head on my chest.

"I love you so much Mark. I can't imagine my life without you."

"You don't have to."

"And Vienna, I don't know what she would do-"

I stopped her with a kiss.

"Sshh. You don't have to worry. Everything is going to be okay."

"Promise?"

"I promise."

We laid there in silence until she found sleep. I stayed awake and struggled with the words I had just spoken to her. I wanted to believe they were true. I wanted them to be genuine. But I wondered, more so feared, that they were not.

I drifted off and dreamt of my wife and Vienna cleaning and bathing me much as the staff did with my father in the nursing home. The fear of ending up as he did, was a nightmare I was not equipped to fight, certainly not with the strength and grace that he did.

Each night my slumber was met with those same images. I kept seeing myself void of bodily control and in need of assistance whenever a visit to the bathroom was needed. I imagined a spoon being pressed to my lips and guided to my mouth and that only being possible with the support of a helping hand. I also envisioned the burden I would be and that I would not be the only one who would be losing the joy of living. I would be taking that from them also. My wife and daughter had spent the previous months serving as caregivers to my in-laws, and now the possibility of continuing that process with me had become real.

As the days passed I grew to dread the idea of resting my head on my pillow. Each night I was forced to consider that when I awoke, I could be as my father was. Fine upon seeking slumber, but not so upon awakening. The task of living each day in an 'unknowing' state was beginning to take its toll on my sanity. All the demons that I had kept at bay for so many years were now back, and at full force. They seemed to have a renewed energy after so much time at rest. It was much easier to push that knowledge away during waking hours, but the fight was too strong when alone in the dark with myself.

The days went by, each filled with the same sense of uncertainty of what they would bring, and I was fixated solely on the repercussions if the worst was to actually be realized. Three months came and went in a blur until it was time for my follow up MRI to see how the artery was responding to the treatment. A few weeks earlier, I was pushed toward another doctor both by recommendation, and also because of a more intimate knowledge of the obscure nature of my condition. Doctor Hill, was a cardiovascular surgeon, with a history of dealing with dissections similar to mine.

I found my way to his office and he greeted me warmly.

He said, "Ready?"

"Sure."

"Okay, go right around there." He pointed down a long hallway. "Just a little paperwork then we'll see what we've got."

"Thank you."

With that, he smiled and left me. I peeked out the window to see a frigid morning in mid-January and in it my resolve to be positive, even my 'wait and see' approach, was hanging on with a fingertip grip.

After the test, I was led to the doctor's office and waited anxiously for him.

"How do you think it went?"

"It went well I guess. I'll wait for the results before I answer for sure."

He laughed. "I wouldn't worry. Either way, I think we can find a solution. Let's just hope for the best and see what happens."

There it was again.' Hope for the best.' 'Let's see what happens.' Doctors all around the world need to remove those statements from their mantra to patients. It means nothing positive to anyone, and only channels into the negative of every person they encounter.

Three days later my phone rang and my emotions were all over the place when I saw who it was. It was Doctor Hill.

"Hey Mark, how are you?"

"I'm good I think. Depends on why you're calling."

"If that's the deciding factor, then I think you'll be happy. I have the results from your MRI and I think you'll be pleased. The artery has opened up one hundred percent."

I wasn't sure how to react or what to say.

"What about the aneurism? Wait... The artery... it's open...a hundred percent? What does that mean?"

"It means we hit a home run. The artery and the aneurism resolved themselves."

"They're gone? Just like that?"

"Just like that."

A home run. That was the second time I heard that verse where a monumental moment in my life was at play.

I was at work when I got the news. I sat at my desk and quietly cried. There would be sleep that night. There would be no fear of what I might find when I awoke. The news also meant, that I still had a future.

My explanation of the news the doctor had given me both to my wife and Vienna consisted of a garbled mess of incoherent words and emotions. I was still given certain restrictions and guidelines to live by, but essentially I was free to resume my life. No more medication, no more weekly visits to monitor Coumadin levels, no more needles.

It would be easy for one to say, if looking at my life from the outside that I had indeed been a very lucky man. Not so much for the circumstances surrounding my life, or the events of the past, but because I was still alive and could move forward and enjoy a beautiful family I often felt I didn't deserve.

That being said, this was a different kind of gift. A different style of luck. I was struck with an illness that so few doctors knew about, that treatment was a guessing game yet just as quickly as it came, it went on its merry way. I taped the results of Doctor Dixon's cat scan on my bedroom wall along with the admission band they strapped to my wrist and I tapped them every morning as I walked by. Results conclusive of a dissection with a pseudo aneurysm it read. Well, not anymore.

Our lives went back to normal, our normal anyway.

We continued to take care of my wife's parents and I still was trying to find my way and fit in to our living arrangements. I would take
long walks on the trail behind their house using the time much as
I did on the track in prison. For personal reflection, and hopefully,
inspiration.

Vienna was due to graduate high school that spring, and I felt a
burning sadness knowing she would soon be to off to school somewhere, and my source, my light for guidance through life would be
leaving with her.

I clung to, and focused on the gift I was blessed with where it came
to my health, and pushed my resolve to find an answer for what to do
with the rest of my life.

Three months passed and although I no longer had my health as
a leading factor in my thoughts, I also didn't feel well either. I mostly
attributed that to our odd and sporadic sleeping pattern do to the
failing health of my in-laws. In addition, the stress and anxiety that
was placed on my wife was difficult to watch. The task of tending to
one parent is difficult enough. Two, was often, too much to bear.   I
was proud of her, and the resolve she showed and the love she felt for
them.

I also couldn't help but to start listening to the gnawing voice
inside my head. I believed there was something more than just exhaustion and distress from daily life going on inside me. I knew there was
something more.

So much focus had been put on me when I was sick, and my wife
juggled all three of us so well. But with the health of her parents deteriorating more so every day, I could not ask it of her again.

I pushed my fears aside, and continued on with life. After all,
results don't lie right? I had nothing to worry about.

I sat at my desk at work one morning, the same desk that tears
of joy flowed so easily just months earlier when I got the news of the
latest MRI. No tears came this time, neither of joy or sadness. What I
felt was fear. I wasn't sure what was making me feel the way I did and
wanted to simply blame it on my body 're-adjusting' as the doctor
called it. He said the artery had been hit with a trauma and although

it healed in a sense of no longer being occluded, it would still need time to adjust to the damage that was caused. I clung to that hope but found myself stepping outside and trying to shake off the numbness in my leg and the tingling in my right hand. I couldn't tell if my speech was clear, but I kept thinking I was over annunciating my words and I didn't know if my sentences were complete or made any sense.

A co-worker finally noticed the pacing and the panic in my face.

"Are you okay?"

I was starting to sweat, and I could feel my body trembling. I rubbed and slapped at my leg, and kept opening and closing my hand and mouth looking for feeling. My response to her was a short and simple.

"No, I'm not."

My boss drove me to the same hospital that my first treatment started. Someone contacted Vienna and she was waiting for me at the entrance to the emergency room. We sat together and waited for someone to call me in for an evaluation, and I did my best to conceal from her how I felt. My right side still felt numb and my hand was tingling more so than earlier in the morning. My speech felt more forced and overstated.

"Are you okay Daddy?"

"I'm fine sweetheart."

"You don't look fine."

I was sweating more and I could feel my heart racing. My father kept circling my thoughts and my mind kept bringing me back to the day my mother first called me after his stroke. I wondered, more so hoped that what I felt within my body, was not how he felt that morning.

I had always loved to engage Vienna in conversation and enjoyed her take on life and the world around her, but that day I only wished to sit in silence and will my body to cooperate and fight off whatever was occurring inside me. The numbness continued and the sense of foreboding stayed with me and stifled the call from the nurse.

"Mark, right?"

Vienna tapped my leg and pointed to her.

"Daddy."

I looked up, and a nurse greeted me warmly.

"Right in here. Have a seat."

She pulled a curtain and pointed to a bed resting in the corner.

"What's going on? How are you feeling?"

I rushed to tell her what happened just months earlier as if the relevance needed to be shouted out before the circumstances of the day changed and I could no longer speak for myself.

"I had a dissection. Right internal carotid artery. Diagnosed in November."

"What is the status now?"

"I was told it resolved itself. Not so sure right now."

She smiled and tried her best to put me at ease.

"Let's not get ahead of ourselves shall we? Give me your arm."

She cuffed my arm with a blood pressure monitor and seemed to try both to assure, and assess me at the same time.

"Any pain? Headache? Anything like that?"

"Headache. Not too bad though. My leg feels strange and I can't stop my hand from tingling."

She released the air from the monitor and didn't do much to disguise her disappointment.

She said, "Your blood pressure is through the roof. That's probably why you have the headache. Are you taking anything?"

"No, absolutely not."

"I meant for your blood pressure. Are you taking anything to keep it down?"

"Oh, sure. Uh, no. Not anymore. Not since my last MRI. Why?"

"When was that?"

"Mid-January."

I barely got the words out when a man, a doctor I assumed, pushed back the curtain.

"January for what?"

The nurse answered for me. "This is Mark. He had a follow up MRI in January for a carotid artery dissection. He was cleared."

He turned to me, and examined my eyes and face.

"How are you feeling right now? Any speech problems? Slurred words? Anything like that?"

I knew where he was headed and my mind was winning the race and was far ahead of him.

"I feel like I have to work harder to get the words out, if that's what you mean. Focus more."

"The MRI showed no occlusion whatsoever? Was there scarring do you know?"

"No. I mean, I'm not sure. I was just told it healed and the aneurism was gone as well."

"Aneurism?"

"Yes, when the dissection occurred it pushed the artery outward they said. I don't know if I'm making any sense."

"Yes, that would make sense. The blood has nowhere to go so it takes the path of least resistance."

He looked down at the chart the nurse was holding. "Your blood pressure is extremely high. Are you taking anything for it?"

The nurse again stepped on my words.

"No, not since he was cleared in January."

The look the doctor gave her assured all of us that she would not be speaking again unless spoken to.

"We're going to hook you up to an IV and give you something to bring it down okay? Sit tight for a while. After we get your pressure down we're going to do another MRI."

My heart went to my throat. I knew the answer to the question I was about to ask but couldn't resist offering.

"For what?"

He lifted the curtain, then turned back to me.

"To see if you dissected again."

There it was. To see if you dissected again. More accurately, to see if your symptoms are stroke related. I laid back on the bed and rubbed my face and said quietly to myself, "I got three extra months anyway."

The nurse must have heard me and attempted to turn my train of thought.

"Was that your daughter out there? I'll go get her."

She disappeared and just as quick, another nurse was pushing a needle into a vein and hooking up a bag meant to drip slowly into my body. Vienna came in and immediately turned away at the sight of the needle.

"Hey Kiddo."

"Hey Daddy. What did they say? Are you okay?"

"Sure, I'm fine. They just said my blood pressure is a little high and they want to do some tests."

"Tests for what?"

"Just to make sure everything is okay. They're going to do an MRI."

"An MRI? Didn't you just have one?"

"That was months ago, and they are so much fun I asked that as long as I'm here, can I take another ride in the tube."

She wasn't buying the attempt at humor, but kept quiet about what she already assumed concerning the test and its intended purpose.

"Did you call Mama?"

"Yeah, she's on her way."

She reached down and hugged me. No words, no sympathetic speech, just a hug. I turned away to hide the tears I knew were coming.

"Thanks Kiddo. I needed that."

"I know."

I laughed. She did know. That was one of the many qualities I always loved about her. She always seemed to know when just a simple hug would cure whatever ails. Children are often so much smarter and wiser and more insightful than we ever give them credit for.

My wife arrived and we all sat and waited as the nurses came through every fifteen minutes testing my pressure until they were satisfied I was down to a safe enough level to perform the test.

The nurse uncuffed the machine from my arm and said, "I think we're ready."

"We love you Daddy."

"Love you guys too. Be back in no time."

I was wheeled, still in bed, through a series of doors by a bored, disinterested orderly and pushed up against a wall to wait my turn.

I was alone now, both in person, and with my thoughts. The same notions I had in November were creeping back in to me about what to do if the prognosis was a negative one. I was also angry. Why would the pleasure and joy of just a few months ago need to be vanquished so quickly? Why tease me with the opportunity of a second chance only to have it be rubbed in my face?

I knew I was feeling sorry for myself. I also knew I had many second chances in life that I didn't take advantage of, so being upset at this one potentially being taken away was just simply a full blown case of self-pity.

That understanding though did not erase all the fears that crept in to me. I was faced again with the possibility of ending up like my father and all the implications that brought not only for me, but also my wife and daughter.

The same speculations of them taking care of me and the simple tasks in life being carried out only with someone's assistance started playing over and over again in my head.

The numbness in my body had subsided and I was starting to feel better, but the idea that things could change so quickly and with no obvious cause made me realize just how little control I, or any of us have over the course of our fate.

For some it could be loss of employment or an accident occurring on any given day, for me it would be the uncertainty of my body failing me in such a way, as to make me an invalid, and a burden to my family. I wasn't sure that was a cross I could bear.

They wheeled me in and the test went quickly. It was the fourth of its kind since my diagnosis and I was becoming seasoned at blocking out the mechanical noises that reminded me of where I was, and why.

A different orderly with the same aloof approach to his profession weaved me back to my room and to my wife and daughter.

"Hey Daddy, how did the test go?"

"Awesome. They were worried at first, but then they did actually find my brain."

She hugged me again, and again I felt the tears coming.

"Silly boy."

"No, I'm serious. It was touch and go there for a while."

She laughed. "No it wasn't."

My wife rubbed my arm and looked me over. The worry was in her eyes and I'm sure some of the same anger I felt as well. She had gotten her husband back, and was once again free to focus on her parents and their health concerns. Now, just as quickly as the good verdict of mere months ago came, it quite possibly went and she was once again faced with the prospect of dealing with three ailing people under one roof.

"You okay?"

"Never better."

She smiled and rubbed my arm.

"I'm sure that's not true."

I ignored her response. "It's going to be a while before they come back with anything. Why don't you go home and check on your folks?"

"I'm not leaving you."

"I'll be fine. Vienna will stay here with me. Right, Kiddo?"

"Sure Daddy."

I wanted her to leave, and not be informed first hand of whatever the tests revealed so I attempted to change the energy and mood of the room.

"Besides, I'm feeling much better now. Wild horses couldn't keep me here much longer. Go on. I'll be home soon."

"Are you sure?"

"Of course, look at me."

I bobbed my head back and forth in a feigned attempt at dancing.

Vienna said, "Don't do that Daddy."

"Why? I told you I feel fine."

"No," she said. "just don't do that because you shouldn't is all, not cause of how you feel."

I turned to my wife in mock disgust.

"You see how she speaks to me? The tone? I am a great dancer."

My wife patted my arm. "Yes dear, Fred Astaire had nothing on you."

"Damn straight he didn't."

She grew quiet and her demeanor changed. She looked at me, really it seemed more like through me. "Are you sure you're okay?"

"Do you want me to get up and show you? I will boogie all up and down these aisles. Just watch me."

I started to rise and was greeted with four arms pushing me back on the bed.

"Easy killer."

"You'll let me know when you know something or if anything changes?"

"I promise. We'll be right behind you. Vienna is gonna get us some snacks from the cafeteria and we'll be home before you know it."

She seemed very unsure of her decision but also knew her parents were alone, and even for a short period of time, that could present a dangerous proposition. She kissed me and made Vienna promise to take care of her daddy.

Vienna and I passed the time between small talk and what I presumed was her leaving the room to update her mother every ten minutes and let her know there was nothing to tell, and that we were still waiting for news.

Finally, the doctor who first examined me pushed aside the curtains.

"How are you feeling?"

"I feel good."

"No more numbness or headache?"

I shook my head. "No, I feel like my old self."

"That's good. You're blood pressure was what anyone in my professional would consider of a critical nature when you came in."

"That's all it was?"

"Unfortunately, no. The good news is you did not re-dissect your carotid artery. That was ours and I'm sure yours as well, biggest concern."

"The bad news?"

"The test was inconclusive as to why you had all the symptoms you did. I don't have a direct answer for that unfortunately."

"Any guesses?"

He sat across from me and seemed to weigh his words carefully. "Well, my best guess and by the way, I hate the idea of grasping at speculation in any form in my profession but if I had to, I would say I think you had some type of TIA or maybe a mini stroke. Nothing that's necessarily going to show on any testing but all the symptoms lead to it."

I knew what a TIA was because my father had one months before his first stroke. It was essentially a warning sign of bigger things to come.

"Is it isolated? I mean, is it a one-time thing?"

"Unfortunately, I can't answer that either. It could be. With the artery being damaged as it was, you could have simply tweaked it in say, your sleep last night, or something you did this morning without even realizing it. I can't be sure. I can tell you that the artery shows signs of trauma consistent only with the dissection you already had, it's inconclusive pertaining any new damage. I recommend that you stay here a few days and we do some additional-"

I cut him off. "No way. I feel fine and if the tests shows nothing new, then I'm leaving. End of story."

He must have heard the determination in my voice and realized a rebuttal would be futile. He stood and said, "Okay, then I suggest you see your doctor and tell him what's happened and at least start up again with some type of blood pressure medication."

"I will. I'll call him today."

He looked at me intently to gauge my sincerity. "I'll start your paperwork. You'll be out of here in a few minutes. Is someone here to drive you?"

"My daughter is right outside." I lowered my voice. "Hey, please don't mention anything to her."

"That's not my place, but you better consider what I've told you. This doesn't just affect you, this concerns your wife as well as your daughter. This is serious Mark, and it's not just going to go away. You really should stay here for more testing to find out what's happening inside your body."

I had read all I needed to about strokes when my father first had his and my view was that all the testing and all the medicines at least in my opinion, did little where this type of affliction is concerned. If the body decides to go in that direction, there is little recourse for any individual. My father was healthy, ate well, slept like a baby, never smoked or drank alcohol and exercised daily, but one morning, despite all his efforts, the sickness won. I didn't need some tests to tell me what I presumed to already know. My body was failing, it was just a matter of when was all.

That was the lone thought in my mind when Vienna found her way back to me.

"Great news." I said. "I'm outta here. Homeward bound we are."

Her smile lit up the room.

"Really? What did they say?"

"They said the test showed nothing new, and that the artery looks the same as before."

She hugged me. "I'll go call Mama. She'll be so happy."

She left me there to change clothes and get ready to leave. I felt guilty about what I told her but I rationalized that I had actually told her the truth. It was fact that the test showed nothing new, and I hadn't re-dissected the artery. The seriousness of what had brought me there to begin was something I needed to live with daily, not her.

I smiled when she insisted on helping me into the car like I was some little old man. As we drove away, I looked back at the hospital, and right or wrong, selfish or not, I knew I would not be returning.

Chapter 18

I returned home with a new resolve whose origin and intensity came on quickly, and was filled with much aspiration. I decided I would do as my father would do, and I would act as I knew he would. Despite my morose outlook on my prognosis, I would take the news the ER doctor gave me concerning the TIA and I would be aggressive about never letting it happen again. Or at least doing everything in my power to prevent it. I was going to fight against everything I believed and held to be true, and would do my best to follow in my father's footsteps. I began exercising and walking more, and I ate only healthy foods. I tried to rest and relax more than I ever had in all my years combined, and I was determined to carry with me the same positive, upbeat attitude he displayed on a daily basis. There was one glaring difference though between my approach and my father's. His mindset and absolute intentions were one of a genuine nature, more something he was born with and which needed little prodding or manipulation. For me, it was foreign, more like a forced labor, or an unnatural rhythm I had to push myself to believe in and coax out its potential energy. I also knew that I had another motive. One that I was neither proud of, nor did I even attempt to hid its cowardly existence from myself. I made the decision that I would make every attempt, do whatever was necessary to be healthy and alive for my family, but should things occur again as they did that day that led me back to the hospital, there would be no tests, no medicines or treatments. I would make the choice that although outwardly seemed weak and perhaps even despicable, it was none the less mine, at least in my eyes, to make. It seemed strange to make such a decision with a clear mind, free of any presence or power, whether it be mental or medicinal in nature, but it was the only choice I believed I had. As the days passed on, and I continued to watch my wife and daughter care for my in-laws I did not see my decision to be one made out of fear or selfishness, but rather out of love and compassion for both of them. They should not have to reach the inevitable end of years of others, only to have to start a new journey taking care of me. I would not allow that. I knew their initial reaction would be one of anger and confusion, but I believed, true or not, that as time passed they would come to understand and even see the consideration that was intended in my action. What I hoped for even more so is that my decision would never come to fruition and that the conclusion I had come to would be one that no one but myself would ever know of its existence.

Life went on each day with one seeming similar, if not identical to the one before. We slept little do to the fluctuation of her parents health, and we did our best to find what little happiness there now was in our routine. I continued each day with the same objective of staying healthy and positive, and it started becoming a habit. Almost to the point where the decision I had made seemed to lack the same energy and intensity it once had.

Life though, as it often does, has a way of challenging us the most the second we let our guard down. Six weeks after I left the hospital, I awoke and was greeted by my own worst fear. I had the same type of headache with much the same intensity as I did when this whole journey started just months ago.

I could feel my chest pounding but what I could not feel, was my right arm. It hung numb and lifeless, as my head beat in rhythm with my heart.

I attempted to stand in an effort to shake off what was happening. I put my feet to the floor but knew that any attempt to stand would not lead to its intended outcome. I also knew with great certainty, and heavy heart that the day had come. The time had arrived where the decision that I made would sadly, come to be reality. I felt oddly cool and calm as I stared out our bedroom window. I believed at that moment, and with great conviction, that I knew what was best for me, and all who loved me. I felt strangely prepared for what was about to happen, and wished only to see it through for what I truly believed was my unconditional love for my wife and for Vienna.

I rolled to my nightstand and pulled out a recorder I kept there for just such a purpose all the while hoping the tape inside would always stay blank and free of my voice.

For the second time in my life I was about to record a message meant to seek forgiveness for something that although painful, was in my eyes, the inevitable and only solution.

Vienna,

By the time you hear this, you will no doubt, know its true purpose. There are no words to express the pain this tape brings me and I'm sure, the pain and frustration it will bring to you as well. Since I was a young child I felt as if this would be my ultimate destiny. I could never be sure of the time or true nature of its passing, only that its inevitability seemed certain. I know you don't understand, how could you? I take great comfort in your lack of knowledge in this part of my life because it means I was able to keep you distant and safe from my past and the pain it caused deep inside me. Please know that whatever has happened in my life, you and your unconditional love has not only kept those demons away, but actually allowed me to live a life, even for a short time, free of their reign. How a small child, and now a young woman, could have such power, is now, and always will be, a mystery to me, but one that has always brought a smile to my face. Do you remember my father? Your grandfather? I promised myself that no matter what, I would never end up like him. Every Sunday after I left him I swore that would not be me. I couldn't live like that. Someone, some stranger cleaning up after me, or worse, maybe it would be you and your mother's burden. Could you imagine that? Could you imagine having to feed me or change me? Or wipe up after me? Is that how you would want to remember me? I know for me, it is not how I would want to be remembered by you. It is inevitable that all of us one day, must leave this world and our lives behind us. The saddest part of that reality is we are forced to leave those we love behind as well. Today, unfortunately, is that day for me. I love you sweetheart, I hope I made that clear throughout the last thirteen years we have spent together. Please understand I wish more than anything to have stayed and watched you grow into the amazing, beautiful woman I know you will become, and hope you somehow appreciate what I have done. Take care of your Mama for me and know in your heart that you gave me more to live for than I could have ever imagined, and even more than I thought I ever deserved. Love you always Kiddo. Please forgive me.

I laid back on our bed and waited until I heard my wife's car leave the driveway. Knowing Vienna had left for school, I once again tested my ability to step from our bed. The walk from our bedroom to the floor below was both slow and challenging, and one made more difficult by the weight of the decision I had made.

I grabbed what I purchased days after leaving the hospital, materials I hoped, even prayed would never find their way out of the bag that held them, then took one last look at my surroundings. I had never really felt comfortable living there, but it had in some ways at least, slowly come to feel like home. This is where my family lived and where Vienna had spent the first eight years of her life. It's where she sat many Sunday afternoons listening to her grandmothers stories or playing outside with an endless array of animals. It held the memories of us as we huddled together as a family and fed the fish in our pond and took shade from the heat under the oak trees surrounding the property. I would miss all that, and I would miss her most.

The concept of not finishing what I started was pulling at me and asking me to re-evaluate my decision. I wanted so much to see how her life would play out. I wanted to see her future children, my grandchildren, and watch her grow into the type of mother I knew she would be. Even as a young child, her affection and love for all living things regardless of their beauty or stature convinced me early on what type of parent she would become.

Still, the idea of me interrupting her life because of the need to tend to me and my worn body made the decision, while difficult and woefully painful, the right one in my eyes.

My emotions still weren't what I would have thought them to be. I felt numb with a glazed focus. Even before hitting the main road I knew where I was going. The car seemed to find its way without my guidance. As if it knew there was no other place for this life to find its end.

I took the dirt road that would lead me back to field five. I drove slowly and looked to my right at the other fields in view. They held memories of times long ago, before Coach even, and before the indelible scar of that day spent with him. They also held precious reminders of what a wonderful family I had and how much promise there could have been for my life.

Even nearly thirty five years later things still appeared largely the same. Field two's big scoreboard still sat high in centerfield, and the grass was mowed and manicured and ready for a day of youthful enjoyment. The sky was clear without even the slightest blemish to disturb the bright blue shade it held that morning. It seemed oddly fitting that the day held the same feel and promise as it did the morning when I sat in the front seat of Coach's station wagon along the very same dirt road so many years ago. I realized that the feeling in my body had recovered some, and the headache had diminished but what did that mean really? Should I spend another day in the hospital? Should I take more tests that would reveal what I already knew? To most I'm sure the answer would be a resounding yes. For me, at that moment, it seemed, foolish or not, to be cowardly not finish what I promised myself.

I found my way back to the field and positioned my car so I could look out over the field and travel back through time and revisit all its memories. I thought of the good times with my teammates and with my brother and his friends. I also thought of Coach and wished I could go back to the day of my encounter with him and somehow make it play out differently. I knew that it couldn't though, for unfortunately life doesn't have a rewind button.

I took my first pull from a bottle of vodka and then lit a joint. I stared at the green back wall of the dugout just below and to the left of my vision. I wanted to be stronger than what happened in there. I wanted more than anything to be above the pain, and perhaps even grow stronger in spite of it. Maybe that could have happened if I had spoken out about the day's events instead of bottling it up inside for so many years, but I didn't. I let it build and fester inside me for all the years that passed, then buried it somewhere where only I could see and feel it. I knew that was a mistake now, but I also believed that too much time had passed to remedy my decision.

I took another long drink then pulled the top from the bottle of pain medication I brought with me. I knew the combination of alcohol and pills would have the desired effect I sought, and I also was aware that it would not be quick or without pain and suffering. Somehow, that seemed the proper combination to me. It had been a life of hidden misery and sadness, how else should it end? It seemed all too appropriate.

I sat with that resolution in my head, and the sounds of Stevie Ray Vaughan playing softly in the background. Pride and Joy, one of my favorite songs came on and I turned up the volume. It was our wedding song. Although I knew it to be true, my wife never would actually admit to me that she didn't particularly care for that style of music, or even the song itself, but I know she understood the words meant her place and meaning in my life were very dear to me. I believe that alone gave our song special meaning.

My thoughts wandered off in the direction of my parents. I was always close with my father, but never in the same way as a child is to their mother. So many memories passed through my mind of endless weekends in the backseat of our station wagon with Mom at the helm leading me to yet another ball game. I closed my eyes and I could see her sitting in the stands wringing her hands, and cheering me on. I missed her more that moment, than I ever had since she passed.

I was starting to feel the effects of my decision and wondered how long before consciousness would cease. I still didn't feel the fear I thought would come, only the sadness of a life never fully lived, and the pain I knew my actions would bring to everyone, but most of all, to Vienna. I rested my head back and thought how much everything had found its way full circle. It all started with Coach, but I also thought of Father Casey, and Shareef and Snowman and even Darnell. I knew I wasn't sitting in my car, at that moment, just because of how sick I felt that morning. If it was that, and that alone I believe my decision would have been different. I was there because I was exhausted. Because I had no more fight, and nothing left to fight with. Thirty-five years of misery passed since the event on the field that lay before me and now here I was, back where it all started.

The combination was beginning to affect my vision, causing clarity and concentration on any one thing no longer possible. I knew what was soon to come and suddenly feared my actions would deny a reunion with my parents. I truly hoped not. That would be a punishment far worse, than any event in my present life. The car seemed to spin and my thoughts were no longer logical or lucid. I reached for the bottle and poured more onto me than into my body. The simple, physical function of consciously raising the bottle to my lips had become far too ambitious a task to be carried out. I fumbled for the pills and was startled back into consciousness, when I saw someone standing at the front of the car.

The attempt to focus brought the nausea I was experiencing to a new, and heightened level. I felt a rush of panic and shame within me. Panic that I would be caught and exposed for my intentions, and shame that even in this endeavor, I would once again fail. The image did not move and made no attempt to come closer to me. It just seemed to center all its attention and intention on me. I forced down the desire to vomit and sat up in an attempt to square my vision on the subject. I could see that the presence was small in stature and felt relief that simply locking the doors would not stop the day's objective. I put my hand to my mouth to hold down my body's attempt at rejection and closed one eye to better visualize the individual. Who it was made no sense logically, for surely it was not possible in the rational sense. Even in my advanced state I knew that, but logic wasn't what was occurring at that moment, that was also clear in my clouded, fucked up mind.

It was Vienna. Not the teenager I saw only the night before, but rather, the little four year old who held my hand that first day at the park. The one who had been the respite for the life I lived before she came to me. She didn't say anything, she just continued to stand motionless as she stared in at me. I knew she wasn't there, not literally anyway, but I still kept up my attempt to see her clearer.

I could see her face, and it was obvious she was crying. Her brown eyes were full with tears and a plea to me. She shook her head slightly as a single tear rolled down her cheek. I could feel tears coming from me also and soon after the contents from within me could no longer be contained. I opened the door and vomited repeatedly outside the car. I foolishly hoped that she couldn't see me, and put up my hand in an attempt to keep her away. Some of the pills came out still whole and intact, and the retching and convulsing was both painful and without remorse. I fell from the car to my knees and continued to reject the contents long after there was anything left to release.

I focused to find Vienna again, and now although all around me was a whirling mass of spinning energy, she was clear and unaffected by the poison working its way through my body.

She was also, not alone. She was holding a hand. She looked up to catch their eyes, then they both set their attention on me. It was my father. Not the man I had witnessed deteriorate and waste away for the last six years of his life but rather, the healthy, larger than life man I had somehow forgotten, or at least let fade from my memory.

I looked away and again pushed my mind to focus on the reality that neither one was actually standing before me. Vienna was at school only miles from the field, and my father laid comfortably next to my mother in a cemetery also not far from where I sat.

Yet, when I looked up, they were both there. I was sure my eyes would meet my father's and reveal disappointment at the choice I had made, but that's not what shone through.

Perhaps, it's only what I wanted to see, I will never be sure, but I believed he was telling me, no, showing me that my decision wasn't mine to make after all. That I could not just decide that I wanted to leave this world and fool myself into thinking I was doing it for others.

His presence before me meant, at least I hoped, that I did indeed possess the strength to overcome not only whatever illness was with me in the present or may invade my body in the future, but also whatever had occurred in all the years past. Especially the memory of the dugout not more than twenty feet from me. I have said it many times and it still holds true that my father was then, and is now, the strongest man I have ever known. Not in the sense of physical prowess although I always believed him capable if need be to handling most people half his age long after his youth had passed him by. The strength that I mean, is one that overcoming anything in life, regardless of its stature or voracity is done within the mind, and the mind only. I knew this in theory of course, we all do, yet he could set its energy in place with the resolve to test it's authenticity over and over only to come out on the other side of whatever challenge he faced, as the victor. Not that things always went his way, obviously they didn't, but his ability to stare them down and rise past, is and will always be part of the legacy he left behind, and the best testament he left to all of us about life, and how it is to be lived. Why it was so prevalent and obvious that day, was a mystery to me until it occurred to me and made itself as clear as the sky above. That's why he stood before me then. That's what he was trying to tell me. This too was the way I must live my life. It wasn't a choice or an option, it was more, a fact. The reality of everything negative or painful, regardless of its strength or intensity, and despite its attempted influence in our lives is powerless if only we perceive it as we should. As something to not only seek out, but also to overcome and conquer. He was there, maybe not in the literal sense or maybe he was, I was no longer so sure, but it didn't matter, real or not, he found a way to get his message through. Even in death, his love for me was simply that strong.

I laid on my side for hours with the sun beating down on me and knew with great resolve, what I had to do.

It was near dark before I felt strong enough to crawl back inside my car. There was vomit spilled all over along with the odor of alcohol and marijuana. Pills were strewn about as well as an opened bottle resting on the passenger floor. I poured out the contents of the liquor bottle, and gathered up all the pills and tossed them from the window.

After steadying my body as best I could, and finally feeling safe to move on, I found myself heading in a direction that only a day earlier I would have thought anyone a fool to even suggest its place in my day.

Chapter 19

I sat alone in the back pew of my grade school church. I don't know why I went there. I could think of no rational reasoning for its purpose other than it was no more than a mile or so from the day's events, and in my current condition, I felt that I had nowhere else to safely go. I'm not sure how long I was there before I heard a door open behind me. I could feel the presence of someone standing at my back, and I hoped my disinterest in even turning around to see who it was, would lead them away. "Am I interrupting your prayer, son?"

I still didn't answer or turn to face the voice, hoping my silence was answer enough. Instead, they stepped toward me and from the corner of my vision I could see the outline that told me who stood before me. Not his name, but what he represented.

"No, you're not Father."

He stood over me, no doubt taking in the condition of not only the clothes on my back, but I'm sure also, my appearance in general.

"I don't think I've seen you around here before, have I?"

"Not for a long time Father. I went to school here but my family always… we went to another church. My Dad was a deacon there."

"Where?"

"Saint Mary's."

"Saint Mary's?" he said. "Are you talking about Ralph? Are you his son?"

"Yes Father, I am."

"I haven't seen him for years. How is he?"

"He passed away Father. In 2007."

He sat down next to me and while he did, he said, "I'm sorry to hear that son. We hadn't spoken much in recent years. I knew he was sick but I didn't realize he had passed. He was a good man."

"Yes, he was."

"And your mom? Rosemary if I remember correctly?"

"She's gone too. Three years before him."

He shook his head. "You're too young to be without both your folks."

I pulled in, then released a long, slow breath. "Yes, I am."

We sat a moment in silence, then he turned slightly to face me. He pointed at my shirt.

"Rough day?"

"Fast food will get you every time."

"Yeah? They're serving alcohol at the drive through now are they?"

I didn't answer his question, but instead tossed out one of my own.

"How do you do it Father?"

"Do what?"

"Have faith. Believe in something you can't see."

"God you mean?"

"Yes."

"I do see him, every day. He's everywhere."

"Yeah?" I said. "White beard and cane?"

"No, I never much cared for that version either. I don't see a man, I see his purpose, his intention for us. I see it all around me."

"But you don't actually see anything, right? You have faith that it's there, but you don't know for sure."

"I do see it. I see it every Sunday in the faces of the small children and the families that come here to worship."

"Yeah, and they are the same ones who are beeping and flipping each other off trying to get out of the parking lot before the last hymn is over."

He laughed and said, "Are they that obvious?"

I laughed back. "I was an altar boy Father."

"There are ones who don't belong. That is true. They stare at their watches or out the window hoping to be home before kickoff. I know that. But most are here for their faith in God, and the sense of rightness it gives them. The peace He brings. Those are the ones I'm trying to reach. Those are the ones who believe."

"What if it's not in you? What if you can't believe?"

"In what? God?"

"In anything? What if you just can't believe in anything?"

He let those words linger for a moment.

"What happened today son?"

I first looked down at my shirt, and in hopes of regaining the composure I knew was starting to fail me, I looked away from him.

"What's your name?"

"Mark."

"What happened today Mark?"

I could feel my tears winning and my voice cracking as I spoke.

"I almost did it today. I'm a grown man with a wife and daughter but-"

"Did what?"

"Chose out. Chose to leave everything behind."

He thought about that for a moment.

"And everyone?"

I didn't answer.

"You said you almost. What stopped you?"

"I don't know."

"I don't believe that. Yes, you do know. Was it something, or someone?"

"Both I guess."

"Well, if you have something and someone to live for then I don't really understand your actions."

"Me either Father."

I kicked at the pew in front of me. "Do you think it's our choice Father?"

"What? To end one's life? I'm the wrong one to ask son. Besides, no one can answer that except you."

"I always thought it was. Our choice I mean."

"And now you don't?"

"I was so sure, but I've lost all my conviction on the matter."

"Why do you think that is?"

"You're going to think I'm crazy."

"Try me."

I knew how ridiculous my words were going to sound but couldn't stop myself from saying them anyway.

"I saw him today."

"Who?"

"My dad. He was there when-"

"Just him?"

"No, my daughter too. I know they weren't there, but I swear, I saw them. I know I did. My daughter was probably walking to class at the time but I promise you they were both right there with me."

"And you think that sounds crazy?"

"Well, it doesn't sound very rational does it?"

"What do you think it meant? Them being there I mean?"

"I don't know. Maybe I was just using it as an excuse to cop out. Maybe I was just too scared to follow through after all."

"You don't believe that do you?"

"I don't know what I believe Father. Right then, right after, I knew what it all meant and why they were there, I just don't know how to hold onto it. To keep it before everything else in my head."

"Here is my take. Your father and daughter were there. Maybe not in the literal sense as you say, but they were still there. What they represent to you was anyway. You experienced first-hand they joy of unconditional love. You are truly blessed. "

"No matter what, I'll never do it again. I don't care what happens."

"Have you ever tried before?"

"Once that I can actually admit to, but I think I've really been trying most of my life."

"Have you ever said to yourself, much like you did just now, that you would never try again?"

"No, I could never make that type of commitment."

"Yet, you just looked me in the eye for the first time and said you would never do it again, just like that."

He let that hang there for a moment.

"Did they say anything to you? Your Father and daughter I mean?"

"No, they didn't. Not a word."

"That's where I think you might be wrong Mark. That's what I think you're missing. I think they said much more than you realize. Words just weren't necessary for their true purpose to be known. Seems to me the mystery before you today, of their presence is not so mysterious after all. The only questions are what do you take from it, and where do you go from here?"

"I don't know Father. I know what I have to do, I just can't even begin to figure out where to start."

"You know you can't go back right? You said that. But you seem to be struggling with how to move forward, that's what you mean?"

"I just don't want to lose the conviction that I feel right now Father."

"Don't underestimate yourself Mark. I think you are ready for the changes you seek in your life, the question is can you find it within yourself to be open to them."

He rose and stood before me gently resting his arm on my shoulder. "Can I give you some advice? It comes in the form of a verse I heard once. It's a saying I read that I think suits you perfectly."

I kept my eyes down and away from his.

"It goes like this. You can't move onto the next chapter in your life, if you keep re-reading the last one. If you really give that some thought, I believe you will know what that means Mark, and how it applies to you and your future. And I do believe you saw your father and daughter today, they were there with you and for you. Believe in their message son, and God bless you."

With that, he was gone. I sat there for hours and did something I hadn't done since I was a small child. I prayed. Not to God, or for a new life or a way to erase the years and all their painful memories, but instead, for strength. I prayed to my father and asked for the courage to start again, and should I fall again, the faith to try again and again until one day, maybe I would land on my feet and simply stay there.

I asked if he would walk with me through that journey, and stay by my side, not to carry me, but to guide me and pick me up should I grow weary of the path or simply stumble off it.

I also prayed for some of his persistence and stubborn determination, for I knew even a small sample of that would be more than I would ever need. My final thoughts were guided toward a deep sense of appreciation, love, and affection for my daughter. I knew more than anything,

it was her love, more so perhaps her will, Vienna's will and strength that guided me toward a different direction that day and would continue to do so through all the years to follow. For that, I will always be eternally grateful.

Chapter 20

My mother and father are buried side by side in a mausoleum near my home. I find myself there often and usually my thoughts are focused more towards my mother, but on this particular day it was my dad that was the center of my reflection.

"That was really something you pulled today Pops. I expect stuff like that from Mom, but you? All that drama?"

I laughed at those words. Although my father could have at times, a flare for the dramatic, if I would have foreseen a visit from anyone, real or imagined that day, my guess would have always been my mother. She had been my source of rescue and relief all her years on this earth that I would have only imagined the same in death.

It gave me great comfort that it was him. I always struggled with and felt the shame of all the pain and suffering I brought him and it gave me much joy that even in passing, there was no judgment, only love.

"I went to church today. Did you see me? Probably made both of you roll over in there. Bad joke, sorry."

I laughed but could feel the tears starting to come. "I prayed Pops. I prayed for what you used to say you always prayed for. I prayed for strength. I prayed for guidance. For acceptance. Acceptance for whatever happens next, for what has already been, and most of all, of myself. I have been blaming others all my life for how I am and how I think. Now I know that that's just a bunch of bullshit. I truly believe that now, I do. I am responsible for who I am and what I am. I am so sorry for everything I put both of you through. I'm sorry for all the pain and suffering, and mostly, I'm sorry I kept everything from you. I know now that more than anything, that was my biggest mistake in life.

"You told me once Pops, to look in the mirror because that is your only competition. No truer words were ever said. I'm not sure how to undo all the years of living and thinking like I do, but I will try. I promise you that.

I knelt down and traced my fingers across the lettering in their names. Across the bottom the word 'always' is etched. That was their favorite song and something that seemed both appropriate and comforting to see at their gravesite at every visit. But that day, even more so.

"Thank you both for everything. No words could ever express what you meant to me in life, and now, perhaps even more so, in death. Thank you Dad, for today. And for everything. For all your unconditional love and support. I love you both and miss you. Pops, today… it won't be in vain, I promise."

I stood and headed for my car, then turned back to them. "Hey Pops, how about this one, its Socrates I think. The secret to change is to focus all of your energy, not on fighting the old, but on building the new. I think I like that one best. What do you think?"

I smiled and turned away.

I found my way back to my car. I pulled up alongside our driveway and looked up at the house my family called home. I got out and leaned on the fence that faced our living room. I could see my wife through the window caring for her parents. I was foolish in thinking that what almost happened that morning would have in any way been for her benefit. She had proven, even through the hard and difficult times we had, even the moments where things seemed there darkest, that she would love me despite it all. It was unconditional and knew no limits.

I snuck into the house through the basement and quickly showered and changed before heading upstairs to greet her. She was standing in the kitchen washing dishes when I approached her.

"Where did you come from?"

I didn't answer her. Vienna came from another room and stood by her mother over the sink. I hugged them as hard as I could and told them through my tears, how much I loved them both.

"What was that for?"

"You say I never hug you enough."

"You're right I do say that. To what do I owe this great honor?"

"No reason. I'm just trying to write my next chapter. Is that okay?"

She looked at me with a confused expression and said, "The last one was no good?"

"You can't start the next chapter, if you keep re-reading the last one."

She kissed me and said, "I like that one."

"So do I."

I pulled them close to me and hoped with all my heart, that my words would prove to be true, and that my next chapter was just beginning. It had been a long road to travel, so turning the page was now I believed, my only true option. My father's presence that day expressed that beyond any doubt. Thanks again Pop. Love you. Always.

EPILOGUE

It has been over three years since that day at field five and I am pleased to say I have had no further health issues where my dissection is concerned, although I do admit to a great deal of anxiety when even the most benign of headaches finds me. As for field five, I still go back from time to time, but the reasoning is different. I feel my visits throughout the years where self- indulgent, masochistic almost in some way. I blamed what happened and reasoned it is why I was the person that I had been all my years. As tragic and senseless as it was, I used it, consciously or not, to carry on and justify my actions.

I go now to understand that what happened was not a reason, or an excuse to live my life as I did.

Now when I go, I still remember its effect on me, and my life, but now I choose to look at the field, and even sit in the dugout that has stayed within my thoughts for almost forty years, and simply say, 'no more'. No more control is allowed over me. No more wallowing in the memory or its cause and effect. I would not wish its aftermath on anyone but I know, I truly believe, I am proof that no matter how long the fight, it doesn't get to win. It can never win. No matter how long it takes to realize, and regardless of the years that pass. That I know now, is the secret. If something controls you, it owns you. And if it owns you, it wins. Whatever our path in life, whatever has happened, whatever will happen, there will always be another chapter and even when that one closes, we must be ready to start writing the next one. That truly is our only option. My final thought to anyone reading this book who may suffer from depression or has experienced abuse whether sexual, physical, or emotional, I cannot express to you strongly enough how freeing it was to finally open up about what I was feeling and what had occurred in my life and I plead to you to do the same. It may very well be the hardest thing you will ever do, but it will, without a doubt, also be the wisest.

In the future I hope to start a foundation to help those who have traveled a similar path as mine, but until that day I will continue working with other organizations that selflessly devote their time and energy helping people through the darkness in their lives. After all, if I have found my next chapter after all these years, it only seems appropriate and fitting to help others do the same. That I know, is what Ralph and Rosemary would want me to do and I know how proud it would make them. It feels good to do that for a change.

THE END

www.ingramcontent.com/pod-product-compliance
Lightning Source LLC
Chambersburg PA
CBHW070416290526
45791CB00005B/1719